I0867272

BRINGING HOME THE WHITE HOUSE

Bringing Home the WHITE HOUSE

THE HIDDEN HISTORY OF WOMEN WHO SHAPED THE PRESIDENCY IN THE TWENTIETH CENTURY

MELISSA ESTES BLAIR

THE UNIVERSITY OF GEORGIA PRESS | ATHENS

Published by the University of Georgia Press
Athens, Georgia 30602
www.ugapress.org
Copyright © 2023 by Melissa Estes Blair
All rights reserved
Designed by Melissa Buchanan
Set in Garamond Premier Pro and Franklin Gothic
Printed and bound by Sheridan Books

The paper in this book meets the guidelines for permanence and durability of the Committee on Production Guidelines for Book Longevity of the Council on Library Resources.

Most University of Georgia Press titles are available from popular e-book vendors.

Printed in the United States of America
23 24 25 26 27 C 5 4 3 2 1

Library of Congress Control Number: 2023940477
ISBN 9780820365107 (hardback)
ISBN 9780820365121 (e-book: EPUB)
ISBN 9780820365138 (e-book: PDF)

CONTENTS

ACKNOWLEDGMENTS

Lots of people deserve thanks for this book's existence. Archivists were the critical first step to telling these stories, since I had no idea most of these women existed before I arrived at the presidential libraries. Many thanks to the staffs of the Franklin D. Roosevelt, Harry S. Truman, and Dwight D. Eisenhower presidential libraries, the Edward H. Nabb Research Center at Salisbury University, and the Wilson Library at the University of North Carolina at Chapel Hill for their help. Valoise Armstrong at the Eisenhower Library deserves special acknowledgment. She prepared a finding aid on women in those archives years before I arrived in Kansas, and the 1950s chapters of this book would be far worse without her work.

Auburn University has supported this project from the very beginning. My research travel was funded by a grant from the university's Office of the Vice President for Research and Economic Development. The Provost's Office granted me a semester of sabbatical to finish drafting the manuscript. I also received a Beeke-Levy grant from the FDR Library, which paid for my time in the Hudson Valley.

The Auburn History Department enabled my work in ways large and small. Dave Lucsko, our department chair throughout the years I was researching and writing, is a strong advocate for our research and the time it takes to do it well. I am grateful for his support and friendship. Monique Laney organizes a works-in-progress brown-bag series where I got wonderful advice from several colleagues at a critical early stage. Kelly Kennington and Christopher Ferguson have talked me through sticky spots over and over again. Outside of Auburn, Jessie Wilkerson and Melanie Beals Goan have heard about this book more times than I can count, and I would be lost without their continual support. Melanie's reading of the introduction just before I submitted the manuscript was especially critical. Stacie Taranto and Leandra Zarnow provided feedback on an early version of some of this research. Writing for their collection made this project many times better. The anonymous peer reviewers from the University of Georgia Press also provided helpful advice, and I am grateful for their time.

I am lucky to have a tremendous team of professionals supporting me. Biggest thanks are due to the staffs of Auburn City Schools, the ACS after-school program, and Creative Discovery Child Care, all of which took wonderful care of my children. During the pandemic my kids had in-person school from August 2020 onward, and I know how lucky that makes me. Thanks to Stephanie Gilmore of Formore Editorial Services for her enthusiasm for this book and for helping to bring just the right words to these pages. Mick Gusinde-Duffy at UGA Press has been a fan of this project from the start, and I am grateful for his support. The team at Eloise Design make me look good with pictures, web design, and all the other things that go into marketing a book these days.

This book would not exist in this form without my agent, Lauren Sharp at Aevitas Creative Management. Lauren contacted me out of the blue in the early months of the pandemic. We spoke, she asked, "Have you thought about making it more biographical?" and off we went. Lauren, thanks for sharing my joy at finding these women, and for your passionate support for me as I tell their stories. Having a cheerleader like you on my team has made a world of difference.

Writing can be lonely, especially during a pandemic. I am lucky to have friends near and far who have seen me through the past few years. A giant thank you to Lacey and Chris, Kathryn and Chad, Sarah and Ferg, Lyn and Alan, Carrie and Erik, Vanessa and Pat, Chase, Kelly, Erin, Jen, Collin, Becca, Angela, Heather, Laura, and Leah. My brother, Michael, and my sister-in-law, Rachel, have been vital sources of laughter and advice for quite a long time now. I'm so grateful to be on this ride of life with y'all.

The unwavering support of my husband, Ross, makes it possible for me to do everything I do, and his joy at my accomplishments is something I never take for granted. Thank you, honey, for washing the dishes, cooking the mac and cheese, tucking the kids in, talking about the book, and still making me laugh every single day after almost twenty years together. This one's just for you.

BRINGING HOME THE WHITE HOUSE

Introduction

In late October 1951, India Edwards met with President Truman in the Oval Office. Such a meeting wasn't unusual. As the director of the Women's Division (WD) of the Democratic National Committee (DNC), it was Edwards's job to connect the president and the party with women throughout the country. By the fall of 1951 she had been part of Truman's team for seven years, since his vice presidential campaign in 1944. When Truman wanted to know what women thought about something, he asked Edwards. In spite of their strong relationship, however, Edwards was shocked by the reason the president had summoned her that day. Truman offered her the chairmanship of the Democratic Party. In 1951, a woman had never led either major party. Edwards was the fourth in a lineage of influential Women's Division directors within the dnc that began with Molly Dewson in 1932. But even Dewson, a longtime friend of Eleanor and Franklin Roosevelt, was never offered the chairmanship of the entire party.

Edwards declined. She believed Democratic Party men would not work for a woman. She told Truman, "Mr. President, *I would be so busy protecting my rear* that I could never move forward." With the hindsight of a quarter century, she called saying no to President Truman that day one of the greatest regrets of her life.[1]

Edwards was part of a small group of white women who, in the middle decades of the twentieth century, held leadership roles in partisan politics. Their goal was to turn women throughout the country into grassroots troops of both major parties. Those grassroots women then did essential work to elect presidents and members of Congress. Women's Division directors politicized the middle-class home, urging American housewives to frequently strike up political conversations with friends and neighbors and giving them facts and figures to use as they did so. From 1930 until 1960 five women—Democrats Molly Dewson, Dorothy McAllister, Gladys Tillett, and India Edwards, and Republican Bertha Adkins—worked with presidents and parties in power to integrate women into party politics during a critical time in American history.

Molly Dewson was the pioneer of the Women's Division and set precedents the other four leaders followed. She established patterns that lasted long after her retirement, and she corresponded frequently with her successors. She was born in 1874, a generation before the other women profiled here, and graduated from Wellesley College in 1897. After graduation she led a life that was typical of many of her peers among the first large generation of college-educated women. In the 1910s and 1920s Dewson was a suffragist and worked for Progressive Era reform organizations, first in Boston and then in New York City. She was an investigator for a state commission on the minimum wage in Massachusetts and the head of the National Consumers League (NCL) in the early 1920s. Like roughly 30 percent of that first college-educated generation, she never married. Her unmarried status, however, was because she was a lesbian; she and her partner Polly Porter were together for fifty-two years, from 1910 until Dewson's death in 1962. In 1925 she left the NCL to work at the Women's City Club in New York, where she met Eleanor Roosevelt. Meeting Roosevelt shifted Dewson's life in a new direction. They were friends for the rest of their lives, and Roosevelt pulled Dewson into party politics.

Dewson led the Women's Division through FDR's first term and retired from an official role after his reelection in 1936. She was followed by Dorothy McAllister. McAllister was born in Grand Rapids, Michigan, in 1899, and graduated from Bryn Mawr College in 1920. After graduation she returned to Michigan, married her husband, Tom McAllister, in 1921, and gave birth to two daughters. Even as a young mother, McAllister threw herself into civic and political work in women's organizations. She was the president of the Grand Rapids Junior League from 1928 to 1931, holding that position both before and after the birth of her younger daughter, Claire, in 1929. In 1931 she became the head of the Michigan chapter of the National Women's Organization for Prohibition Reform.[2] After FDR rescinded Prohibition she led Michigan's Reporter Plan, one of Dewson's innovations to bring women into politics and into support of the New Deal. Through that work she got to know Dewson, and Dewson personally chose her to take over the WD.

McAllister was one of two women who juggled running the WD with raising children in these decades. When she became WD director her daughter Mary was twelve years old and Claire was eight. She moved her daughters with her to D.C. and was functionally a single mother for most of her time as WD head, because her husband was elected to the Michigan Supreme Court in late 1937.[3]

Tom McAllister was offered a federal judgeship in December 1940, and McAllister did not believe it was appropriate for a judge's wife to be doing partisan work for the president while her husband was on the federal bench. She was also undoubtedly ready to reunite her family. Gladys Tillett took over from McAllister at the beginning of 1941. Tillett was born in 1891 in small-town North Carolina. As a student at North Carolina State Normal College in Greensboro she was an active suffragist, and once the Nineteenth Amendment passed, she became a founder of both the North Carolina League of Women Voters (LWV) and the Mecklenburg County LWV chapter in Charlotte. Tillett spent her life working for feminist causes. In 1974 and 1975, in her eighties, she was the chairwoman of North Carolinians United for the ERA. Tillett's story is unique in many ways from those of the other four women. She was the only southerner. She was the only one of the five who spent her life working in feminist politics. Tillett was also a working mother, but her children were slightly older than McAllister's—her daughter Sara, the youngest of her three children, was fifteen in 1941. But instead of moving Sara with her to Washington, Tillett divided her time between Washington and Charlotte, keeping a secretary in her Charlotte house and commuting weekly when she wasn't on the campaign trail.[4]

McAllister and Tillett's tenures as WD directors were critical steps to moving the job out of the Roosevelts' personal orbit and into the regular functioning of the DNC. But that transition wasn't fully realized until after Roosevelt was no longer president. When FDR died in April 1945, several years of infighting within the DNC ensued. The woman guiding the WD's ship through the tumult was India Edwards, who became Tillett's second-in-command after the 1944 campaign and the Women's Division director in 1948. She was a relative newcomer to party politics, having spent over two decades as a journalist focused on women's and society news in Chicago before moving to Washington, D.C., when she married her third husband in 1942.

A year later, her son was killed in action during World War II, and Edwards threw herself into political work. She was known throughout Democratic circles for being hard-working, thorough, and someone who would do everything in her power to get her way and get the job done. Party women described her as "not afraid of work" and someone who would "not take 'no' too easily."[5] Her hard-working, hard-driving personality served Edwards very well as she helped Harry Truman secure one of the biggest upsets in presidential history. She and Truman were close. She rode with him on his famous whistle-stop train tour during his campaign, and she never wavered in her belief that women voters would turn out for Truman if he appealed to them directly. And she was right. The gender gap in the 1948 election favored Truman, and both Republicans and Democrats acknowledged women as a critical factor in his surprising win.

Because Republicans agreed that women were vital to winning back the White House, they revamped their outreach to women and hired Bertha Adkins as the director of the RNC's Women's Division in 1950. While her party politics differed from that of the other women, Adkins admired the structures that the Democratic Party had built to reach women voters and make them active party members. She immediately began building the kind of robust programs for Republican women that Molly Dewson created in the early 1930s among Democrats. Adkins became the right-hand woman to a president who both valued women coworkers and believed that women voters were essential to his success at the ballot box. She was an important part of the team that helped Eisenhower become the first Republican president in twenty years. Women voters' swing from the Democrats to the Republicans was one of the shifts that enabled his victory. Even though she disagreed with their politics, Adkins always admitted the degree to which she patterned her work on what Democratic women had been doing the previous twenty years. In the West Wing's approach to women, there was a lot of continuity throughout these decades, in spite of the transition to Republican from Democrat.

Adkins was also a lesbian, the second queer person known to lead a WD in these decades. But working for the federal government in the 1950s, rather than the 1930s, meant that she had to be much quieter about that fact than Dewson had been. She and her partner, Winifred Helmes, met in the early 1940s and were living together by 1954, if not before. The timeline of their relationship is somewhat murky, as Adkins excised all mentions of Helmes from her papers at the Eisenhower library and an oral history she gave in 1967. These omissions are not surprising. Given the context of the 1950s "lavender scare," in which LGBTQ men and women were being fired from government work for their sexuality and one historian has estimated that someone in the country was arrested for homosexual behavior every ten minutes, Adkins had to stay mum about Winnie (as she called her).[6] They both had government jobs—Adkins with the RNC, and Helmes in the Women's Bureau of the Department of Labor. But Helmes kept a diary of their time in Washington from 1954 to 1958, which reveals a couple not entirely in the closet. They socialized with other D.C. power brokers, including Ambassador Ted Wailes and his wife and Anne Wheaton, who was also on Eisenhower's staff and a good friend of Mamie Eisenhower.[7] When Adkins left political work as John F. Kennedy became president, she became headmistress of the Foxcroft School, a girls' boarding school in northern Virginia, and Helmes joined the faculty. The two were together until Adkins's death in 1983.

These five professional women—including two working mothers and two lesbians—do not fit comfortably into most people's vision of white women in the middle of the twentieth century. Nor do their close relationships with presidents and their positions in party leadership square with our narratives of women's formal political power. Opening up their working world reveals the centrality of white middle-class women to national politics in an era during which popular culture still largely depicts them as stuck at home.

Once Edwards declined Truman's offer of the DNC chairmanship, more than twenty years passed before a similar offer was made again. There was not a female head of either the DNC or RNC until 1974. And after one three-year term by Republican feminist Mary Louise Smith at the RNC in the 1970s, neither party was led by a woman again until the 2010s. So how do we understand the extraordinary opportunity that India Edwards had? Edwards and the others reveal that white women were influential politicians in these decades. Those women politicians sought to bring other women into politics, especially suburban white housewives. Campaigns believed women were critical swing voters, especially during and after World War II. They spent enormous amounts of money to gain women's votes. Headlines from the 1940s and 1950s such as "Both Parties Woo Women as Decisive Election Factor" and "Key Political Force—the Ladies" do not make sense within our usual picture of women and party politics in the middle decades of the century.[8] Many midcentury political women feared their work would be forgotten, and they were right to worry. In contemporary characterizations of the midcentury as a time of restrictive domesticity, their stories have been lost.[9]

Contrary to the popular twenty-first century vision of white women's lives in these years, WD staffs spent decades connecting women nationwide to the halls of power in Washington. Women who were on the mailing list of the Democratic and Republican Women's Divisions received reams of material giving them talking points to use in political conversations with their friends and neighbors. Women were told it was their duty to persuade others to support their party, and women were praised as the essential grassroots workers of both parties. Forgetting these stories has obscured the role of local women in campaigns and elections in these decades, when they were among the most important tools in getting out the vote.[10]

By losing sight of women as party workers, many people have misremembered middle-class midcentury homes—the iconic split-levels and ranches of the early Cold War and the Baby Boom—as spaces free from politics.[11] The leadership of both parties believed that the home was an essential local site of politics. Women were described as the saleswomen of the party by both Republicans and Democrats from the 1930s through the 1950s. Presidential campaigns simply could not run without the work of armies of grassroots women informing their communities about what was going on in Washington and getting out the vote. Partisan politics was part of daily life for hundreds of thousands of middle-class white women through these years, and they were doing more than stuffing envelopes. They were charged with shaping local understandings of each party's beliefs.

Before World War II, Molly Dewson and Dorothy McAllister built up the DNC Women's Division into a vital piece of FDR's first three campaigns. They created virtually all of the print media distributed by the DNC, ordering millions of copies of small fliers that outlined the administration's position on various issues. In 1936, those fliers made up 90 percent of all the print media used in the campaign. When FDR was reelected for an unprecedented third time in 1940, he sent a thank-you note to McAllister declaring that "a great deal of credit for the result [of the election] is due you."[12]

Dewson and McAllister operated largely behind the scenes. They did not give keynote addresses at nominating conventions or appear frequently on radio and television news programs. Instead, they created networks of women the DNC used to get material into voters' hands. In the 1930s women were not seen as an important voting bloc. Rather than targeting women voters specifically, Dewson's and McAllister's WDs created material that could be used to persuade *any* undecided voter to support FDR. They built a national network of women to distribute that material and report back on how the New Deal was being received in their area.

Dewson used women to build her networks for reasons that were more structural than ideological. The middle-class white housewives who were her main audience had the free time to work for the party. Dewson also targeted women outside of the nation's biggest cities, which helped the WD amass a power base that was geographically distinct from the areas of men's strength within the Democratic Party. Dewson and her successors also believed that women worked better with other women, and that separate structures allowed women to do their best work for the party.

Unlike women, working-class and African American voters *were* specific targets of campaigns during the Great Depression. Democratic activists believed women within those groups were reached most effectively through their class and racial identities. Crystal Bird Fauset, an African American politician from Philadelphia, was tasked with organizing the campaign work of Black women during FDR's 1936, 1940, and 1944 campaigns. She worked with both the WD and the "Negro Division" of the DNC in order to mobilize voters who fell into both of those categories, but she was not officially part of either office. Similarly, working-class women—especially those in union households—worked for FDR through union political action committees and, especially, women's auxiliaries.[13]

World War II and the Cold War changed the calculus of many aspects of women's participation in politics. Both events led to an increase in public statements supporting traditional gender norms. The resurgence of those beliefs could have led to a political arena that shunned women. Indeed, most scholars have implicitly argued that that is what happened—the conventional story is that politicians (who were always men) were happy to have women's labor but did not pay attention to women as voters in the 1940s and 1950s.

In fact, just the opposite was true. Women's Division leaders were suddenly visible members of party leadership, constantly appearing on the radio (and eventually television) and giving speeches all over the country. By the 1950s, thinking about women as an important voting bloc was so ingrained at the highest levels of politics that one RNC staffer described holding that position as natural as "like being against sin."[14] But when "women" became a focus in 1944 and after, the structure that was in place to reach them had been designed to reach and mobilize middle-class white women. Tillett, Edwards, and Adkins did not alter the patterns Dewson had established. WD leaders in both parties always envisioned the "woman voter" they were trying to reach as white. During the early Cold War years, they also explicitly saw her as a housewife, using the words "woman" and "housewife" interchangeably during the late 1940s and 1950s. Women of other races or classes were assumed to be mobilized through those other identities and not through the WD.

The WD system—focused on and structured to suit middle-class white women—therefore replicated the longstanding segregation of women's political organizing. Since at least the 1870s politically active women worked in racially segregated groups, with a few exceptions (primarily the YWCA and the Women's Christian Temperance Union).[15] This pattern emerged out of disagreements among women's rights activists about the intersection of race and sex after the Civil War, disagreements that led famous women's rights leaders like Elizabeth Cady Stanton to campaign against the Fifteenth Amendment because it only gave the vote to Black men.[16] Even groups that partially challenged this segregation at the turn of the century, like the YWCA and WCTU, were segregated at the local level while including Black and white women in the same national organization.[17] Partially in response to their exclusion from white women's national groups, Black women developed their own clubs. The National Association of Colored Women's Clubs, African American sorority alumni chapters, Black women's Republican clubs, and beginning in 1935, the National Council of Negro Women founded by Mary McLeod Bethune all organized the political and civic activism of African American women.[18] Those groups continued to thrive into the Cold War era, and they were the spaces, along with mixed-sex civil rights groups, where most Black women engaged in organized political work. Political action coming out of those spaces rarely intersected with WD work or other official party actions, and at times considered both major parties targets of activism, especially as the civil rights movement burgeoned in the 1940s and 1950s.

The segregation of women's organizing mirrored the broader segregation of American society. Restrictive covenants and redlining worked together to keep neighborhoods segregated, which in turn ensured segregated public schools. In the workplace African Americans and other racial and ethnic minorities were routinely assigned to the most dangerous and dead-end work, which usually paid less.[19] While fewer Jim Crow laws were found outside the South, segregation was everywhere in American society in the nineteenth and twentieth centuries. Women's politics was no exception.

No WD director seems to have considered the difference that race made in any systematic way. Theirs was not an intersectional feminism but rather one that made fundamental assumptions about both race and class and then grounded its work in those assumptions. This reluctance to integrate women's politics is particularly unsurprising among the Democrats. The Democratic Party of these years still included the white supremacist southern politicians who embodied the nineteenth-century vision of the party. The party was therefore not as progressive as one might assume, given the massive move of Black voters to FDR in 1936 and Eleanor Roosevelt's very public support of civil rights. As chapter 3 will describe, Fauset found working for the Democratic Party so frustrating that she publicly endorsed Thomas Dewey in 1944 and began working for the Republicans in 1945.

Segregation was also paradoxically reinforced by midcentury political culture. Beginning in the 1930s and increasingly during and after World War II, an influential group of politicians and media leaders emphasized "the American Way," which they defined as "the ability of diverse individuals to live together harmoniously."[20] Diverse voices were important in the consensus politics of postwar America, but only to the extent that they contributed to a peaceful and coherent whole. The focus was on ensuring pluralism, rather than equality. People were sorted into groups to ensure each group had a spokesperson. African Americans, workers, and women should all be represented by people who were assumed to represent those entire groups. Integrated meetings and organizations were still run by middle-class and elite whites. Male political leaders valued giving women their own structures, in part, because they believed that acknowledging difference made the nation stronger.

In this context, the difference feminism of WD leaders, the emphasis they placed on women as housewives, and the time they spent politicizing the home, make perfect sense. All five WD leaders who worked in the White House believed that men and women were fundamentally different from one another and, therefore, brought different strengths to the table. Those differences made women's participation critical to politics. WD leaders believed women's separate structures could be leveraged to gain women equal opportunities. If women had spaces where they could thrive, and jobs and positions set aside for them, they could then engage with partisan men on equal footing. Difference feminism was prominent not only in the WD in these decades but also in women's civic organizations and among women within the labor movement.[21] But while WD leaders grounded their activism in gender difference, they were blind to the difference that race made. WD leaders happily worked with Black women who fit into their vision and structure. But they never considered making their process more open to a diversity of opinions or perspectives.

Other strains of feminism were also present in midcentury America. Some women politicians and party women were proponents of equality feminism. Those women believed that women should have equal treatment because they were men's equals—that it was their sameness with men, rather than their difference, that made their political inclusion essential. Equality feminists called for the passage of the Equal Rights Amendment (ERA) and equal pay legislation throughout these years, but they never passed any feminist bills. WD leaders never worked in favor of the ERA, believing it would do more harm than good because it did not acknowledge the different roles men and women played in society. WD leaders wanted more women in politics and wanted to improve their treatment in that arena. But they did not seek to alter women's primary role as wife and mother, nor did they question the belief in women and men as fundamentally different. Their entire political structure was built around acceptance of that idea.

Questioning women's primary identity as housewives or their difference from men would have cost women influence in the context of consensus-era pluralism. Or so WD leaders thought. But in spite of a pluralist ideology that gave women a seat at the table, WD leaders' influence over campaigns slowly but steadily declined in the postwar era. Many male party leaders appear to have been unconvinced that women really did deserve special, separate structures. Indeed, once the Democrats were out of power, the DNC dissolved its Women's Division in early 1953. There were multiple ways for women to work for the Republican Party in the 1950s, but that meant no single woman in the party had the kind of power that Dewson or Edwards had. And ideological divisions among women in both parties became more visible in the 1950s. Speaking for "women" became an increasingly difficult goal to achieve as the Cold War years progressed. By 1960, professional party women had lost their influence over presidential campaigns. The DNC no longer had a Women's Division at all. Bertha Adkins recalled that Richard Nixon ran his campaign largely outside of existing Republican structures and did not reach out to her or anyone else who had worked in the RNC on women' issues. And so the era of women at the center of presidential campaigns ended.

In spite of all its limitations—the lack of attention to race and class differences, the glass ceiling, the inability or disinclination to advance policies specifically focused on women—the Women's Division created an influential space for women within both major parties. Telling this story highlights a time when difference feminism was influential in national politics. It shows how the racial segregation of women's politics persisted from the late nineteenth century into the era of the civil rights movement. It forces us to think differently about the women who lived in the suburban middle-class homes of the postwar era, who did vital work to make American democracy function at the grassroots level while their children were at school, ballet, and Little League. That work was cultivated by a small group of successful professional women in midcentury Washington. In all of these ways, the story of the WD illuminates and challenges what we thought we knew about middle-class white women in these decades and about women in midcentury politics.

I

"An Instrument to Attain Their Hopes and Dreams"

DEMOCRATIC PARTY WOMEN, 1928–1935

At a spring 1936 meeting of senior Democratic Party leaders, Molly Dewson outlined all the ways in which women had become integrated into the work of the Democratic Party from the 1932 campaign on. They had become active party members, she argued, because they saw the party as "an instrument to attain their hopes and dreams of a measure of economic stability and security of every-day persons."[1] In other words, women believed that the Democratic Party was the right tool to solve the crisis of the Great Depression and the economic havoc it had wreaked.

According to Dewson, the New Deal had changed women's ideas about what politics could do and their relationship to the party. Unlike in earlier economic crises, where women would have been more likely to use charity or other private methods to help suffering people, now they were using the government and a political party. Many women, Dewson argued, had discovered during the New Deal that "since it is the parties that pass or do not pass desired legislation, the effective place to work is from the inside."[2] Beginning during the fight for women's suffrage, many women's political groups had argued that being nonpartisan gave women a political advantage, because they could pressure both parties and not feel required to compromise.[3] But the national disaster that was the Great Depression moved women out of that delusion, according to Dewson. Because parties pass legislation and legislation was what the moment called for, women integrated themselves into the Democratic Party.

The foundations for women's incorporation into the Democratic Party began in the late 1920s, when Eleanor Roosevelt ran the Women's Division for Al Smith's 1928 campaign. Over the course of the next eight years, Roosevelt's close friend Molly Dewson became the leader of Democratic women, designing programs to attach women to the party and make them the party's most reliable grassroots workers. She also articulated a rationale for women's involvement that straddled the line between difference and equality feminism. Dewson believed women and men had the same political interests but also that women were fundamentally different from men. Women should organize separately, therefore, but work on everything. That belief, paired with tactics Dewson developed to achieve her vison of women's political engagement, became the foundation of women's partisan work at the highest levels of both parties for the following twenty-five years.

While earlier generations of female activists had believed their greatest political power lay in nonpartisanship, many women who came into politics in the 1920s began to embrace the party structure. Women who sought leadership within the parties found receptive male audiences among male party leaders because "party leaders believed that women were best able to mobilize women."[4] That belief led to the creation of women's bureaus in both parties during the 1920 and 1924 campaigns.

Many younger activists who came of age at the end of the suffrage fight valued working within the parties for ideological reasons, as well as practical ones. Historian Mary Trigg has argued that women activists born around the turn of the century who became adults as the Nineteenth Amendment was ratified saw working with men as the next important feminist battleground. Many self-identified feminists among this generation believed that attempting to "assimilate into male institutions and forge close relationships with men" was the most effective way to improve women's lives in the modern era.[5] All of the WD leaders except Dewson were part of this generation. None of them described themselves as feminist, as that term was used exclusively by equality feminists in these years. But WD directors were all invested in working with men to advance women's standing. These women strove to build up women's strength within separate women's spaces and then to use that strength to engage with powerful men on more equal terms.

In the first campaigns after the Nineteenth Amendment's ratification, women voters were pursued by both parties. Both the Republican and Democratic National Committees adopted rules to include women in the national committees and organized women's bureaus to rally women voters during presidential elections. The Democrats were particularly energetic in building structures to bring women into the party. They did not believe in gender equality more than Republicans but pursued women more aggressively because, throughout the 1920s, the Democrats were the minority party and needed every vote they could get.[6] While both parties and the media paid attention to women voters in 1920 and 1924, it was largely because they were unknowns. Their mystery was what gained the headlines, as in a 1920 *Boston Globe* article titled "How Will Women Vote?"[7] Because they were in uncharted waters, party leaders' efforts to bring women into the parties were haphazard. Women's Bureaus were formed for presidential elections but quickly withered away between campaigns. Women's Republican and Democratic clubs were formed, but their connection to the party leadership was minimal, especially on the Democratic side.[8] Even in 1928, the effort put into securing women's votes did not translate into permanent structures within the parties' leadership.

The 1928 presidential campaign was the first one in which women voters were believed to be a decisive factor, not merely a question mark. Prohibition was one of the central issues in the campaign. Al Smith, the Democratic candidate, was a Catholic who opposed a national Prohibition law, while Quaker Republican nominee Herbert Hoover supported a federal ban on alcohol.[9] Many American women had been lobbying to ban alcohol since the revival of the Women's Christian Temperance Union in the late 1860s; for most of the late nineteenth century, the WCTU was the largest women's organization in the country. The Hoover campaign, therefore, believed that women would support him and help keep the White House in Republican hands, as it had been throughout the 1920s. As one female Hoover supporter put it, "If Mr. Hoover is to be elected . . . it will be largely due to the votes of great numbers of women who have never taken part in politics. . . . Churches and women's magazines are most direct contact" to mobilize women to vote for Hoover.[10]

Women were more involved in this presidential campaign than any since the passage of the Nineteenth Amendment eight years earlier. County clerks throughout the country reported the highest rates of women's registration ever. By the first Tuesday in November, some 28 million American women had registered to vote, the largest number of women voters in any country in the world.[11] The Hoover campaign organized many groups to drum up support for its candidate, including a Hoover-Curtis Women's Activities Division.[12] As had been true of women's bureaus within the parties throughout the 1920s, however, the Hoover-Curtis Women's Activities Division was seen as temporary and dissolved in late November 1928.

However short-lived, the group established models that were used by women's groups of both parties in coming decades. It focused on voter education, showing women how to split their ticket so that they could support Hoover for president but still, perhaps, vote for a Democratic House or Senate candidate. The Hoover-Curtis Women's Activities Division believed that grassroots work was very important and prioritized developing programs that functioned on the local level.[13] In this regard especially, Democrats were aiming for the same target.

Beginning in April 1928, before Al Smith was even the nominee, his team was working on the women voter issue. Because of women's perceived support for Prohibition, Smith's team knew it would need to turn out every Democratic woman it could find to help close the gap. To help with that task, they brought in a rising political star. Eleanor Roosevelt had taken on more independent political work in the seven years since her husband Franklin had contracted polio, working both as his surrogate and to satisfy her own interests and abilities. In the spring of 1928 Al Smith asked her to organize women's activities on behalf of his candidacy and the Democratic Party. Roosevelt threw herself into the work. According to her most recent biographer, she worked on the job "every day, from eight in the morning till midnight," between April and the nominating convention in June.[14] She dealt with correspondence, assigned volunteers to committees, organized regional meetings, and hosted visiting Democratic women for tea or luncheon at campaign headquarters in Manhattan. She reported to Belle Moskowitz, Al Smith's publicity director and one of his most trusted advisors.[15]

Roosevelt learned many important lessons in the 1928 campaign that informed the work of the Women's Division that supported her husband. Even though she was the head, other women in the office remembered her as a colleague who worked alongside them, rather than a boss. Moskowitz taught her that women politicians functioned best behind the scenes and allowed men to take credit for women's work so as not to offend those who would be bothered by women doing the work in the first place.[16] While Roosevelt herself did not take that advice once she was First Lady, a friend she drafted into party work in 1928 took the maxim to heart.

Dewson and Roosevelt met earlier in the 1920s, when they were both active in New York City reform circles alongside Frances Perkins and others who would become leading women of the New Deal. In 1928, Roosevelt asked Dewson to go to St. Louis to organize the women of the area on behalf of Smith's campaign.[17] Dewson did the job, and although Smith was not elected, her first foray into partisan politics provided her with lessons she drew on four years later. But like the Hoover-Curtis Women's Activities Division, the Democratic women's activities office closed its doors once the election was over.

Even if the committee had remained operational, Roosevelt would have had to leave her leadership role because she had a new job: First Lady of New York state. FDR was elected governor of New York in 1928, and over the next four years Dewson was a frequent guest at the governor's mansion in Albany, visiting with Eleanor and lobbying Franklin on bills that she believed deserved his support. Usually she was there to talk about legislation regarding wages and working conditions. Her training as a social worker and her leadership position in the National Consumers League, a bastion of middle-class women's activism to improve working conditions since the turn of the twentieth century, led her to focus on those issues. She did not see anything gendered about that activism—she did not believe these were "women's" bills—but rather would visit the governor to talk him into signing a bill that she believed anyone, male or female, should support.[18]

The New York governorship was only a two-year term, and so FDR ran for reelection in 1930. That year, Molly Dewson took a more formal leadership role in his campaign. She worked alongside Eleanor Roosevelt, future New York state legislator Caroline O'Day, and Roosevelt's close friend Nancy Cook to run the state Women's Democratic Committee. Dewson was the lowest-ranking member of this four-person team. While the other three planned strategy and managed the office, Dewson was essentially the corresponding secretary. She answered every letter that came to the office from women who had questions or offers of support. Dewson responded to each one in detail, as she would in 1932, because she believed that "every letter was an opportunity for winning a couple of votes."[19] She also preferred this behind-the-scenes office work to a more visible role. Even at the height of her power, Dewson rarely made speeches and never sought the limelight.

After the success of the 1930 campaign, Frances Perkins summarized the approach that Eleanor Roosevelt, Dewson, and the others had taken. They had, she declared, "done a grass roots organizing job and haven't depended upon big, overall banners and slogans . . . they have known that the real work is done in smaller meetings, in the house to house visitation, and in the organizing."[20] This description fits Dewson's vision for the WD perfectly. The 1930 campaign established Dewson's beliefs about the best way to mobilize women voters. She took all of that campaign's lessons—answering personal letters, focusing on small meetings and door-to-door grassroots work, creating robust organizational structures—to the national level in 1932. The women who followed in her footsteps for the next twenty-five years would repeat every move.

Securing the Democratic Party's nomination for FDR in 1932 was not easy. While pictures of him in a wheelchair were kept out of the press, and the newspapers generally reported that his health was improving, powerful men within the party knew that he had never completely recovered from his battle with polio. His friends and allies, therefore, began working in the summer of 1931 to secure the support of Democrats throughout the country. In this era before primary elections, this kind of personal campaigning was essential. FDR's proponents had to ensure that a majority of Democratic Party convention delegates would support his nomination at the 1932 Democratic National Convention in Chicago through their votes on the convention floor.

Jim Farley, FDR's campaign manager from 1930 to 1940, began this process in the summer of 1931. He spent several months touring the country, ostensibly speaking as a national leader of the Elks fraternal organization. But everywhere he went he met with local political leaders about FDR. That winter, Molly Dewson was sent by Farley and Louis Howe, another close FDR advisor, on a tour of western states, where she met with male and female Democratic leaders. In states where the women's side of things was not well organized, Dewson chastised the male party leaders and urged them to recognize and support hardworking women. This trip, which lasted a full month, was not a speaking tour. Rather, Dewson attended meetings of the party and smaller gatherings, gauging opinions of FDR and drumming up support.[21] She was also making contact with Democratic women in each location, building up a mailing list that grew steadily over the next five years.

She and Farley's trips established a division of labor within the party that served the Women's Division well in the coming years. Farley's job was to keep the male heads of the state and big city political organizations active. Dewson worked more at the local level. She recalled, "It was my job, as I conceived it, to get the women organized, informed on the issues, and 'grasstramping'; to convert to the point of voting those previously too uninterested to go to the polls, or those too uncertain about Roosevelt to make him their candidate."[22] The women who did this "grasstramping" work never reported to Farley. They were the foot soldiers of the WD, and Dewson was their general.

This separation of the Women's Division from the overall leadership structure of the campaign gave Dewson crucial independence. She operated in her own way and did not have to seek approval or consent from Farley or anyone else except FDR himself. This independence proved critical to the Women's Division throughout the Democrats' time in the White House, and future WD leaders fought tooth and nail to maintain it. But establishing it was easy, in part because of Dewson's relationship with the Roosevelts. She was friends with both Eleanor and Franklin. They had complete faith that she would do her best to help Franklin achieve their mutual goal and so saw no need to have men oversee her work. Dewson baked the liberty she gained through her friendships into the structure of the WD, and so it persisted long after she and the Roosevelts left the West Wing. Personal relationships created the WD as a vital part of midcentury campaigns. But the work of WD leaders maintained that status for almost three decades.

The WD's role in creating publicity for campaigns was also set before FDR entered the White House. The Women's Division was part of the campaign staff overseen by Louis Howe, which Dewson dubbed "the brain work."[23] The "brain work" included research, publicity, and correspondence—exactly the kind of work Eleanor Roosevelt's women's activities division had done in 1928. Because the WD was closely related to publicity from the beginning, it maintained a tight hold on the creation of most print material for Democratic presidential campaigns throughout the 1930s and 1940s.

Most of that publicity took the form of rainbow fliers, one of Dewson's most important innovations in presidential campaigning. Rainbow fliers were single-sheet broadsides, each of which addressed a particular issue. The format was first used by Dewson during the 1930 gubernatorial campaign and were an update of women's suffrage fliers she had used in the 1910s.[24] Although they had been successfully used in 1930, it was not guaranteed that the format would be adapted to a national campaign in 1932. But the material prepared by men to mail to undecided voters that year was twelve pages long, and Eleanor Roosevelt, Dewson, and others were appalled. Dewson recalled Roosevelt looking at the men who had written the lengthy pamphlet and declaring, "Women have no time to waste reading through stuff like that."[25]

With titles like *The Forgotten Farmer* and *Your Electric Bill*, rainbow fliers laid out basic facts about the Hoover administration's actions on a particular issue and how a Roosevelt-Garner administration would act differently. The electric bill flier, for example, had two subcolumns; one was headed "Roosevelt Sees the People's Needs," while the other read "Hoover Heeds the Power Trust."[26] There were nine different fliers for the 1932 campaign, and during the heart of the campaign, from Labor Day to the end, roughly 6 million were printed and distributed. The fliers were the primary print media produced by the Democratic Party in 1932, and they were written entirely by women on the Women's Division staff, mostly by Mary Chamberlain.[27]

While one of the fliers was titled *Why Women Want Roosevelt*, none of the others were gendered in any way. In fact, Dewson disagreed with what she saw as Hoover's overt appeals to women voters. Just a few weeks before the election, she told women campaign workers throughout the country that "the Hoover appeal for women's support is so blatant and so cunning that we feel every Democratic woman should answer it." Each woman was instructed to mail five enclosed postcards to "women Republicans whom you know or, better still, to women 'on the fence.'"[28] A postscript at the bottom noted that more rainbow fliers were still available and that women could receive them "in any quantity—large or small" to see them through the last few weeks of the campaign.

The enclosed postcards have not survived, but it is likely that they included talking points similar to those on the *Why Women Want Roosevelt* rainbow flier. That flier shows how material created by Dewson's Women's Division dealt with differences between men's and women's political preferences.

"Roosevelt has known pain and hardship," the flier began. "He can understand the man and woman who is today struggling and he can be trusted to put his heart as well as his mind into the battle." The flier then briefly mentioned the Democratic Party's traditional support of child welfare and "enlightened foreign policies" that would keep children from "the menace of war" and closed by arguing that the "life partnerships" of the Roosevelts and Garners "symbolize all that is finest in American home life."[29] The topics chosen for this flier reflect what Dewson and her staff believed would persuade American women to vote for FDR. And the thing the staff found most important was simply that FDR could empathize with men and women struggling during the Depression. By touching on children, peace, and the candidates' marriages the rest of the flier dealt with more traditional "women's" issues. But it opened with a point that it explicitly stated applied to everyone in the country regardless of sex.

This was the only gendered flier of the nine produced for 1932. The rest were completely gender neutral, talking about issues like tariffs and taxes. Dewson believed that anyone could be persuaded by short, factual presentations that made the case for supporting FDR in clear terms. As she recalled a few years later, "In 1932 Roosevelt made no special appeal to women to support him. He saw no interests that were not their interests and by this simple act he testified to his belief that whatever has to do with the general welfare, be it the problems of children or of economics, are of common concern to men and women."[30] The belief that there were no specific "women's issues" influenced FDR's interactions with the political women who worked with him throughout his presidency.

Despite this philosophy of political sameness, virtually all of the rainbow fliers were mailed to women. Dewson focused on Democratic Party county chairwomen as the main vehicles of distribution for campaign literature.[31] By using county chairwomen as the distribution point for campaign literature, Dewson crafted her most lasting contribution to the Democratic Party. Women all over the country received mail from Dewson, and she was a particularly eager correspondent with women outside of the biggest cities, which were traditional locations of Democratic strength. By tapping Democratic women in small towns and rural counties to distribute campaign literature, Dewson made those women into the grassroots of the Democratic

Party. Dewson formed these women into a connected, national network of Democratic Party workers. There was no analogous group of men working for the party throughout the country. Women, therefore, became the grassroots of the party not only because they had the time as housewives, as later activists and subsequent historians would argue, but because they were deliberately created that way. Molly Dewson believed that women were valuable tools to serve the Democratic Party. She believed that if the party took the time to explain its policies to them and gave them the facts necessary to have political conversations with others, they would work hard for the party. She believed that working through women increased the geographic reach of the party. Because Farley and the other men of FDR's campaign were not connected to truly national networks that reached every corner of the country, Dewson built up her power base by growing this grassroots network.

She grew that network not only by mailing mass-produced postcards and fliers but also through personal correspondence. As she had done in 1928, Dewson spent a huge amount of time answering mail in 1932. She did not give a single speech during that campaign, believing that her time was better spent behind the scenes, building up her team. Every day, the Women's Division staff would gather for lunch at the Biltmore Grill, the restaurant of the Biltmore Hotel in Manhattan where the Roosevelt campaign had its offices. The staff would talk through any problems or events of the day, and any Democratic women who were visiting New York were welcome to join the lunch table. Dewson saw these lunches as another effective way to connect grassroots women to the party, by giving them a glimpse of how the WD worked. As she recalled in her unpublished memoirs, the visiting women "caught the spirit."[32]

In spite of all her work during the campaign, it was unclear what role, if any, Dewson would play in the Roosevelt administration or the Democratic Party after FDR's election. Traditionally the women's divisions closed once a campaign ended and then reorganized themselves again four years later. Dewson herself wasn't sure what she wanted to do. She spent most of the time between the election and the inauguration lobbying for jobs for other women, especially a cabinet position for Frances Perkins. She told Franklin that every political woman she talked to was in favor of Perkins's appointment as secretary of labor. She also reported that leaders of departments of labor in the various states supported Perkins, as did women's groups like the General Federation of Women's Clubs and the American Association of University Women. Dewson concluded the letter by noting, "I am counting on a quiet talk with you sometime before too long about the Democratic women."[33] That quiet talk would determine whether or not Dewson joined the administration's team.

During the interregnum FDR told Dewson that he wanted to build a women's organization within the Democratic Party that was "lasting and effective."[34] But she was not sure that she was the person to do that work. She was fifty-eight years old in 1932 and had been working hard—for women's suffrage, for workplace reform, and for the Democratic Party—for twenty years. Her partner, Polly Porter, wanted them to build a quiet life together in Connecticut as they moved into their later years. Dewson's sister died at the beginning of 1933, a stark reminder of her own mortality even though her health was good. Porter wanted her at home, and Dewson was tempted.

But not too tempted. Throughout the first six months or so of FDR's presidency, Dewson remained in close correspondence with both Franklin and Eleanor and lobbied the president on issues she was passionate about. But she took her time returning to full-time work for the Democratic Party. Jim Farley and the president offered her the directorship of a new, permanent Women's Division in the spring of 1933. She turned them down. Only after she spent the summer in Maine with Porter did she return with a counteroffer: she would take the job on the condition that she could maintain an office in Manhattan as well as one in Washington. She would commute back and forth each week, spending the midweek in the capital and then returning to New York and her home with Porter for long weekends. Her staff in Washington would keep things going in her absence.[35] Farley agreed, and Dewson became the permanent Women's Division director in October 1933.

As she contemplated what the WD directorship looked like outside of campaign season, Dewson focused on two areas, both of which grew out of the philosophy of women's politics she had used so effectively during the 1932 campaign. First she had to refine her understanding of how and why women should be involved in politics. Was it simply because they should care about all the issues, just like men did? That was FDR's rationale. Dewson recalled that the president's practice of "treating us as people without special feminine interests [was] more in tune with his whole program."[36] Roosevelt was not alone in this position during the 1930s. The Equal Rights Amendment and other policies guaranteeing women equality under the law became more popular during the Great Depression. The protective labor laws that Dewson, Perkins, and their Progressive Era peers had spent years writing and passing had done little to cushion the blow of the Great Depression for women, and some people were willing to consider trying something else like the ERA. Getting rid of protective labor laws, which often dictated things like women's total hours of work per week or the times of day they could work, seemed like a logical response to the Depression crisis to many.[37] And passing the ERA would, in the minds of its supporters, guarantee women equal status in society.

Dewson disagreed. Like many other supporters of protective labor laws, she supported legal equality for women. But she believed that the Equal Rights Amendment was not the best way to achieve that goal. Dewson continued to reject the ERA because she believed that women *were* fundamentally different from men. Rather than drawing a hard line between "equality" and "difference," however, Dewson wanted a truly separate but equal structure within the party. Women would have their own base, where they could do things their way. They would not have to justify their actions to men or wait to get men to agree. They would simply, as women, make plans to reach other women and put them to work for the Democratic Party.[38] This vision of the WD—a separate base of power for women that would, ideally, give them an equal voice within the party—remained the model in the White House for almost thirty years.

Dewson was not the only person in the West Wing or Democratic Party leadership who favored such a separate arrangement. Jim Farley was supportive of a permanent Women's Division, partially because it enabled him to minimize his own work for and with Democratic Party women. This rationale would be repeated by other DNC leaders over the years. But there were also more positive reasons for adopting the structure. Eleanor Roosevelt, coming from the same educational and political background as Dewson, was a firm believer in separate spaces for women. She organized her first women-only press conference for female reporters just days after FDR's inauguration and held roughly 350 press conferences for women reporters only throughout her time in the White House.[39] Dewson and Roosevelt believed that separate women's spaces worked and dedicated themselves to making those spaces as robust and effective as possible.

As Dewson proved throughout FDR's first term, having a permanent framework for women's work on behalf of the party made women better, more effective party workers. A few months after she took on the directorship full time, Dewson began her most ambitious project. At one of the women-only press conferences in January 1934, Dewson announced a program called the Reporter Plan.[40] The Reporter Plan asked women throughout the country to serve as sources of knowledge about the New Deal's impact in their communities. Each reporter was assigned a specific New Deal agency and then tasked with learning everything she could about the program's goals and its implementation in her community. A summary of the program declared, "The Reporters do not need to be leaders or speakers or organizers, but just plain citizens who will say in this crisis 'I want to understand thoroughly at least one of the many things the Government is trying to do and to keep continuously in touch with this particular agency.' If a Reporter has the ability to tell her neighbors about it over the teacups or on her feet so much the better, but at least she herself will be informed and not 'leaving everything to Roosevelt.'"[41]

This summary encouraged reporters to keep clippings about agencies "in a ten cent notebook" so that they had the facts and figures at their fingertips when they were in conversation with their neighbors. "Who can be an authority," the summary asked, "without accessible facts, and who can carry every statistic in her head?"[42]

The emphasis on facts creating authority was not only a critical part of the Reporter Plan but also one of Dewson's biggest contributions to the developing political culture of the middle decades of the century. Many political historians tie the rise of facts and data as a major political force to the World War II era and the increasing complexity of technical knowledge that politicians needed. But through the Reporter Plan, Dewson was building this type of expertise at the local level among Democratic women. The League of Women Voters was involved in a similar project. The structure devised when the National American Women's Suffrage Association reorganized itself into the LWV after the Nineteenth Amendment's ratification required careful factual study of an issue and a consensus among group members before any action could be taken.[43] Molly Dewson always believed that "education and issues" were women's main interest in government, as opposed to "patronage and power" that attracted men to the political arena.[44] And many other women in politics and civic organizations agreed. While scholars looking at male politicians have argued for a new political style growing out of World War II, those male politicians were likely also influenced by the political culture women had formulated since the passage of the Nineteenth Amendment.[45] Rather than creating something new out of whole cloth to deal with the technical complexities of the postwar world, men (perhaps subconsciously) reached for the style that the women around them had been using effectively for twenty years and adapted it into the political culture of Congress and the White House as well.

The Reporter Plan was well received from the beginning. Dewson informed Eleanor Roosevelt days after the plan's launch that "I am getting some awfully nice notices of my Reporter Plan" and particularly mentioned a supportive article in the *Boston Globe*.[46] Dewson understood the plan to be a critical piece of the Democratic Party's success, especially among women. She believed that women needed to be actively engaged in the party at all times and not simply asked for their vote every two or four years. One of her maxims of politics was that elections were won between campaigns. In a letter to Louis Howe, she explained that working constantly for the party not only yielded better results but did so at a lower cost. "Every dollar spent NOW in developing enthusiastic women workers down to the grass roots," she told Howe, "will be more effective than 25 times as much just before the election."[47] Dewson focused on women because she believed they were the party's best weapon. "I told Mr. Farley," she recalled, "that I have no particular feminist leanings but I am trying to build up the party."[48] The party was strongest, Dewson believed, with an active national network of women.

As the Reporter Plan developed, local women began requesting an easier way to get information than making their own clipping files. Early in 1935, Dewson and her staff began producing a monthly magazine, the *Democratic Digest*, which provided reports on every agency's actions in Washington.[49] The magazine was a smash hit. On its first anniversary FDR noted that "the *Digest* has proved its usefulness abundantly during its first year. It has given valiant and faithful support to the administration, support which I am happy to acknowledge at this time."[50] A Democratic man from Washington state suggested working to increase male subscribers and declared that the *Digest* "should be in every home that supported the New Deal and unless those living in the homes that opposed President Roosevelt are entirely unreasonable, they could jolly well benefit by becoming subscribers."[51]

Armed with the *Democratic Digest*'s facts and figures, the Reporter Plan grew by leaps and bounds. By the eve of the 1936 campaign, there were 15,000 women signed up with the program.[52] A clear structure emerged that developed leadership among grassroots women at every point of the system. Each New Deal agency was assigned several "junior reporters" in each city. Those junior reporters divided the research—one would call heads of local agencies to see what they were doing, another would subscribe to the *Digest* to know what was going on at the federal level, and so on. The junior reporters then gave their material to a senior reporter for each agency, who synthesized all their material. The senior reporters then held "round tables," open public meetings where they presented the work of each New Deal agency to the community and connected it to what the Roosevelt administration was doing in Washington. The roundtables were open to "all interested women in the precinct." If the Democratic women's group was small in a particular area, they did away with the "senior/junior" distinction and simply assigned one woman to each agency.[53]

All the reporters (or senior reporters, in large communities) reported to their precinct vice-chair. In the structure Dewson developed, the precinct vice-chair was the critical piece. She was the conduit between the DNC and her community. One woman who served in that role, Mrs. John P. Kirby of Williamsport, Pennsylvania, described it eloquently:

> The Precinct Vice-Chairwoman or Committeewoman, as a direct connecting link between county organization and the voters is, in many respects, the most important one in our political system. As the party salesman, she brings to the voter knowledge of party principles, advantages of voting for the party's endorsed candidates, and, by frequent and personal contact, continually strives to increase registrations and awaken the interest of the regular and the new voter in her precinct. . . . The success of the party as a whole depends almost entirely

upon the individual thoroughness with which these party salesmen in the field perform their work.[54]

By the end of 1935, Molly Dewson and her colleagues at the WD had made women feel empowered and connected them into an effective grassroots network for the party.

Dewson used the Reporter Plan structure to build up the party with women by embedding education and issues—which she believed were women's strengths—at the center of women's partisan work. In doing so, it made women the party's most effective workers, and other DNC officials took notice. By the spring of 1935 other groups within the DNC were trying to incorporate or duplicate the Reporter Plan's success. In a letter to the president, Dewson pushed back on efforts to incorporate the Young Democrats into the Reporter program. She was proud of the success of the WD and did not want anyone interfering in the systems she had developed. "I still believe the Women's Division is on the most fertile ground for winning independent, stay-at-home, and possibly Republican voters," she wrote to FDR. "Moreover, the plans I have, do not in any way cross with the plans for the Young Democrats. I hope, Honored Chief, that this seems sensible to you."[55] As FDR's reelection campaign plans took shape in the early months of 1936, the WD was at the heart of the action.

II

"Women Have Indeed Come of Age Politically"

THE DEMOCRATIC WOMEN'S DIVISION, 1936–1940

One woman brought into Democratic Party work during FDR's first term was Harriet Elliott, a professor of political science and dean of students at the Women's College of North Carolina (now the University of North Carolina–Greensboro).[1] In 1935 Molly Dewson recruited her to join the Women's Division as one of its first national speakers, traveling the country to give speeches drumming up support for the New Deal.[2] Elliott served in that role full time for the first half of 1935, then returned to her faculty position while remaining engaged in Democratic Party politics. In 1940 Elliott returned to the DNC and summarized the changes regarding women in politics that had occurred over the course of the 1930s: "Under President Roosevelt women have indeed come of age politically. No longer are they pleasantly pampered in election year and then forgotten until another election year rolls around. Today their recognition is positive and permanent, for President Roosevelt not only talks equal opportunity but makes it a reality as well." Elliott further declared that "we women do not believe that the voter's interests and responsibilities can be divided into masculine and feminine areas. Not at all." But toward the end of the speech, she also noted several policy areas in which women took a particular interest: "youth-home-peace. Or peace-youth-home. Or however you list them. Much of the time these three walk abreast."[3]

Elliott eloquently articulated the WD's philosophy and approach. WD activists occupied a halfway point in feminist politics, neither fully espousing women's difference nor articulating a belief that no such difference existed. Both Dewson and her successor, Dorothy McAllister, tended more in the latter direction. Very little of the material produced by the WD from 1936 through the end of 1940 was explicitly gendered. They—and President Roosevelt—frequently declared that one of the hallmarks of women's politics in the 1930s was their full inclusion as equal citizens, as Elliott did in this speech. But they did believe that there were certain issues—the trio of peace, children, and "the home" mentioned by Elliott—which spoke to women in specific ways. This belief appears to have been less ideological and more of a simple reflection of most women's lives. In the 1930s the majority of American women were wives and mothers. That was becoming less true as the Depression dragged on, but it was still how most Americans thought about women's role in society. Pairing these kinds of statements, then, is not as contradictory as it seems. And for many politically active women, it was liberating. They could speak about and be active on everything, including home and family issues, without feeling pigeonholed into only those topics. They had the support of the president in approaching politics in this way. Throughout the second half of the 1930s, FDR praised women's efforts to become active, equal workers for the Democratic Party and celebrated them as some of the people most responsible for its success.

Everything Molly Dewson had done during FDR's first term, from the success of the rainbow fliers in 1932 to the establishment of the Reporter Plan and the *Democratic Digest*, paid off as the 1936 campaign began to heat up. That January the campaign's "high command," as Dewson called the president, Jim Farley (the DNC chairman), and Louis Howe (FDR's closest personal advisor) had agreed that the rainbow fliers should be the "bulk of the literature issued in the campaign." Dewson believed they were relied on so heavily both because of "the reception given the fliers in the 1932 campaign" and because "the country is hungry for these short, well-phrased, factual statements."[4]

With this decision made early on, Dewson maintained control over much of the campaign. In midsummer, as campaigning efforts expanded, she informed DNC publicity head Charlie Michelson that the WD would not pay the printing bill when men wanted direct shipments of the fliers.[5] Those costs would be borne by Michelson's department; the WD did not provide its material for free. She also encouraged Michelson to establish a system in which an individual man (such as a state or county chairman) could order no more than five hundred sets of fliers at once, then reorder as necessary. Such a system ensured that all the fliers were actually used, according to Dewson, and avoided the party paying for fliers that were not distributed. "If you did this," Dewson told Michelson, "I believe that conceivably eight to ten million sets could be used to great advantage" by the men.[6] The rainbow fliers, all written and designed by women on the WD staff, made up 90 percent of all the print media distributed by the Democratic Party to support FDR's reelection. There were fourteen different titles, covering tariffs, agricultural policy, conservation, and other topics.[7] More than 80 million of them were mailed throughout the country during the summer and fall of 1936.[8]

While men asked for and used the fliers, women remained their primary distributors. They were tasked with getting fliers in front of every single voter. The Women's Division kept lists of creative methods that women came up with to spread the fliers throughout their communities. A woman in Lexington, Kentucky, reported that "I had eyelets and a cord put through them and hung them in the lunch room of the biggest tobacco factory" in the town.[9] An Iowa woman informed WD headquarters that it was "not practical, or at least tactful," to go door-to-door in small towns and rural areas of her state, so she used the same eyelet-and-cord system to hang the fliers in store windows in downtown Williamsburg, Iowa.[10] And the vice president of the Los Angeles Young Democratic Club, Eunice Schmidt, praised the fliers and their format: "Your Rainbow Fliers were truly a great success. They tell all the story we need to know in brief, concise, and intriguing form. Put all available money into them, give us lots of them, and *spare us the dissertations*."[11] This praise for the fliers' brevity echoed Eleanor Roosevelt's statement four years earlier that, when it came to campaign literature, shorter was best.

Not only did the WD account for almost all of the campaign's print literature, Dewson and her right-hand woman Carolyn Wolfe also innovated a new way to use the WD structure to raise money.[12] Starting at the end of 1935, readers of the *Democratic Digest* were encouraged to buy donkey banks, small donkey-shaped piggy banks. The goal was to get each donkey bank owner to deposit a nickel a week, then turn the money into their county party office at monthly "Donkey Bank roundups" that also served as monthly meetings. The money stayed at the county level, funding the travel of women speakers and office costs like telephone bills.[13] By the beginning of 1936 twenty thousand donkey banks had been distributed.[14] An additional thirty-seven thousand were shipped throughout the spring. Since the money stayed local, the banks made each county's women self-sufficient. After the donkey bank plan was fully established, "county leaders either paid for their own gasoline or stayed home."[15] As they self-funded grassroots initiatives and created almost all the campaign literature, the Women's Division and its local members were the vital core of FDR's reelection campaign in 1936.

In 1936 Dewson also expanded the WD's services by setting up a Speakers' Bureau. She hired Gladys Tillett to run the bureau from the party convention in July till the end of the campaign, matching women trained by the bureau with requests for speakers all over the country. Tillett had been a student of Harriet Elliott's at the Women's College, and it is likely that Elliott first suggested her to Dewson. In 1936 Tillett was the vice-chairman of the North Carolina state Democratic Party.[16] She was also the North Carolina director of the Reporter Plan.[17] Running the Speakers' Bureau in 1936 was her first work in the national party office; she served in that role again in 1940 and then became WD director at the beginning of 1941. In 1936, her main job was to secure speakers in every state and provide them with facts for their speeches. Within a week of moving to New York and starting the job, Tillett had sent letters to each state's vice-chairmen, asking for the names of at least "your five best woman speakers" so that they could be added to the national files. Those women registered with Tillett, so she could contact them when she got requests for speeches in their area, and also received a speakers' kit, which contained a full run of rainbow fliers and additional materials. "These women," Tillett informed state leaders "will have a great opportunity to serve the Democratic Party. They will have, too, a great responsibility for building up the Democratic Party and creating a tidal wave of enthusiasm for the administration."[18]

Some of the women Tillett recruited were African American, in one of the only documented places where Black women worked within the WD structure in the 1930s. Just days before the election, Mamie Geraldine Bledsoe, a member of the Michigan division of the National Negro Democratic Campaign Committee, thanked Tillett for sending Elizabeth Ross Haynes, an African American woman, to speak in the state. Haynes's day in Michigan included meetings in the Detroit suburbs, a tea with professional women, and an evening mass meeting attended by "seven or eight thousand" Black Michiganders. Bledsoe concluded, "The Negro women of the country are pleased to see significant Negro women like Mrs. Haynes in the national set-up. We are all glad to have even a small part in molding a fuller life for the masses of this country."[19] Although there is no clear mention in the archives, it is highly likely that African American women around the country were distributing rainbow fliers and knocking on doors to get out the vote for FDR. Considering the massive movement of African American voters to Roosevelt and the Democrats in 1936—in Chicago, to give one example, the Black vote for Roosevelt increased 132 percent over 1932—it could hardly have been otherwise.[20]

In addition to creating the Speakers' Bureau, Dewson gave speeches in 1936 for the first time in her career. Because the WD was the center of the campaign, she could no longer stay completely behind the scenes. She recorded five radio speeches, all of which highlighted her belief that women should consider a broad range of issues when voting. There were speeches on farm policy, social security, "relief" programs like the Works Progress Administration, and the federal home loan program.[21] But the speeches all discussed women in a uniform way: as wives. Early in the agriculture speech, for example, Dewson said that "I want to talk to you today about some of the fine things the present Administration has done for the farm woman." The next sentence began, "Every wife should be."[22] Using "woman" and "wife" as interchangeable terms was not new in 1936, although WD material during the New Deal did not discuss women as wives very often. But such language showed up in speeches in particular, when Dewson and other WD speakers were addressing a mixed audience of men and women and trying to appeal to everyone. In those circumstances, leaning into traditional gender roles—roles that also reflected the majority of American women's lives at the time—helped win over undecided voters.

When she was speaking directly to her troops, Dewson used no such language. And she made sure that grassroots party women knew just how central they were to the overall campaign and to FDR's success. In the spring of 1936, Dewson and Carolyn Wolfe put together a sixteen-page pamphlet titled *Dedicated to Mrs. County Leader*. The document outlined all the ways women worked for the campaign to reelect FDR, declaring that, "You, Mrs. County Leader, are the keystone in the arch of Democratic victory. If you are inactive or flying around in circles, your county will be the stone that lets the arch collapse."[23] Through bold graphics, varying fonts, and a lot of exclamation marks, the pamphlet stated that the work of women at the county level was critical to Roosevelt's reelection. Finding volunteers, getting new voters registered and to the polls, door-to-door "visiting" to persuade undecided voters, and organizing listening parties to hear radio speeches by the president were all discussed. The rainbow fliers were also highlighted; a full list of titles was included in the pamphlet, and women were encouraged to order them. Under a drawing of two women fishing from opposite sides of a stream—one labeled "Born Democrat land" and the other "Rock Ribbed Republican land"—the pamphlet stated, "From the twenty percent of independent voters must come the extra votes necessary for any party to win. Your bait is our record!"[24] The pamphlet empowered women to make their own plans and choices and insisted that they do so. Next to a drawing of a woman crank-starting an old-fashioned car the text read, "Be a self-cranker! For the Democratic Party has no automatic starter. Don't wait for permission from any high up chiefs to go out and WIN VOTES. We can't expect—and we don't deserve—VICTORY if you and the other Mrs. County Leaders wait to be told."[25]

Dewson was well known for not accepting obligations to husbands and children as an excuse for not working for the party. At the end of the *Mrs. County Leader* pamphlet, she declared, "After All—Mrs. County Leader, your county is your responsibility and there are no alibis. If John has lost his job or Mary has the measles or you have broken your leg, you can resign and the sooner the better. . . . If you carry your county, HOORAY! Then you can rest happy and wear the crown everyone wears who sees her duty and does it."[26] Her WD system was built on strong leadership spread throughout the country. Without it, the whole WD and the influence it garnered for women within campaigns might collapse. And so the women had to show up and work hard.

Dewson was just as firm with the women who worked with her in the national WD office. She had prevailed on Carolyn Wolfe to come work for the WD in spite of Wolfe's initial refusal due to her husband and five children at home in Utah. Those reasons "didn't seem to bother her [Dewson] so much," Wolfe recalled.[27] Nearly a decade later Dewson had mellowed a bit in these opinions, but not very much. In 1944 she told Gladys Tillett, "I always feel a little shame-faced when I see Jim Wolfe or Tom McAllister or your Charlie, [for] luring their wives from the fireside." But not too shamefaced. The rest of the letter dealt with Dewson's disappointment about Henry Wallace being dropped as vice president, how Tillett should deal with ERA advocate and influential Democrat Emma Guffey Miller, and other business of politics.[28] Even professional excuses were unacceptable. She pushed Harriet Elliott into coming to work for the WD in 1935 when Elliott initially declined due to her responsibilities at the Women's College.[29] If Molly Dewson wanted you, in other words, she got you. And she wanted every single woman in the WD structure, from the national office to a rural county chairwoman, to have that same level of commitment.

Dewson's high expectations stemmed from her overarching goal: to make women a fully equal part of American politics and the Democratic Party. She also achieved that goal in 1936 by creating a Women's Committee for Suggestions on the Democratic Platform. That spring Dewson rounded up a group of fourteen nationally prominent women who would be "recognized as representing women's point of view."[30] The women spent several months corresponding with each other and hearing from organizations that wanted their issues represented. The National Women's Trade Union League and the National Council for the Prevention of War, for example, sent letters to the main Platform Committee, which were routed to the Women's Division for consideration by the Women's Committee.[31]

The fourteen women met in late June to draft a set of recommendations. Their final list recommended eight planks, including statements about child labor, peace, employment discrimination against women, and housing.[32] The list was a fairly predictable statement of women's politics in the 1930s; the peace and child labor sections, topics women had been lobbying about for decades, were by far the longest. But the preamble again illustrated the blend of ideas about women's difference from and sameness to men and how that was reflected in politics. The first two paragraphs read, "During the past three years women have widened their interests from isolated individual laws to broader social and economic trends and are looking at America as a whole. They have come to realize that human welfare is inseparably integrated with economic conditions. Possessed of a broader social outlook, aware of the broader responsibility of the Federal Government—women commend this administration for taking the lead in solving these modern human problems."[33] Women were interested in everything now, this document declared.

They were not restricted to "women's issues" any longer, although those issues were still present.

Very few of the recommendations of the committee made it into the 1936 platform, and none were incorporated in exactly the form women suggested, a reflection of the long way women had to go before being seen as true equals by men in the party. But Molly Dewson was still pleased: "The Democratic Women's Committee for Suggestions on the platform were delighted because the platform did not mention women even once," she told a friend. "We are now persons."[34] Not mentioning women even once meant that the platform did not include the committee's plank opposing employment discrimination against women, particularly married women. Such discrimination had become a major problem as the Great Depression continued to rage.[35] The Democratic Party did not endorse the most clearly feminist recommendation of its women's platform committee, the one that would have made the most immediate tangible difference in women's lives. But Dewson focused instead on what she believed was a sign of fuller power within the party. She chose to interpret the lack of mention of women not as a failure to act on feminist policy but as a triumph of women's equality.

FDR won an overwhelming victory in 1936, securing nearly 61 percent of the popular vote and all but two states in the Electoral College. It was the most lopsided Electoral College tally since the uncontested election of 1820.[36] Never one to rest on her laurels, Molly Dewson contacted every county leader in February 1937, just a month after FDR's second inauguration. The cover letter read simply, "We are proud of the effective work the women did in the campaign. We are determined to do even better in 1938 and 1940."[37] Dewson outlined a plan in which all the WD structures and programs of the previous three years—the *Digest*, the Reporter Plan, the donkey banks, the Speakers' Bureau, the "Democratic Visitors" program of door-to-door canvassing—became permanent.[38] A flow chart illustrated leadership roles for nearly twenty women at the state level, and close to thirty in each county.[39]

But Dewson no longer wanted to be the woman in charge. She was in her sixties, had dedicated more than five years to getting her friend Franklin Roosevelt elected and reelected, and was ready to retire.[40] She chose as her successor Dorothy McAllister, who had been the head of the Reporter Plan in Michigan. By mid-April 1937, McAllister was working in the DNC offices in Washington; one of Dewson's last official tasks was asking FDR to help McAllister's husband get a federal job so that the couple could "afford to live in Washington."[41]

Apparently the efforts to get Tom McAllister a job in D.C. were unsuccessful. Later in 1937, Tom, a judge, ran for and was elected to the Michigan Supreme Court.[42] For the next three years, the family lived apart, and daughters Mary and Claire were with their mother in the Washington suburb of Alexandria, Virginia. In the 1940 census, Dorothy is listed as the head of household in Alexandria, living with her daughters, who were then fourteen and ten. When the family was still together in Michigan, the 1930 census showed a live-in domestic worker as part of the McAllister household. It is probable that Dorothy had paid domestic workers who were at the house when her daughters got home from school and who cooked and cleaned for her. But no domestic worker lived in. So it was likely McAllister who got Mary and Claire up every morning, made their breakfast, and got them out the door to school before heading across the Potomac to run a crucial piece of the campaigns to reelect a Democratic Congress in 1938 and get a third term for FDR two years later.

McAllister immediately began working to implement the plan Dewson had outlined to keep all facets of the WD operational at the local level on a permanent basis. After six months on the job, she reported that more than half of the states still had a state-level director for the reporter program, three-quarters had a state radio director, and nearly all had a state-level coordinator for the *Digest*. Through McAllister's first year the WD remained the main source of print material for the entire party. The division shipped nearly 200,000 pieces of material to male Democrats nationwide regarding FDR's controversial court-packing plan, and that was just a portion of the "assistance to the men's division" provided by the WD.[43]

McAllister emphasized throughout the 1938 campaign that the WD was essential to Democratic victory and that Democratic victory was vital to continuing to fight the Great Depression. The August 1938 issue of the *Digest* included an article by her titled "What Women Can Do for Their Party," which the WD also sent to grassroots activists as a single-page flier. McAllister declared that women were needed to help the Democratic Party fulfill its goals of "protection of the family and the home, aid to those overtaken by disaster, and establishment of a democracy of opportunity for all the people." To achieve those goals, women had to take the facts to the voters. Of the five steps McAllister outlined for women party activists, all but one focused on getting the facts out. Women were encouraged to use rainbow fliers, the *Digest*, and study clubs to "spread the facts" about the New Deal.[44] That emphasis on spreading facts became a hallmark of McAllister's time as head of the WD.

Roosevelt and McAllister's working relationship provides a valuable window into FDR's role in campaigning while he was president. Once his friend Molly Dewson was no longer in charge at the WD, it would have been easy for the president to disengage from the group's activities. Instead, the opposite seems to have happened, and he regularly chimed in on WD plans. In August 1938, FDR signed off on McAllister's plan to use rainbow fliers for the midterm campaign, declaring that "they have proved their value. Also, I hope the Women's Division will send speakers to the key states." He closed the letter, "I hope to see you soon."[45]

A year later, as preliminary plans were being made for FDR's unprecedented third campaign, McAllister sent him drafts of several new fliers to be used in 1940. He enthusiastically signed off on the material: "Dear Dorothy, I like the new fliers very much. Go to it!" At the bottom, he added a postscript: "I suggest getting into each 'flier' something like this: 'What substitute or improvement do the Republicans in your county or state, or your Congressmen or your Senators offer? Ask them questions. Pin them down!"[46] This letter is revealing in several ways. After two years of working together, McAllister has transitioned from "Dear Mrs. McAllister" to "Dear Dorothy." Also, FDR's letter was sent from Hyde Park. He was working on WD matters while he was away from Washington and, presumably, supposed to be relaxing at least a bit. It was in that downtime that he chose to really engage and suggest text for the fliers—the only record I found of him ever doing so—because he believed they were important.

FDR was always deeply convinced that the WD's work was important to both the Democratic Party and American democracy, and he told McAllister so repeatedly. Roosevelt was especially effusive with his praise in April 1938:

> The New Deal has given abundant evidence of its confidence in the leadership and ability of women. The women in their turn, have, by loyalty and

> ability, understanding and discernment, justified fully the expectations of the Administration. They are a factor in our family, social, economic, and political life, and an instrumentality for peace whose influence can in many instances have the determining power.
>
> Government can be no more than the collective wisdom of its citizens and I welcome these regional conferences. They will afford a forum through which the Women's Division can, by encouraging discussion and common counsel, increase the collective wisdom which we all seek and which we must attain in order to make Government representative and effective.[47]

This letter summarizes FDR's belief about women in politics, and his was very much an equality vision. Women should be involved in politics, according to the president, because they were citizens. And as citizens, their voices were essential to representative democracy. More than a year later, he hit a similar note, responding to a St. Louis editorial column that McAllister sent him by saying "the women of today are really interested in the specific programs of the government, and this interest is swiftly supplanting the old-time torch-light parades and Fourth of July style speeches."[48]

In these discussions of the collective wisdom of citizens, of the need to talk about concrete programs rather than the "old-time" partisanship of earlier eras, FDR was articulating what scholar Sid Milkis has identified as one of his central goals during his second term: making the Democratic Party a party with programmatic (liberal) consistency rather than one simply tied together by partisan history. Milkis cites the court-packing plan and an executive reorganization bill, both of which were sent to Congress in the summer of 1937, as the main expressions of this goal.[49] Roosevelt's correspondence with McAllister shows that he saw the WD as another tool that he could use to turn the Democratic Party into a liberal party that supported the totality of the New Deal. The WD was more focused on the substance of the Democratic Party than many of the male structures like big-city machines that Jim Farley and the other male party leaders worked through, and which FDR had criticized early in his career.[50] Every part of the WD's structure—from the reporter plan organized around specific agencies to the rainbow fliers—oriented the WD toward policy and its effects. According to the WD, people should vote for the Democratic Party because of its actions, not because of its name and their attachment to that name and history.

FDR was also drawn to the WD because it reflected his preferred style of politics. Historian Jeremi Suri has described FDR as "a joiner, an organizer, and a community builder."[51] Those traits were at the core of the WD's structure and mission. Every piece of the rather elaborate organization was designed to get women into the Democratic Party, get them organized, and put them to work. Women's political power within the Democratic Party, then, was dependent on a mixture of many different factors. The Roosevelts' friendship with Molly Dewson, their feminist belief in the value of women as political actors being equal to that of men, and the need to have an efficient way to spread the gospel of the New Deal to every corner of the country all contributed to the powerful position that the WD held in the late 1930s. The WD's perfect fit with Roosevelt's goals and political personality may be one reason why he became so engaged when Dorothy McAllister took over. While she had run state-level organizations in Michigan with aplomb, and Dewson thought she was the right woman for the job, FDR needed to make sure. If the WD had faltered as Dewson stepped back, it would have been a serious problem for how Roosevelt envisioned the party. McAllister did not let him down.

It was a good thing McAllister was up to the task, because in the middle of her tenure, global events shifted Roosevelt's attention and altered his rhetoric about women. In 1939 FDR had to back out of a promise to speak as part of the WD's annual radio fundraiser, Democratic Women's Day. The event was held in late September, and the outbreak of World War II in Europe forced the president to back out. He apologized to McAllister, stating, "A week ago I might consistently have spoken words addressed primarily to our Democratic women." But now, the war,

> render[s] it imperative that every utterance of mine in these days of tension be addressed to all of our citizens, regardless of sex, age, or political affiliation.... One essential duty which lies within the power and influence of our American women is maintenance of the American home.... We must protect [our children] from every evil force which would shake their faith in our fundamental institutions of democracy.... Although our women, as homemakers, have a

> special task, the present duty of all of us—men, women, and children—is to keep this nation safe and to throw all of our weight into the cause of peace.[52]

This is an important letter, both for illuminating Roosevelt's concerns as World War II began and for highlighting the ways in which women's traditional roles became more emphasized in his rhetoric as he moved toward becoming a wartime president. This letter hints at the changes within most of the political communication targeting women once the United States entered the war in late 1941.

As foreign policy began to consume the president's thoughts and days, Dorothy McAllister was determined to keep the WD working smoothly on his behalf. Her greatest strength as a politician lay in her ability to discreetly avoid problems without angering the people she was trying to sidestep. This habit, which she demonstrated most clearly in her interactions around the ERA and the 1940 Democratic Party platform, shows her focus on achieving the task at hand and not being distracted by issues that could bog her down. In her first two years as WD head, the job had been to keep women engaged with the party, keep growing the WD structure, and maintain the forward momentum that the division had been building throughout the 1930s. In 1940 she had to turn that momentum to achieve something almost unthinkable: electing a president for a third term.

While FDR was somewhat less engaged in the day-to-day of the 1940 campaign than he had been four years earlier, Dorothy McAllister knew exactly what to do. She used the established, successful programs that the WD had developed and added new components. This approach proved highly effective. First on McAllister's agenda was ensuring that the Reporter Plan was still going strong. Historians who have written about the Reporter Plan have depicted it as a program run by Dewson and targeted at the New Deal. The implication is that it stopped when Dewson left. In fact, it was a point of emphasis for McAllister, who had led the Michigan Reporter Plan before joining the WD staff. Under her leadership the national Reporter Plan covered eleven different areas of study, and she encouraged reporters to speak to nonpartisan women's groups and local media in addition to sending material back to Washington.[53] In the fall of 1939 she informed Reporter Plan county leaders that her goal was to have a Reporter Plan active in "every one of our 3,074 counties" by the end of the year. Those reporters were vital in McAllister's organization of the WD because they were tasked with not only gathering data on how government programs were working in their area but also communicating that information to the general public. McAllister instructed all county leaders to organize public meetings, "at which there will be an opportunity for the exchange of opinion between the people of the cities and the rural districts, and for the presentation of the points of view of youth, the wage-earners, the employer, and the businessman. In this way," McAllister concluded, "we can spread a wider understanding of the New Deal."[54]

As always, the reporters needed facts about the national programs they were investigating at the local level, and so the rainbow fliers were revived once again. Seventeen different fliers—the most ever—were produced for the campaign, touching on some of the same topics as previous fliers, such as agriculture, trade policy, youth, and conservation work. But the context of 1940 brought new issues to the forefront. Four of the seventeen fliers dealt with foreign policy or national defense. And, since Roosevelt was seeking an unprecedented third term, one flier dealt with that issue specifically.[55]

The third-term flier—titled *That Third-Term Bugaboo*—and a flier on the Tennessee Valley Authority (TVA) titled *Life Lines vs. Spite Lines* offer fascinating evidence of just how central women's work was to the campaign. For both of those fliers, handwritten drafts have been preserved along with the printed fliers. While freelance journalist Bess Furman assisted McAllister with several of the fliers, the draft of *That Third-Term Bugaboo* is in McAllister's handwriting. She conceptualized a flier of historical quotes about presidents seeking third terms, including some from Republicans who had pushed Calvin Coolidge to run a third time just twelve years earlier. As with the TVA flier, the handwritten draft and the final, printed flier are almost identical.[56] McAllister and Furman crafted the talking points that were used to defuse what could have become the biggest issue of FDR's campaign.[57]

The fliers were important, but McAllister also wanted Democratic women to meet with one another in order to share ideas and build the national operation. That goal led her to organize a series of regional conferences designed to bring women together from several states. These conferences gave Democratic women a chance to network on the regional level and provided an opportunity to inform the public about Democratic Party policies. The conferences were, "*Open to all women interested in political questions.* There are Round Tables on social, economic, and political issues and on the 6-point program for Democratic women. . . . Introductions are *brief*; speakers present facts relating to the policies and programs of the Democratic Party, or take part in discussion summarizing previous effective work in party organization."[58] McAllister and her staff saw these conferences as yet another way to bring women into the party as well as connecting committed party activists. In addition to regional meetings, McAllister also organized a national gathering, an idea that had originally been proposed by Carolyn Wolfe for the 1936 campaign. In this three-day meeting of party women in Washington, the Institute of Government intended to give those "on the firing line in the campaign an opportunity to secure the information they will need to answer the propaganda of our opponents and to win votes for our party."[59] Attendees heard from multiple cabinet secretaries, the First Lady, and Democratic Party officials including Chairman Jim Farley. The Institutes of Government—more often called Schools of Government—became a fixture of women's politics for the next two decades, repeated by McAllister's successors on the Democratic side and copied by Republican women.

McAllister also revived the Speakers' Bureau for the 1940 campaign. Each state leader was instructed to appoint a state Speakers' Bureau director by the end of 1939. Those directors were responsible for recruiting speakers not only from women involved in party politics but also from community leaders who were not party activists but who "are for the New Deal." The League of Women Voters, the AAUW, and the General Federation of Women's Clubs were all suggested as good sources for speakers.[60] Speaker recruitment was an area where the ties between women's civic groups and party politics remained tight throughout the middle decades of the century. McAllister believed that having a team of speakers ready to go as the campaign began would help get the facts out to voters as FDR sought his third term.

The slogan of the WD's 1940 work, "Fortify for '40 with Facts," shows how vital McAllister believed that work was. As the campaign kicked into gear, she reminded her troops that "it is our duty from now until election day to use the organization we have been building during recent years to see that every voter knows the record of accomplishment in the nation of seven years of Democratic leadership."[61] In addition to speakers, meetings, and fliers there were newly available films and slide strips women could order. Democratic women were also, for the first time, told to write into their local newspapers "in answer to misleading editorials or news articles which distort the facts."[62] The emphasis on letters to the editor came straight from the president. McAllister had sent him a draft of the 1940 WD plans, which included letters to the editor as one of the new aspects of WD work. FDR replied, "I think your program for the Women's Division is excellent, and I can only suggest that you pay a lot of attention to number three—letters to the editor, preferably from home owners, wage earners, farm women, and others, to answer misstatements of fact and to tell how they have benefited from New Deal programs. . . . I think your rainbow fliers are fine but I hope you will get our far more than one million of each in the long run."[63] FDR continued to take a particular interest in the fliers. He had asked Jim Farley at the beginning of the year to hold off distributing them until at least May 1, but in early April, he changed his mind and asked Farley to give the WD the "green light" to begin distribution. "They have some excellent material," the president declared, and the fliers should be "sent out right away without any more delay."[64]

The work of the WD was so successful and so visible in 1940 that the group faced pushback from Republican newspapers. The *Chicago Tribune* accused the WD and, especially, the Reporter Plan, of being illegally subsidized by the government, run outside of "regular Democratic organizations" and, in McAllister's rendering of their claims, "a devious and nefarious Communist plot." To refute the "propaganda against the Women's Division," McAllister declared that "there is nothing mysterious about it [the Reporter Plan]—nothing sinister. It is not a threat to our democracy—it is in truth a technique of democracy."[65] The range of claims that McAllister was forced to rebut in her response to the *Tribune* suggests the efficacy of the WD. The newspaper didn't know where to aim to try and discredit the group, and so it tried a little bit of everything—that the WD was misusing taxpayer money, or perhaps was bringing the "red shadow of Moscow" across the country. Nothing stuck.

As the WD's visibility grew, McAllister also tried to increase the number of female Democrats in elected office. In February she became the first WD director to publicly encourage women's office holding. "With assurance of support from the women of our party," McAllister declared, "it should be possible to have in every state, on the Democratic ticket, at least one woman candidate for Congress and ten for the [state] Legislature."[66] McAllister was likely disappointed by the 1940 election results for women candidates. While it is unknown how many women ran, when the seventy-seventh Congress gathered in January 1941, there were only two Democratic women in the House, neither of whom were newly elected. The Republican delegation had three women, two of them new members. Those two new Republican women went on to have storied careers. One, Frances Bolton, represented the eastern suburbs of Cleveland for nearly three decades. The other was Margaret Chase Smith, who spent almost a decade as part of Maine's House delegation before being elected to the Senate in 1948. She served in the Senate until her retirement at the end of 1972. Democrats would not start sending women to Washington for similarly long tenures until after World War II.[67] In the state legislatures, however, McAllister's push for women candidates was more successful. Eighty Democratic women served in state legislatures in 1941, and more than 40 percent of them were newly elected.[68]

McAllister's encouragement of office holding shows that she valued women in politics in both a voluntary and professional capacity. Her successors at the WDs of both parties also emphasized growing the ranks of professional political women, and after World War II, doing so became almost as important as organizing grassroots party activists. WD directors in the 1940s and 1950s rarely advocated for feminist legislation. But they believed in the importance of women having power in politics. Their efforts to increase the number of women holding elected office and working in policy-oriented civil service jobs demonstrated their consistent belief that these positions and women's local, voluntary work were two sides of the same coin. Getting power for women at every step of government, they believed, improved American democracy and women's daily lives.

In addition to encouraging women to run for office in 1940, McAllister also orchestrated steps to formalize women's equal inclusion in Democratic Party structures. Early that year McAllister informed her lieutenants that the DNC executive committee had unanimously endorsed a resolution requiring that 50 percent of platform delegates be women. This was a different situation than had occurred in 1936, when women were named only as alternates to the platform committee and therefore had very little influence. Women making up half of the regular platform committee members was a huge step forward, and one which the party's leading men endorsed. McAllister noted that, while the change would not become official until the national convention, "we have the President and Mr. Farley on our side."[69]

In order to maximize the effectiveness of the women on the platform committee, McAllister revived the Platform Advisory Committee structure that Dewson had used in 1936. She assembled a group of eighteen prominent women, including Congresswomen Caroline O'Day and Mary Norton, former WD assistant director Carolyn Wolfe, and future WD director Gladys Tillett. All the women who made up the committee had participated in the May 1940 Institute of Government, and several of them made speeches there. One part of the institute was a roundtable titled "What Do Women Want in the 1940 Democratic Platform?" The striking thing about the speeches that have been preserved from that session is their unanimity. Five different speeches are in the files, and all focus on two issues—peace and full employment.[70] These topics are hardly surprising ones in the spring of 1940. World War II had begun in Europe the previous autumn, and while institute attendees did not know it, the Nazi invasion of Western Europe began just a week after the women's meeting concluded. The lingering effects of the Great Depression were also still present; President Roosevelt's "Arsenal of Democracy" speech and the full effects of wartime mobilization on the American economy did not come until after the 1940 election, and so continued discussion of employment made sense.

Given the uniformity of these speeches at the May institute, the breadth of recommendations that the committee eventually made is surprising. The report issued by the women's platform advisory committee recommended planks on fifteen different topics. While peace was listed first, and discussed in far greater detail than the other issues, the recommendations were wide-ranging. Part of the reason for this breadth may be the fact that all eighteen members of the committee could recommend planks, which they circulated in advance to their fellow committee members.[71] McAllister's goal in assembling the team and asking them to speak on so many issues, she explained to Gladys Tillett, was to enable women to present a full slate of planks at the convention. Doing so would prove women's seriousness and persuade any reluctant men to vote in favor of the resolution requiring women's equal representation on the platform committee. Showing that women had done their homework and were ready and capable of engaging in the entirety of platform committee deliberations "will be helpful in our effort to have women made full-fledged members of the Platform Committee at this year's convention and will give them definite recommendations to present if they have an equal voice with men in shaping the platform."[72]

One part of the women's proposed platform had the potential to create tremendous controversy within the party. The women included a civil liberties plank, the majority of which focused on defending freedom of speech and assembly. "Fear should not lead us," the women wrote, "to place in jeopardy those civil rights and liberties without which we should cease to be a free people."[73] That statement was important in the summer of 1940. The months between the women's institute meeting and the Democratic national convention saw Holland, Belgium, and France fall to the Nazis and the Battle of Britain begin. Speaking up for freedom of speech was not an empty platitude in such a context.

The plank continued, however, with a proposal that had the potential to truly rock the boat within the party. The advisory committee recommended abolishing the poll tax. "The right of suffrage is the essential guarantee to our economic way of life," the committee declared. "We believe that the requirement of the payment of taxes as a prerequisite to the right to vote is contrary to the basic principles of Democracy."[74] It is likely that this plank was suggested by advisory committee member Delphine Thomas of Auburn, Alabama, one of three white southern women on the committee. Thomas had been an outspoken opponent of the poll tax for several years, writing an article titled "Some Facts about Alabama's Poll Tax Laws" that appeared in many Alabama newspapers in 1938. Thomas argued in that article that removing the poll tax was imperative to increase the number of Alabama voters. "At present Alabama has about 400,000 registered voters," she stated. "For the population there should be almost 1,000,000 white voters alone."[75] More voters would increase the state's power within the Democratic Party, Thomas argued, and increase its influence in Washington.

At the end of the 1938 article, Thomas emphasized that she was not suggesting a civil rights approach. According to her, "Southern states which have eliminated the poll tax have had no trouble in maintaining 'white supremacy.' Florida, Louisiana, and North Carolina have had no increase in negro [*sic*] voters while they have practically doubled their overall number of voters."[76] Abolishing the poll tax, in other words, would increase the *white* vote in the South. It was a way to strengthen southern influence in a party that was beginning to move away from many white southerners' policy preferences.[77] Because the text of the platform recommendations does not include this kind of detail, it is impossible to determine how many of the women agreed with Thomas and how many hoped that eliminating the poll tax would enable more African Americans to vote. What is clear, however, is that not everyone who supported including this plank did so on civil rights grounds.

The lack of explicit discussion about race in the women's platform fits with the only other time African American voters or civil rights issues came up in the Women's Division's papers for the 1940 campaign. In September 1939, more than a year before the election, McAllister informed a select group of state leaders that Crystal Bird Fauset, an African American Pennsylvania state legislator from Philadelphia and a friend of the First Lady's, would be taking charge of the work of Black women during the 1940 campaign. The letter was sent to women in states where the African American vote was "important," and McAllister was asking the state leaders—all white women—to forward the names of Black women who are "the leaders in your state" to Fauset.[78] The fact that McAllister did not already have these names suggests that Black women were not included in the WD structure in between campaigns. After all, Gladys Tillett had a list of prominent Black women for the Speakers' Bureau in 1936. But African American women were not serving as county vice-chairs or directors of the *Digest*. While they had almost certainly done grassroots campaign work in 1936 and 1938, that work had not been a focus of McAllister's WD. Instead, a separate structure was being built to organize Black women's work in the Democratic Party in 1940, parallel to the WD.

After this letter, neither Fauset nor Black women are ever mentioned again in the official WD papers, although Fauset did at least occasionally touch base with McAllister. She met at least once during the height of the campaign with McAllister and Ed Flynn, who had taken over from Jim Farley as DNC chairman.[79] Gladys Tillett, who was again directing the Speakers' Bureau during the 1940 campaign, worked more closely with Fauset, who suggested at least some of the Black women used by the Speakers' Bureau.[80] Six weeks after the election Fauset told Tillett she had "enjoyed so much working with you" during the campaign.[81] It appears that Fauset worked more closely with Tillett (the southerner) than McAllister. But exactly how Fauset's work dovetailed with that of the WD, and every aspect of what she did, remains unclear.

That lack of clarity, however, is telling. There can be no doubt that the WD failed to fully and equally incorporate Black women. In a letter to Tillett, Fauset corrected her mailing address, noting that the WD had been using the wrong house number "for some time."[82] The lack of attention to this kind of detail, and the lack of effort to include Black women as equal parts of the WD's work, reflects the tendency of all of the WD leaders studied in this book who welcomed African American women who wanted to help with the projects the WD organized. But WD leadership did not explicitly seek Black women's input into designing projects or consider how race might affect the work the WD was doing.

There was little public discussion about race among white Democratic women, but that was not the case regarding the Equal Rights Amendment (ERA). When the Women's Platform Committee issued its report, it did not support the ERA. Instead, the last point of a five-point labor plank declared, "The Democratic Party will continue its efforts to achieve equality of opportunity for women and men without impairing the social legislation which promotes true equality by safeguarding the health, safety, and economic welfare of women workers. The right to work for compensation in both public and private employment is an inalienable privilege belonging to women as well as men, without distinction as to marital status."[83] This language, which spoke out against the marriage-based discrimination women had faced throughout the Depression but stopped well short of an endorsement of the ERA, was the result of lots of behind-the-scenes negotiations. The group of women within the party who supported the amendment, led by Emma Guffey Miller, were pushing to have the party support it. Women's nonpartisan groups proposed compromise language. The National Association of Business and Professional Women's Clubs (BPW) tried to drum up support for a plank that used ERA-style language but stated merely that "the right to work for compensation should not be denied or abridged" on account of sex, race, or marital status.[84] The American Association of University Women (AAUW) supported a ban on discrimination in government employment on the basis of sex or marital status.[85] In the end, the language adopted by the advisory committee stopped short of even these more modest statements.

McAllister had no patience for the ERA fight, which had been raging within women's politics for nearly twenty years by the summer of 1940.[86] She told Dorothy Crook of the BPW that the best way to get her group's position on the ERA heard at the convention was to "make certain that one or more prominent members of your organization are chosen as delegates to the National Convention in Chicago."[87] But she refused to put strong ERA partisans on her platform committee. Given that the committee was made up of some of the most prominent Democratic women in the country, the ERA litmus test is most clearly seen by Emma Guffey Miller's exclusion. Miller was the national committeewoman from Pennsylvania and had seconded FDR's nomination at the 1936 convention.[88] When she found out about the platform committee's position on the ERA, she fired off a furious letter to the president. The "unofficial" advisory committee, she fumed, was "chosen by Mrs. McAllister [,] met in secret session and later notified the Committee on the Platform that Democratic women disapprove" of the ERA.[89] As Lorena Hickok, Eleanor Roosevelt's lover and confidant who had become assistant director of the WD at the beginning of 1940, told the First Lady: "Emma Guffey Miller blasted out at Dorothy and her advisory committee today, but Dorothy didn't issue a counter-statement and for once I'm in accord with her." But Hick (as everyone called her) was also somewhat troubled by the secrecy of the proceedings. "I do think," she continued, "that the suggestions of her advisory committee should be discussed at an open hearing of the platform committee, and this they apparently are not going to do."[90]

Regardless of how much Miller blasted or what Hick thought she should do, McAllister refused to get into the ERA fight. She knew that Democratic women were divided on the topic, and divisions among Democratic women were the absolute last thing she wanted. Women had to be unified and working hard to elect FDR, and doing nothing else.

McAllister worked tirelessly throughout the 1940 campaign, and Roosevelt knew it. After the campaign was over, he sent her a heartfelt note from Hyde Park: "I want you and those who worked with you to know how much I appreciate all you did during the past busy weeks. A great deal of credit for the result is due you and I am tremendously grateful for your untiring efforts."[91]

III

"The Consensus Is That Women Will Swing the Pendulum"

THE WOMEN'S DIVISION IN WARTIME

The election of 1944 was unlike any the United States had seen for generations. Not since 1864, eighty years earlier, had a president been chosen during a war. FDR, aware of the crucial role soldiers' votes played in reelecting Lincoln, pushed early in the year for legislation to allow soldiers to vote absentee on a special federal soldiers' ballot. He faced a great deal of resistance. Southern Democrats wanted to maintain their Jim Crow voting restrictions on African Americans, even those in uniform. Republicans wanted to deny FDR a fourth term. The result of this combined opposition was a bill that enabled almost no deployed soldiers to vote through the special ballot. Instead, the vast majority of soldiers had to figure out their county or state's requirements for absentee voting and fulfill them, regardless of whether they were in a stateside army camp, on a naval ship in the Leyte Gulf of the Philippines, or fighting their way into Germany.[1] Roughly 4 million soldiers eventually voted. But the total number of service members in 1944 was 11.6 million.[2]

To commentators at the time, the absence of so many men from polling places led to a somewhat obvious conclusion: women would be the most important voters in 1944. In February of that year the *Washington Star* declared "Both Parties Woo Women as Decisive Election Factor," adding that "the consensus is that women will swing the pendulum in the 1944 elections."[3] Four months later, the *Chicago Daily News* featured the headline "Both Parties Change Tune to Win Votes of Women." Such a pivot was necessary, the paper reported, because of the "realization that the women's vote in November may be several million more than that cast by men for the first time in the country's history."[4] Both parties gave women high-profile speaking spots at their conventions—the Republicans featured Connecticut congresswoman and playwright

Clare Boothe Luce, while the Democrats highlighted former actress and 1944 congressional candidate Helen Gahagan Douglas. While political historians have ignored the role of women in this campaign—neither of the books focusing on the 1944 election published in the past twenty years mention it at all—everyone at the time recognized 1944 as "the women's year."[5]

The increased attention to women voters led to major changes in how the Democratic WD worked. The changes created in response to wartime conditions established patterns that both parties followed throughout the early Cold War. The 1944 election, therefore, was a pivotal one in the history of women in electoral politics for all kinds of reasons. From increasing rhetoric about what women voters wanted to new forms of communicating with voters to a decline in work with African American women, precedents were established that would be followed for the next fifteen years.

The WD director overseeing all these changes was Gladys Tillett, who had taken over at the beginning of 1941. Dorothy McAllister had told the president shortly after his 1940 victory that she did not want to continue at the Women's Division, due to her husband's pending federal judgeship. FDR also informed the DNC chairman Ed Flynn that McAllister "wants to go home," an unsurprising request given her three years as a single working mother in Alexandria.[6] Lorena Hickok hoped that, as McAllister's right-hand woman, she would become the next director. Less than a week after the election, Hick recorded that Charlie Michelson, the DNC publicity head, agreed with her assessment that "I was the only woman he knew who was qualified to take over that job as director of the women's division!" Hick acknowledged that Eleanor Roosevelt and Molly Dewson would be consulted, but she hoped Roosevelt would speak up for her. While their relationship had cooled somewhat by 1940, they still wrote to each other daily, and Hick closed this letter noting that the Women's Division work was "the most satisfactory job I've had since I left the AP" in 1932 in order to be with Roosevelt on the campaign trail.[7]

Just a few days later, however, Hick realized she did not get the promotion. Molly Dewson had come down in favor of Gladys Tillett. "I thought Molly would want Mrs. Tillett," Hick lamented to Roosevelt, "and I think she is probably right." Hick continued, rather damning Tillett with faint praise: "Mrs. Tillett isn't very colorful but she is a nice person, sane and even-tempered with lots of experience and, Molly says, ability. And Molly, I suspect, thinks she ought to have the recognition. She has come up 'the hard way'—League of Women Voters into precinct work for the party."[8] Dewson herself put it more kindly when writing to Tillett. "You see," she told Tillett in December 1940, "there is no one but you who would work first and last for the New Deal. I could not be bothered to suggest anyone else. . . . You have the essentials—interest, stick-to-itiveness, and drive."[9]

Dewson also preferred Tillett to Hick for more pragmatic reasons. "I see we are all afraid of Hick's appearance for the adverse impression it might make on the unsophisticated leaders," Dewson wrote. "Alas there are few valuable instruments that are perfect or serve *all* purposes. I bet you 100 to 1 you can minimize that defect."[10] Hick was valuable, in Dewson's mind, and a good member of the team. But she was not right as the head of the Women's Division, the public face of women within the party. Hick stayed on as the executive secretary of the WD until early 1945, and she and Tillett worked well together for four years.

What exactly was it about Hick's appearance that created the wrong impression? Pictures of her show a woman who clearly was not worried about makeup or current fashion but rather favored practical choices in both clothing and hairstyle. More likely, however, is that Dewson was referring to Hick showing up places, rather than her look, and that her somewhat public relationship with the First Lady and her relatively open lesbianism would upset the "unsophisticated leaders" within the party. Merely the fact of her and who she was, in other words, had the potential to create controversy. In either case, Dewson's instincts were likely correct. Once the United States entered World War II at the end of Tillett's first year on the job, there was increasing emphasis on femininity among American women. Historian Melissa McEuen has argued that the focus in media and official propaganda on keeping American women looking feminine was intended to counteract any long-term changes to gender norms that could have emerged from millions of women entering defense factories and hundreds of thousands joining the military.[11] Stylish, blond Gladys Tillett with her southern accent proved to be a perfect fit for the moment in a way that Hick likely would not.

But Hick was part of the president's inner circle, and while Tillett had held leadership roles in the WD in two campaigns, that work was always temporary, restricted just to the campaign. She and the president did not know each other. Dewson, therefore, filled her in on the most important people she would be working with:

> Now a word on your main stays. FDR you'll rarely see and will get no ideas from, but if you do sit by him at dinner, boil down the one thing you want him to do for you into a few words. He expects you to seize the opportunity. He loves the bar room style of jokes and joshing. A sly little poke of fun at him on a not sore point is his favorite mode of relaxation . . .
>
> ER: get into a quandary every so often and ask to be allowed to come over and get her advice. NOW DO THAT. Some days you won't be able to exist without her help and you want an open road to her. Otherwise she is so busy you'll never see her. . . .
>
> *Eddie Flynn. Go to him regularly for a terse report.* Also when there is anything worth taking to him take it but he does not want to be bothered really. He plans to give you a free hand. . . . You should keep up your contact by reporting regularly "all's well" so he won't forget you. Never will you be so free or so forsaken. BUT there are 85,000 women looking to you from all over the country.[12]

In three paragraphs, Dewson laid out everything Tillett needed to know to effectively manage the relationships between the White House, the DNC leadership, and the WD. The rest of it—how to deal with her staff and those 85,000 women who were the grassroots of the Democratic Party—Dewson knew Tillett could figure out on her own. Otherwise, she never would have recommended her for the job.

Dewson's comments about how disconnected FDR would be from Tillett's work is surprising, given his hands-on approach with McAllister during the campaign that had concluded just weeks earlier. Since she was retired, and living in Connecticut with Porter, it is likely that Dewson did not know how much feedback McAllister had gotten from the president on issues like the timing and number of the rainbow fliers. As a friend, however, Dewson may also have been attuned to FDR's increasing focus on the war. Now that he had been reelected, Roosevelt was free to pursue the more aggressive position of support to the Allies that he had wanted ever since World War II began. This letter from Dewson is not dated beyond "On the train—Tuesday," but within six weeks of her writing it—and possibly as little as two weeks—Roosevelt gave his famous "Arsenal of Democracy" speech announcing the United States' intention to provide Britain with supplies to fight the Nazis. Foreign policy was his overwhelming focus. Domestic politics slid to the back burner.[13]

Tillett, then, was left on her own to continue the work of McAllister and Dewson. There is very little material in any archives regarding Tillett's first couple of years on the job at the WD. The archival record picks up in the middle of 1943, when the war had created big changes in the WD structure. Gasoline and rubber rationing meant that countywide meetings and long speaking tours were things of the past. The relocation of millions of Americans for military service or defense work meant that existing networks of women at the local and state level had been altered, or perhaps shattered altogether.

In June 1943 Tillett announced a new WD publication, created at the state level and designed to respond to wartime conditions. More women were in the paid labor force or had moved, and so in-person meetings had become more challenging. So the WD created a new publication to connect with women. "A number of state and county leaders," Tillett reported, "have adopted the plan of having a newsletter to make contact with party workers in their organization. Most of these newsletters go out monthly and give party workers information with which to answer questions and criticisms which may be made by voters in their communities." Most of the material in the newsletters was taken from the *Democratic Digest*, supplemented with state-specific information.[14] These newsletters enabled women to get facts to the women in their communities, which could then be used in conversation or in writing letters to the editor in their local newspapers. Getting the facts to the grassroots remained a focus of WD work, but the war made innovation in how to do that a necessity.

Around this same time, Tillett was working on the second prong of her approach to motivating women to vote for Roosevelt. In the spring of 1943, Tillett warned the president that the "interest and enthusiasm" of Democratic women was waning. This decline, she argued, was due to the administration's "lack of recognition" of women's abilities in policymaking. In order to get women to turn out for the Democratic Party, Tillett insisted that "it is going to be necessary to give women more voice than they have now in the wartime policies of the Administration." She singled out the Office of Price Administration, the rationing office whose head, Leon Henderson, had become a lightning rod of controversy. "If some woman, who actually had to adjust her household to the program, had been given a chance to pass on the way the program was put into effect and handled," Tillett argued, "mistakes which became an issue in the [1942] election might have been avoided." But instead, "no woman was apparently consulted in the matter."[15]

In response to Tillett's indignant plea, FDR instructed his corresponding secretary, Marvin McIntrye, to "bear in mind" placing some women on "every board we can think of."[16] In the spring of 1943 Tillett also worked with Sumner Wells, the undersecretary of state, to create a roster of women qualified to serve on international committees. Wells requested Tillett give him the names of "five or six women who, in your judgement, are qualified to serve on official delegations." The undersecretary noted that he had received Tillett's letter asking for these appointments and also heard from the First Lady that she wanted him to do what Tillett asked. But he needed help to find the right women.[17] In 1944 Tillett organized a conference where the women who had been appointed to these international boards shared their experiences and advice with other women who wanted to do this kind of work. The conference, which featured opening and closing remarks by Eleanor Roosevelt, was called "How Women May Share in Postwar Policy-Making."[18]

Not only did Tillett work to place more women in policymaking positions, her WD also developed strong relationships between women journalists and the division. One new program for the 1944 campaign provided women radio personalities around the country with exclusive reports. The project, which began in June 1944, sent a bulletin featuring "general human interest items, homemaking news, personality sketches, and items about the American woman's INCREASINGLY important role in government" to one female journalist in each community.[19] The demand was so high that the WD quickly began creating three different versions of each week's bulletin, so that they could give exclusive content to three different women reporters in each media market. This program helped develop the journalist-politician connections beyond the women of the D.C. press corps (who were part of the women-only press conferences) to include female journalists nationwide. Together with Tillett's work in getting appointments for women in policy positions in Washington, this project highlights a new focus for the WD, which grew during the postwar era. Not only were WD leaders developing a grassroots network of women to work for the party, they were also supporting women leaders who could take on more formal roles in public life.

As the 1944 campaign shifted into high gear, WD staff and male party leaders knew that they would have to shoulder much of the burden of campaigning themselves, without much active involvement from FDR. It was obvious to anyone who saw him that the president's health was poor. Had the war not been at such a critical juncture, he likely would not have run at all. A week before the Democratic convention in July, Roosevelt lamented to Bob Hannegan, the DNC chairman, "For myself, I do not want to run." But he felt that he had to, declaring that he had "as little right to withdraw as the soldier has to leave his post in the line." However, he made it clear to Hannegan that he would not be campaigning in the usual way. While he would accept the nomination and serve if elected, "I will not run, in the usual partisan, political sense."[20] Running, then, fell to the staff of the DNC. And given the focus on women voters during the wartime election, the WD was center stage.

Tillett formally kicked off the WD work at that year's Democratic convention. Many of the women with leadership roles in the WD throughout the country were also delegates to the convention, so Tillett held a "campaign school" in Chicago, the site of the convention, on two mornings just before the convention began. In 1940, the campaign school had been in May and held in D.C. in order to allow women to hear directly from cabinet officials and other government figures. After World War II ended, that format returned. But wartime conditions made a change necessary, and combining the school with the convention enabled Tillett to reach her most important grassroots leaders efficiently without requiring multiple long-distance trips. As she explained in her remarks opening the event, "because war-time restrictions will make it harder to campaign, the Women's Division is holding this Campaign School. Through this school we are trying to give you some new techniques to meet some of the new conditions you will face."[21]

Over two half-day sessions, there were speeches from more than a dozen women active in the WD and the Democratic Party. The speeches were a mix of addresses on particular policy issues, like the GI Bill and agriculture policy, and more practical talks about how to run a good campaign under wartime circumstances.[22] Jean Poletti, a veteran WD worker from New York, gave a speech on "street corner speaking." She described the tactic as they had used it in New York City in 1940, where they decorated a car with FDR signs and parked in business districts at lunchtime and residential areas at night. They unloaded a stepladder and a megaphone and began speaking out for Roosevelt. As Poletti put it, "from 8 to 10 [p.m.] we were the main attraction in the residential districts!"[23] Dorothy McAllister's speech emphasized the importance of giving speeches and the need for "a speakers' bureau in every county," since gas rationing meant that "we cannot depend on a few star performers to cover the state."[24]

Another new tactic became a staple of women's partisan politics in the postwar era. In reaction to gasoline rationing, the WD began promoting neighborhood meetings as a substitute for large gatherings in central locations. Helen Gahagan Douglas, a candidate for Congress in 1944, outlined this approach. She described meeting with the residents of the district she sought to represent, "in the homes of volunteer hostesses, sometimes making as many as two or three speeches in an evening. We welcomed questions and discussion, and got plenty. The resultant intimacy and informal discussion developed interest and enthusiasm in the audience that would never have been brought out in a larger group." Douglas's district was predominantly working-class, and many of her potential constituents were new to the area, having moved to Los Angeles to take jobs at defense factories. Meetings with those groups took place not only in private homes but also "in the foyers of apartment buildings, and on street corners."[25] Douglas described the small, home-based meetings as a crucial way to both generate votes and find new volunteers at a time when gas rationing made driving long distances impossible. During the baby boom, such home-based meetings became the primary way women gathered to pursue partisan politics.

For those who did not attend the convention, the WD provided a booklet reminiscent of *To Mrs. County Leader* from the 1936 campaign. *The Campaign School Book* laid out everything women were expected to do for the Democratic Party. Heavy emphasis was placed on registering voters. Millions of Americans moved during the war, for military service or to take jobs in defense industries. Getting them registered was a crucial first step in getting out the vote. And it was a task that, historically, men had handled. In a press release from April 1944, Tillett noted that men had traditionally done most of the work of registering voters, and also of providing access to absentee ballots. But with so many men gone, Tillett stated, Democratic women were "taking off their party dresses and doing overall work in party organization" and "doing a greater share than ever before of this essential work which assures a maximum expression of the people's opinion on election day."[26] The implication that women were just now getting down to the hard work was disingenuous, and Tillett knew it. But she also knew that the press was fascinated with women's role in the election in 1944. By emphasizing the new work they were doing and playing up gender stereotypes, Tillett made this press release good copy. Good newspaper coverage was essential. It alerted women who might not be plugged in to Democratic Party networks that there were women working on partisan politics and doing their utmost to shape this "woman's year."

WD staff also wrote radio scripts focused on registration. Tillett stated that the scripts "have been kept reasonably nonpartisan, so that a friendly station could give you free time without violating the general agreement among radio companies not to give free time to a political party following the convention."[27] Registration and voter turnout were a focus partially because they had been so poor in the 1942 midterms. That year less than one-third of registered voters cast ballots, a low that has never been repeated. The low turnout, Democrats believed, was at least partially responsible for their big losses in both the House and Senate.[28] Polling throughout the spring and summer of 1944 showed FDR in his closest contest ever. Only in a poll published the day before D-Day did Roosevelt enjoy more than a 3 percentage point margin over his opponent (on June 5, he led 52 percent to 48 percent).[29] In order to maintain control of the White House in such a tight election, the DNC had to come up with new ways to get voters registered and to the polls. The slogan of the campaign highlighted this emphasis on voter turnout. In speeches, on the back of fliers, everywhere one looked in Democratic material for 1944 was the hard-hitting slogan: "If democracy is worth fighting for, it's worth voting for."[30]

In order to ensure that every woman could vote, the WD developed an innovative Election Day tactic: the childcare committee. In dozens of cities and town, groups of Democratic women volunteered to be on call to go to homes and watch young children while their mothers went to vote. The Republican

Party added this service in 1948, and both parties maintained it through at least the 1952 election. Such a labor-intensive program demonstrates just how important women's votes had become in the minds of leaders of both parties over the 1940s and 1950s.

Because women's votes were so vital, the WD used gendered language in its materials far more frequently than it had in the 1930s. Gendered language or approaches designed specifically for women were not part of Molly Dewson's or Dorothy McAllister's WD. But the heightened focus on traditional gender norms during the war, combined with the focus on women voters, led the WD down a new path in 1944. After the war, woman political leaders in both parties continued to articulate gender-specific reasons for women to support either the Democrats or the GOP.

Gladys Tillett's speeches highlighted this new need to speak to women voters as women. In one stump speech she gave several times throughout the campaign, she focused on the fate of women working in defense industries, "When the war is over, many of these women will return to their homes and many will not; but all of them will have had the experience of enjoying for themselves and their families the high standard of living made possible by their wages. They will not be content for themselves and their families to return to the meager standards of living that they were accustomed to before the war."[31] Including the lives of those women in postwar planning was essential, Tillett argued, and the Democratic Party was best positioned to meet that need. They were the party that supported workers and the social safety net. While she tied working women's needs back to broad party policies, earlier WD leaders would never have singled women out in this way. The visibility of women voters led to an increase in rhetoric discussing their lives and targeting them as a voting group.

Many of Tillett's speeches had an even more gendered aspect to them, speaking not merely about women but asserting that women had particular interests in common. At a July 1944 breakfast in honor of Congresswoman Mary Norton, Tillett outlined themes she returned to throughout the rest of her time as WD director, well into the postwar period. Women were deeply interested in the shape of the postwar world, she argued, and were also the ones most able to start that planning while the war continued. "Many of our men today are in action or poised for action on the war fronts," she noted. "They haven't the time to give thought of the post-war world. Part of the service we can render our men is to do some thinking and planning for them." Women wanted a postwar world free from poverty and inferior education, because those factors had provided "the more fertile ground for the seeds of Hitler's subtle propaganda."[32] Both of these themes—the relationship between poverty and totalitarianism and the need for women to be engaged in politics and policy because they were the ones with the time to do so—became staples of the postwar politics of both parties.

Print materials by the WD also focused on women's perspectives. One radio script, for example, began by stating that the speaker was coming to talk with listeners "about our homes, about our children, about our country." The script continued: "We women always felt ourselves pretty important to our families.... We're USED to carrying the responsibilities of a home, and a family. We LIKE it. And, as a matter of fact, we DREAD the day when we have to give it up." The script then asserted that women understood that one of the ways they were responsible for their homes in 1944 was to vote Democratic in order to ensure "the health, the security, even the LIVES of millions of people all over the world."[33] Being a good wife and mother in 1944 meant voting for FDR, according to Tillett's WD.

Because women's votes were so important and women voters were being targeted for the first time, Tillett gave a speech during the convention's opening evening, which was broadcast live as part of the radio convention coverage. It was the first time a WD director had given a nationally broadcast speech targeted at a general audience and not just Democratic women. Dewson had given some speeches that were recorded and sent to radio stations in 1936, and the WD director usually gave a kickoff speech on Democratic Women's Day, the party's annual September fundraiser. But never before had the WD director been highlighted as part of the convention proceedings. Tillett's speech was a highly gendered one, laying out why women should support the Democratic Party. The women of the country, Tillett said, "wish to be heard. From the depth of their experiences, from the depth of their sharpened emotions, they say: 'Out of this war, out of the suffering of this war, let there be a better world.' They say, 'we did not risk our peace and family happiness for a government of timidity and reaction.' They say, 'we have sacrificed much, and we will sacrifice more, but for our sacrifices we demand a just return. We demand a future of opportunity and peace. We want our coin in human good."[34] Toward the end of the speech, Tillett stated that women were terrified of what would happen to these demands if the responsibility for fulfilling them "should suddenly be placed in the hands of inexperience." Only Roosevelt, in other words, could be trusted to bring about the postwar world that women wanted. Tillett thrived in this new version of the WD director, taking a more direct role in making the case for the president. Thirty years after the fact, she described her work on the 1944 campaign as "fascinating."[35]

Tillett was not the only woman featured at the national conventions. The GOP, meeting a few weeks before the Democrats, made extensive use of Connecticut congresswoman Clare Boothe Luce. Luce had gained prominence in the mid-1930s both as the author of the Broadway smash hit play *The Women* and as the second wife of Henry Luce, the publisher of *Time* and *Life* magazines. Clare Luce had a long interest in politics, and in 1932 had attended the Democratic National Convention with her friend Bernard Baruch, a confidant of FDR. That year she had cheered FDR's election, but by 1940 she had switched parties, convinced that the New Deal had gone too far. In 1942, she ran for the House of Representatives and won. In her first press conference as the congressional term began in January 1943, Luce outlined her support for women's rights, her interest in foreign policy, and her support for free-market capitalism.[36] She and her husband (and his magazines) had been major supporters of Wendell Wilkie in 1940, and Luce continued to promote her vision of what the Republican Party should stand for—an active engagement in the world but, in her telling, a clearer plan to end the war, as well as an end to the New Deal.[37]

Journalists were fascinated by Luce, and she was happy to oblige their interest. By the time the 1944 campaign season kicked off, she was the most famous Republican woman in the country. That spring, she gave numerous speeches castigating what she called FDR's lack of a "coherent" foreign policy. She also wrote several articles on the importance of women playing a substantive role in politics and shaping the postwar world. With titles like "Why We Should Have a Woman at the Peace Table" and "How a Woman Can Get Along in State Politics," these pieces could have come straight from Gladys Tillett.[38] Recall that one of Tillett's major projects in the summer of 1944, in fact, was organizing a conference at the White House titled "How Women May

Share in Post-War Policy Making."[39] Political women's focus on the postwar world crossed party lines—just as everyone agreed that 1944 was the year of the woman, everyone agreed that postwar policy was one of women's primary concerns as they considered their vote.

At the Republican National Convention, Luce gave a speech that electrified many women into making that vote choice, although not in the way she intended. GOP leaders wanted Luce to give the keynote address, believing that having her in such a prominent position would "constitute recognition of the part women have taken in politics." Thomas Dewey, the presidential candidate, rejected this suggestion and gave the keynote spot to his running mate, California governor Earl Warren. Searching for a way to use Luce, the convention committee asked her to introduce former President Herbert Hoover. Hoover, however, knew better than to shove one of the party's best speakers into such a thankless role. He offered to swap places with Luce, having her speak after him to close out the convention's first night.[40]

Luce's speech was inflammatory. She claimed that soldiers fighting in World War II had died because of Democratic mismanagement of the war. According to her, electing Dewey was the only way to ensure the sacrifices of America's young men were not in vain. "A fighting man," she declared, "dies for the future as well as the past, to keep all that was fine of his country's yesterday, and to give it a chance for a finer tomorrow." Only Dewey and the Republican could bring about that "finer tomorrow," according to Luce. The speech was derided throughout the media. The *New Yorker* called it a "staggering breach of taste."[41] A *New York Times* editorial intoned that "in love and loyalty to the dead we had better not make [their deaths] partisan."[42]

In spite of the outcry over Luce's speech, she remained an in-demand stump speaker throughout the campaign.[43] The media also manufactured a rivalry between her and Helen Gahagan Douglas, the Democratic congressional candidate and former actress. The headline for an article in the *Christian Science Monitor* that announced Douglas's candidacy, for example, bore the headline "Competition for Clare Luce? Democrats Pick Ex-Actress." The substance of the article dealt with Douglas's innovative campaign tactics and mentioned that she defeated seven men in the California Democratic primary to become the nominee. But the headline set her up as a foil for Luce and stated that the Women's Division was "rejoicing" at the idea of having an equally glamorous and well-spoken woman on their side of the aisle to spar with Luce.[44]

Articles pairing the two women became a feature of campaign coverage. Newspapers' Sunday magazines featured long profiles of both women. Some of the comparisons were positive and substantive, such as Mary Hornaday's *Christian Science Monitor* piece that described Luce and Douglas as leaders of a new type of political woman, who made personal, emotional speeches that were "less distasteful" to many listeners and who "play up their personalities, their looks, and their depth of feeling as political assets."[45] Others had headlines like "Helen vs. Clare: Torch vs. Icicle," a hackneyed, "cat-fight" approach to covering the women that belied the positive assessment of Douglas's true commitment to politics that the article contained.[46]

Throughout the campaign Douglas presented herself as a serious, committed politician. A lengthy profile in the *New York Post* was titled simply "DON'T Call Her the Democrats' Clare Luce."[47] Another article, which appeared in the *New York Times* on the same day the "Torch vs. Icicle" article ran in Chicago, was titled "'Fencing' with Mrs. Luce Barred by Miss Gahagan." That piece, which used her married name throughout in spite of not using it in the headline, detailed Douglas's claims that she was not interested in "sparring" with Luce. "I have a great respect for Mrs. Luce," she told reporters. "I'm not a fencer. I'm not a wit. . . . I just feel very deeply about the situation we're in and I hope I can help if I get elected to Congress."[48]

All of these articles appeared after Luce's convention speech, and all of them used Douglas, to a greater or lesser extent, as an example of what women politicians should be like. The "Torch vs. Icicle" piece was the most hard-hitting. Its author, Hazel MacDonald, claimed that while Douglas had prepared to run for office by working for the Democratic Party—as an alternate delegate to the 1940 Democratic convention, then as the vice-chair of the California Democratic Committee and the head of the state WD—Luce's preparation for political office had "consisted of writing for fashion magazines and the Broadway stage, with a dash of foreign correspondence thrown in."[49] Luce was a lightning rod, and while the Democratic Party was clearly happy to have a woman on their side who could also deliver a speech with passion, Douglas was not interested in participating in the kind of cat fight so many reporters were trying to create.

The clearest evidence of Douglas's preference to stick to the issues was the speech she gave at the Democratic National Convention. She spoke on the second night, the night after Tillett. Her speech, while passionate, stayed away from both explicit rebuttals of Luce's speech weeks earlier and from explicitly gendered reasons why women should vote for FDR. Instead, Douglas talked about what all Americans had at stake over the next four years: "The people of America cannot afford to make a mistake. We cannot afford to endanger our future by muddy thinking or limited vision." Later she made her only indirect response to Luce's address of three weeks earlier, stating that "you belittle your son, your daughter, your husband, and I belittle my husband and we imperil our children unless we see our dear ones now serving overseas in relation to their country, their world, their future." In order to secure the future that everyone wanted for their soldiers, Douglas said, voters "must not commit the lives and the future of the American people to inexperience and negation."[50] On Election Day, WD leaders were thrilled to celebrate Douglas's congressional victory as well as the president's. She became an important ally for the WD in Congress for many years.

All of the media attention on women voters and prominent political women like Douglas, Luce, and Tillett did not extend to African American women. And the WD's work with Black women in 1944 was even less well developed than it had been in the previous two elections. The lack of outreach to Black women, and the lack of discussion about how Black and white women should work together, had nothing to do with the southern Tillett's leadership of the WD. It was a direct order from the president.

In early 1944, Crystal Bird Fauset began working for the DNC again, expecting to resume the sort of work that she had done in the previous two campaigns. She had been castigating the Democratic Party privately throughout the war for its lack of meaningful work on behalf of African Americans and its evident prioritization of keeping white supremacist southern Democrats happy. A directive from the president in the summer of 1944, therefore, was the last straw. Fauset had been discussing plans for a "new interracial approach to women" with Eleanor Roosevelt, and had organized a meeting between several African American women and the First Lady in early June 1944.[51] After that meeting, Fauset outlined her plans for bringing politically active Black and white women together, with several small conferences culminating in a "tremendous" interracial meeting, to be held at Madison Square Garden or Central Park at the end of the summer, "around the theme of American Unity—emphasis being laid on the activities of women."[52] Fauset was excited by the idea of leveraging the authority of the Democratic Party to forge a new interracial movement among American women.

The president, however, immediately quashed these plans. Tucked among the correspondence between Fauset and the First Lady is a small, handwritten note. It reads, in total: "Memo for Mrs. Roosevelt. I would not encourage any announcement of future meetings on the interracial subject. The less said about it for the next few months, the less loss of life. FDR."[53] It is unclear what the "loss of life" statement refers to. Was the president referencing stateside race-based violence, which had been happening throughout the war, from Los Angeles to Mobile and everywhere in between?[54] Or did he mean that antagonizing southern Democrats would cost him the election and, therefore, possibly lengthen the war, causing more soldiers to die? In either case, the message was clear, and the First Lady communicated it to Fauset, "The President feels very strongly that anything we do in the next few months should be done very quietly and should have no publicity. He thinks that your work for the Democrats should, if possible, be on the side of peace and understanding because, if we get people too much excited, there will be trouble, particularly in the South."[55] Fauset got the message, and the plans for a series of interracial women's meetings was dropped. But she was not happy about it.

Fauset kept trying to be involved in the campaign. But the DNC chairman, Bob Hannegan, did not utilize her. She pressured Roosevelt to speak up for her, but in late August the First Lady told her no: "I am sorry to say that I have absolutely no influence with Mr. Hannegan, and he does run the National Committee." Roosevelt suggested scheduling a meeting with Hannegan, "telling him you want to do whatever will coincide with their plans, and then if they do not work out something you feel you can honestly do, I would resign and find a job somewhere else."[56] It was good advice, but Fauset apparently did not take it. She continued throughout the rest of the campaign to draw a salary from the DNC—a topic that had been a sore spot since the beginning of 1944, when Fauset felt she was not being paid promptly. By October, Tillett was fed up with Fauset's demands for money. She suggested that DNC chairman Bob Hannegan talk to Eleanor Roosevelt about previous sums paid to

Fauset and also get a statement from the WD's bookkeeper about her salary. "For this amount of money," Tillett stated, "she has done nothing whatsoever and was instructed not to do anything."[57] Tillett had reason to be angry with Fauset—a month earlier, Fauset joined Thomas Dewey on a stage in Philadelphia, and after Dewey concluded his speech, Fauset publicly endorsed him for president.[58] Yet she still expected the DNC to pay her. Some portion of the resistance to organizing African American women voters through Fauset, therefore, may have been difficulties with Fauset herself.

Regardless of Fauset and Hannegan's personal conflict, however, FDR's quashing of a focus on interracial women's work, combined with the DNC's refusal to do any work specifically with African American women, is a lost moment and set problematic precedents. Women's politics had been segregated for nearly a century by the mid-1940s, and the First Lady seemed intrigued by the possibility of working with Fauset to begin breaking down those boundaries. But in the absence of such high-level support, the primary site of women's interracial work after the war was unions and a handful of religious groups. The YWCA, for example, ordered its chapters to integrate in 1946, but more than twenty years later they were still having to dispatch national staff members to deal with recalcitrant chapters around the country that refused to do so.[59] How differently might things have gone had FDR not come down hard on his wife and refused to let her give her name and prestige to an effort to integrate women's political activism?

Without the kind of major push Roosevelt and Fauset envisioned, the WD and other women's middle-class political groups continued to be largely segregated. This segregation was never absolute, and Gladys Tillett and her successor, India Edwards, tried to ensure that Black women who did work with the WD were acknowledged by the group and treated fairly. But increasing the number of African American women active in the Democratic Party's WD was never a priority for either Tillett or Edwards. The pluralist politics of the postwar period reinforced this existing segregation—there was a place for women, and a place for African Americans, but where did Black women fit? As has so often been the case, the answer seems to have been nowhere.

Molly Dewson sits at her desk with donkey banks, 1936.
Image courtesy of Bettman Archives / Getty Images.

Mrs. County Leader

Be a self-cranker!

For the Democratic Party Organization has no automatic starter.

Don't Wait for permission from any high up chiefs to go out and WIN VOTES.

We can't expect—and don't deserve—VICTORY if you and the other Mrs. County Leaders wait to be told.

Supposing no one ever told you to start!

Suppose you were wakened from your knitting some day by the radio saying "Democrats defeated in YOUR COUNTY."

15

Page from the DNC Women's Division's *Dedicated to Mrs. County Leader* pamphlet, written by Molly Dewson for the 1936 campaign.

Image courtesy of Franklin D. Roosevelt Presidential Library, Hyde Park, New York.

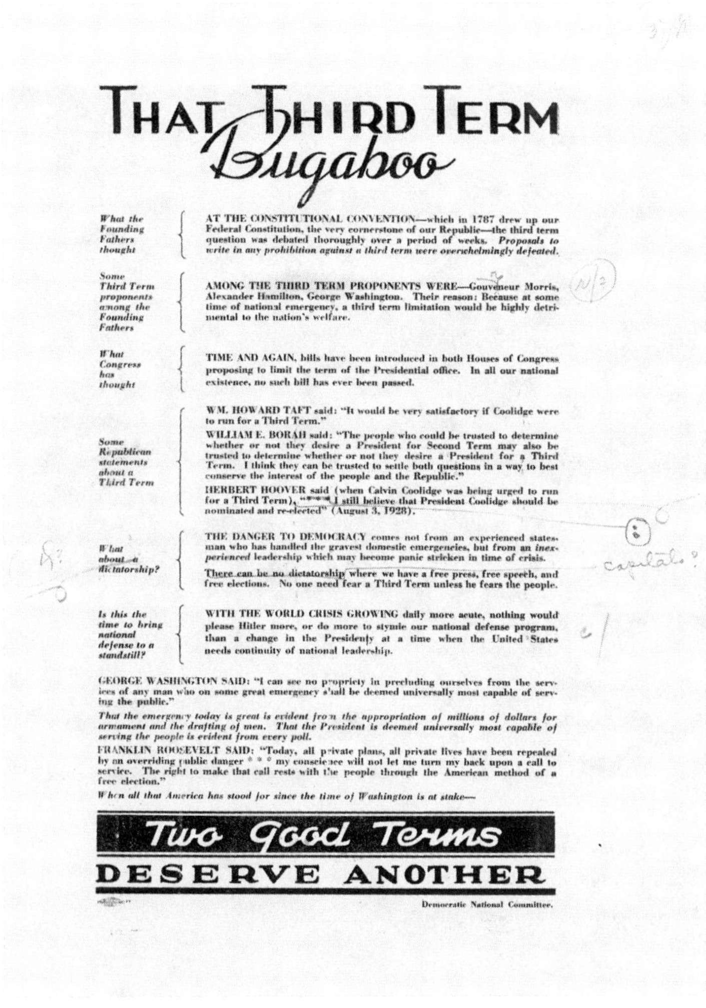

THAT THIRD TERM *Bugaboo*

What the Founding Fathers thought

AT THE CONSTITUTIONAL CONVENTION—which in 1787 drew up our Federal Constitution, the very cornerstone of our Republic—the third term question was debated thoroughly over a period of weeks. *Proposals to write in any prohibition against a third term were overwhelmingly defeated.*

Some Third Term proponents among the Founding Fathers

AMONG THE THIRD TERM PROPONENTS WERE—Gouveneur Morris, Alexander Hamilton, George Washington. Their reason: Because at some time of national emergency, a third term limitation would be highly detrimental to the nation's welfare.

What Congress has thought

TIME AND AGAIN, bills have been introduced in both Houses of Congress proposing to limit the term of the Presidential office. In all our national existence, no such bill has ever been passed.

Some Republican statements about a Third Term

WM. HOWARD TAFT said: "It would be very satisfactory if Coolidge were to run for a Third Term."

WILLIAM E. BORAH said: "The people who could be trusted to determine whether or not they desire a President for Second Term may also be trusted to determine whether or not they desire a President for a Third Term. I think they can be trusted to settle both questions in a way to best conserve the interest of the people and the Republic."

HERBERT HOOVER said (when Calvin Coolidge was being urged to run for a Third Term), "* * * I still believe that President Coolidge should be nominated and re-elected" (August 3, 1928).

What about a dictatorship?

THE DANGER TO DEMOCRACY comes not from an experienced statesman who has handled the gravest domestic emergencies, but from an *inexperienced* leadership which may become panic stricken in time of crisis.

There can be no dictatorship where we have a free press, free speech, and free elections. No one need fear a Third Term unless he fears the people.

Is this the time to bring national defense to a standstill?

WITH THE WORLD CRISIS GROWING daily more acute, nothing would please Hitler more, or do more to stymie our national defense program, than a change in the Presidenty at a time when the United States needs continuity of national leadership.

GEORGE WASHINGTON SAID: "I can see no propriety in precluding ourselves from the services of any man who on some great emergency shall be deemed universally most capable of serving the public."

That the emergency today is great is evident from the appropriation of millions of dollars for armament and the drafting of men. That the President is deemed universally most capable of serving the people is evident from every poll.

FRANKLIN ROOSEVELT SAID: "Today, all private plans, all private lives have been repealed by an overriding public danger * * * my conscience will not let me turn my back upon a call to service. The right to make that call rests with the people through the American method of a free election."

When all that America has stood for since the time of Washington is at stake—

Two Good Terms

DESERVE ANOTHER

Democratic National Committee.

That Third-Term Bugaboo, a rainbow flier written by Dorothy McAllister for the 1940 campaign.

Image courtesy of Franklin D. Roosevelt Presidential Library, Hyde Park, New York.

Dorothy McAllister (*seated far left*), Eleanor Roosevelt (*center*), and Crystal Bird Fauset (*standing left*) attend the Women's Centennial Congress, 1940.

Image courtesy of Bettman Archives / Getty Images.

Gladys Tillett (*right*) working with her secretary in her Washington office, circa 1944.

Image courtesy of Elizabeth Avery Thomas / Wilson Library, University of North Carolina at Chapel Hill.

Gladys Tillett (*left*) and Eleanor Roosevelt with Democratic congresswomen, including Mary Norton (*center*) and Helen Gahagan Douglas (*far right*), January 1945.

Image courtesy of Elizabeth Avery Thomas / Wilson Library, University of North Carolina at Chapel Hill.

India Edwards and President Truman aboard the whistle-stop campaign train, 1948.
Image courtesy of Harry S. Truman Library and Museum.

Housewives for Truman trailer,
Amsterdam, New York, September 1948.
Image courtesy of Harry S. Truman Library and Museum.

HOUSEWIVES FOR
TRUMAN
HOUSEWIVES...
For TRUMAN

India Edward and Helen Gahagan Douglas hug after Douglas's speech at the 1948 Democratic National Convention.

Photo by Acme Photography. Courtesy of Bettman Archives / Getty Images.

General Eisenhower confers with (*left to right*) Mary Lord, Bertha Adkins, and Ivy Baker Priest during the 1952 campaign.
Image courtesy of the Associated Press.

President Eisenhower and Bertha Adkins laugh in the Oval Office, 1956.

Image courtesy of the Eisenhower Presidential Library.

IV

After Roosevelt

THE POSTWAR FATE OF THE DEMOCRATIC WOMEN'S DIVISION

After the triumph of FDR's unprecedented fourth electoral victory in 1944, Gladys Tillett was ready for a new challenge. She remained director of the Women's Division and vice-chair of the DNC, but she began spending more time drumming up grassroots support for the United Nations. She attended the first planning meeting for the United Nations in April 1945. After that trip, the Women's Division began writing radio scripts and pamphlets focusing on what Tillett saw as the imperative of a new international organization. In explaining this shift, Tillett hit many of the same notes she had throughout the 1944 campaign. Women were deeply interested in peace, she claimed, and the United Nations was "the only plan we have before us at this time to prevent another war."[1] Although she remained Women's Division director until early 1947, she shifted her attention away from turning out women's votes.

As part of this shift, Tillett continued to focus on securing government jobs for qualified women in newly forming UN agencies and other international bodies. She informed DNC chairman Bob Hannegan in August 1945 that "it is important to have a woman delegate on each United Nations Conference. The women of the country are interested in international affairs and they want a voice in them." Tillett needed Hannegan's support, as she was rarely in the room when final appointment decisions were made. "I should like your complete backing on my recommendations of qualified women to the Department of State," she wrote. "When the re-organization takes place, I hope you will back me up on this with our contact person."[2] Tillett was right to be worried about the lack of women on these boards. Eighteen months later India Edwards, then the WD assistant director, protested women's exclusion from important international business: "It is disgusting that no woman was included in any of the conferences that led up to the signing of the satellite treaties, and now none is in this [economic conference]."[3]

Tillett's pivot to UN work, while certainly sincere, also enabled her to steer clear of the turmoil that swept through the DNC in the middle years of the 1940s. After President Roosevelt died in April 1945, President Truman's team began remaking the national committee's staff. It was not an easy process, and the top leadership of the DNC was chaotic for years. When Truman became president, Bob Hannegan was the party chairman. Over the next three years, the committee had two chairmen, two executive directors, and a tremendous amount of tension among all of those men. Each chair or executive director had his own power base within the party, and the men clashed frequently. By pulling the Women's Division away from partisan activity to some degree, Tillett kept the division, and herself, out of this chaos. Doing so also maintained the division's historic independence, an independence that her successors fought hard to keep.

Shifting her focus also helped Tillett make her schedule more manageable. From late 1940, when she became director, until after FDR's death, Tillett often went on weeks-long campaign trips around the country. A year into the job she told Molly Dewson that running the WD "takes every day and Sunday too, but it is exceedingly interesting and I enjoy it immensely."[4] Her schedule was particularly daunting during the 1944 campaign, when gas rationing sidelined many women speakers and required Tillett to carry more of the speaking load. She kept up a schedule that, as Lorena Hickok said after one trip, "would kill an ordinary woman."[5] Unlike previous WD directors, Tillett also commuted back and forth between Washington and her home in Charlotte, North Carolina. Both Molly Dewson and Dorothy McAllister had moved to Washington when they became the director (Dewson's plan to go home to New York and Polly Porter every weekend was short-lived). But Tillett's husband, Charles, maintained an active law practice in Charlotte, and Sara, the youngest of the Tilletts' three children, was fifteen years old at the end of 1940 when her mother became Women's Division director.

From the start of her time working for the DNC, Tillett blended her professional life and her motherhood to a level rarely seen among women in politics at the time. Dorothy McAllister's children never come up in the archives, even though they were living with her.[6] But Tillett's children appear often. During her first tenure as Speakers' Bureau director in 1936, she spent the summer working in the Women's Division's New York office with Molly Dewson. Tillett's older daughter, Gladys, seventeen years old in 1936, accompanied her mother to New York and was given "a little job" in the office by Dewson. Fifteen-year-old Charles Jr. had spent that summer working in his father's law office, and eleven-year-old Sara was sent to camp.[7] But three months away in the summertime was one thing; a full-time job working for the party was something quite different. And so Tillett always commuted. In fact, she made her ability to do so one of the requirements for taking the job. When she accepted the position as Women's Division head, she announced that she would be in Washington two days a week and do "the rest of the work from Charlotte."[8] That schedule was fine a month after a presidential election. But during 1942 and 1944, Tillett was away from Charlotte far more than she was home. By 1945, she was ready to tackle new issues and also ready for a break. And so she pulled the Women's Division directorship back from the break-neck pace of activity the job had entailed ever since 1932. Even after she stepped down as director in early 1947, she remained vice-chair of the DNC until 1950. That job required less work than running the Women's Division.

When Tillett pulled away from the Women's Division, India Edwards, whom she hired in March 1945 to replace Hick as executive secretary, stepped up to lead—but not without a fight. The executive secretary was the director's right-hand woman, and Hick had worked tirelessly since early 1940 in that capacity. She had worked through two presidential campaigns, and with her health declining, she was ready to retire to her home on Long Island. Tillett's efforts to get Edwards hired in 1945 hinted at the trouble brewing for women in the upper levels of the Democratic Party. In order to persuade DNC chairman Hannegan to let her hire Edwards, Tillett wrote a three-page single-spaced memo outlining all of Edwards's strengths and her contributions to the 1944 campaign. She also included testimonials from Democratic women around the country singing Edwards's praises. Never before had so much effort been required for a Women's Division director to hire her own executive secretary. It seems like overkill, but a memo from George Killion, the DNC treasurer, to Chairman Hannegan explains why Tillett had to fight so hard. "Mrs. Tillett plans to employ a Mrs. Edwards as a successor to Miss Hickok, whose resignation becomes effective March 3," Killion wrote. "She proposes to pay Mrs. Edwards $115.38 per week. I recall during a recent conversation that you questioned the advisability of hiring anyone to replace Miss Hickok."[9] It seems that the party chairman did not find staffing the Women's Division to be money well spent.

Since 1932, the WD director had been able to hire her staff as she saw fit and never faced a DNC chair questioning the necessity of an executive secretary for the division. During Roosevelt's presidency, the value of the Women's Division was undisputed, and Dewson and her successors had the autonomy to run things as they wished. But during the Truman years, India Edwards had to battle to maintain that independence and influence. Her difficulties highlight the divergent ideas about how best to reach women voters—and the role of women in politics—that were flowing through Democratic Party circles in the years after World War II.

It is hard to imagine someone more suited to the task of fighting for the Women's Division than India Edwards. She had a reputation as a hard-charging, hard-working woman who refused to back down. Throughout the second half of the 1940s, Democratic women around the country sent letters to President Truman and top DNC officials praising her. They described her as "not afraid of work" and someone who would "not take 'no' too easily." She had the "vigor and 'know-how' to get things done" because she refused to be overlooked or underestimated.[10] Edwards cultivated this image throughout her life: the title of her 1977 memoir was *Pulling No Punches*.

Edwards's drive came in part from a privileged but tumultuous early life. Her mother divorced her alcoholic father in 1899, when India was four years old and her sister just two. After the divorce, India's mother moved with the girls back to her hometown of Nashville. But after a fire in the house they shared with India's grandmother, India, her mother, and her sister moved to Chicago. Her mother later remarried, and Edwards's school years were spent moving around the Midwest until the family settled in St. Louis when she was about ten.[11] There, the family grew prosperous and stable. But the upheaval of her early childhood returned to Edwards as a young adult. On December 22, 1917, she married Second Lieutenant Daniel Sharp just weeks before he shipped off for basic training as part of the American Expeditionary Force of World War I. Lieutenant Sharp was assigned as a liaison officer with the British Army and deployed in Belgium. In January 1919 Edwards received a telegram informing her that her husband had been wounded in a mustard gas attack in late October 1918, three weeks before the end of the war. He succumbed to his injuries on December 20, 1918, two days before the couple's first wedding anniversary. She had only spent a few months with her husband, and now she was a widow at the age of twenty-three.

She did not remain a widow for long, however. In March 1920 she married Jack Moffett, a World War I veteran. For the next twenty years, Edwards raised her and Jack's two children, John and India (called Cissy). For most of that time she also worked as the editor of the society page for the *Chicago Tribune*. She took a seven-year hiatus from the paper, from John's birth in 1924 until 1931, to be home with her children. But she returned to work in 1931, at the depths of the Great Depression, and stayed with the *Tribune* until she moved to Washington, D.C., in 1942. Edwards's memoir is very thin on details about her marriage to Moffett, although at least one episode of infidelity is recounted.[12] The couple had separated by 1933 and divorced in 1937.

In 1942 India married her third husband, Herbert Edwards, with whom she had had a relationship since 1936. Herbert worked in the diplomatic corps, and so after their marriage India left the *Tribune* and moved to Washington, D.C. To that point in her life, Edwards had done no organized political work of any kind. And she might have settled into the role of Washington hostess had tragedy not struck in 1943. Her son, John, had enlisted in the air force in 1942, on his eighteenth birthday. He dreamed of following in his father's footsteps to fly during a war. He was assigned, however, to train other pilots rather than deploy himself, which was a huge relief to his mother. But on December 29, 1943, he was on board a bomber that was training for night flight when his airplane "touched wings" with another training plane, causing both planes to crash. All twenty-five people aboard were killed. In her memoir, published more than forty years after the crash, Edwards confessed that she never got over John's death but only learned to live with it.[13]

One way she learned to live with her grief was by throwing herself into political work on behalf of the Democratic Party. Clare Boothe Luce was largely responsible for this choice. Luce's 1944 convention speech, blaming FDR for the death of John and all the other casualties of the war, enraged Edwards. She recalled that a friend suggested that she volunteer at Democratic headquarters, "but I didn't do it until I heard Mrs. Luce's speech."[14] During that campaign she volunteered with the Women's Division and worked at the campaign headquarters. She eventually became one of the point people for publicity and radio when the previous volunteer leader resigned. In spite of the fact that the job was "dumped in [Edwards's] lap," Gladys Tillett told DNC chairman Hannegan that "too much cannot be said" about the work Edwards did.[15] When Hick retired from the Women's Division in early 1945, Edwards was a logical pick for her successor.

Because Tillett's own work and interests were moving toward the United Nations, most of the day-to-day work of running the division fell to Edwards. She was the one, for instance, who invited Bess Truman to make a brief statement during the 1946 Democratic Women's Day radio broadcast, as Eleanor Roosevelt had done since the early 1930s.[16] Beyond organizing Democratic Women's Day, the only other thing the WD seems to have done in that midterm election year was send out scripts of speeches to be given by specific people—a "first voter," the oldest Democrat present, a veteran, and so on. These speeches could be either for local radio or for community meetings. The most interesting was a speech suggested for a county vice-chairwoman, outlining why women should work for the party. "What concerns me," the script read:

> is that so many Democratic women who want success for the party do not realize how much they could do to help. Some are busy with a thousand and one household tasks. Their children demand most of their attention. Their church or club work absorbs the time they can spare for group activities. They know that all such duties are important, and part of the American way of life. But what is more important in its effect on the American way of life than voting for the party of the people? . . . Let us show these women how they can help and how they can be of service without slighting their other duties and obligations.[17]

WD leaders were worried about a letdown in women's political activism as the baby boom swung into gear. They believed that women were vital to the party and that women benefitted from political work. But over the next fifteen years, the concerns in this speech increasingly came true. While the WD structure remained robust until the late 1950s, especially among Republicans, its influence slowly but steadily declined as children, church, and club once again became the focus of middle-class white women's lives.

In 1946 the DNC was still chaotic, which hindered Edwards's and Tillett's efforts to rally their troops. Chairman Bob Hannegan was in poor health. There were huge fights within the party over whether it would continue pushing the boundaries of liberalism, as it had during the New Deal, or retreat to a more moderate platform. Most people sensed Truman's preference was for the latter, but the president was not terribly forthcoming.

The 1946 midterms were a disaster for Democrats. The party lost control of Congress for the first time since 1930. The relationship between liberal New Deal Democrats and conservative white supremacist southern Democrats had grown more contentious, foreshadowing the rupture of the 1948 presidential election when South Carolinian Strom Thurmond led a southern break from the party and ran as a white supremacist Dixiecrat candidate. This was not purely a regional problem, however. The tension between the liberal and moderate factions of the party could be seen nationwide. An article in the *Kansas City Star*, President Truman's hometown newspaper, reported that some party members blamed Hannegan's "insistence on tying the party to the left-wingers and labor organizations" for the 1946 losses.[18]

India Edwards proposed another reason why the party had failed. In a letter to Hannegan, she analyzed the party's failure with women in stark terms: "We lost the independent women's vote this year, and it is a big factor in winning every election. The women's vote is more important every year but apparently we Democrats do not recognize this, for as far as I know no woman ever was consulted during the campaign when decisions had to be made that would affect the women's vote. . . . We must recognize our mistakes and then push forward. There is a tremendous job to be done among woman voters, and in order to do it, we must have a program, a long-term plan of action."[19] Edwards believed that the party needed to be focusing on women voters as a distinct voting bloc, and she did not think that party leaders had done enough to court women's vote. In her mind, that was a major reason why the party lost the midterms.

In early 1947, a new long-term plan was undertaken for the Women's Division, but it was not the one that India Edwards wanted. On Valentine's Day 1947, the DNC announced that Chase Going Woodhouse, a Connecticut

Democrat who had lost reelection for her House seat in the 1946 midterms, was the new director of the Women's Division. Gladys Tillett would stay on as vice-chair of the DNC, and Edwards would continue under the new title of associate director.[20]

To Edwards, this was a flagrant slap in the face. Woodhouse had no history of national campaign work. She was an academic and a legislator. She was strong when it came to policy, but she was not a party worker and did not understand politicking. Just a month before Woodhouse was announced as Women's Division director, Edwards had recommended Woodhouse for an open seat on the Federal Communications Commission.[21] The party clearly wanted her to stay engaged in politics, and she regained her seat in the House in 1948. But Edwards, and party women around the country, were incensed that she was given the directorship ahead of Edwards. After several months of Woodhouse's leadership of the division, one influential Indiana Democratic woman, Mary Rickett, wrote to the DNC chairman that Woodhouse "has so many things wrong with her that I hardly know where to start to enumerate them."[22]

A major reason that Woodhouse was so disliked by rank-and-file Democratic women, and by Edwards, was that she was clearly in over her head. But there is no evidence that she asked for help from the strong WD network or reached out to Edwards. At the end of the year, Edwards told new DNC chair Howard McGrath that she could not turn in the breakdown of the WD's 1947 expenses because Woodhouse "has all the Women's Division copies with her" and was out of the office for the holidays. The letter also revealed that Woodhouse was using her daughter Margaret as her secretary, rather than a professional secretary or a woman with a history of party involvement.[23] Mary Rickett's letter critiquing Woodhouse specifically mentioned that she "has no sense of administration and seems unable to adapt herself to work either in a group or with a group, or to delegate authority to another."[24] Edwards recalled that the only reason she stayed on through Woodhouse's tenure was because Woodhouse wasn't in the office: "She and her secretary-daughter started off on a motor trip that took them across the continent not long after her appointment. We got nothing from her except expense accounts for several months, which did not at all please the new chairman, Howard McGrath. Her ambition to be reelected as a representative from Connecticut seemed to outweigh all other considerations."[25] In short, Woodhouse lacked the kinds of skills or interest necessary to run a national organization.

The Women's Division was also an uncomfortable fit for Woodhouse ideologically. She was a supporter of the ERA and opposed to the kind of difference feminism that justified the existence of a separate organization for women. Woodhouse did not believe that men and women should be treated differently, as voters or anywhere else in life. What the tension between Edwards and Woodhouse was really about, then, was the fate of the World War II shift within the Women's Division toward more explicitly gendered appeals to women. Had that shift occurred merely in response to the wartime crisis? Or would the WD continue to target women *as women*, not merely as voters like they had in the 1930s?

Woodhouse clearly believed that appealing to women in a gender-neutral way was best. When the Equal Rights Amendment was discussed in the House of Representatives in 1945, then-Congresswoman Woodhouse stated that she supported the amendment because society should not "lump people together in categories" but instead should look at every woman as "an individual American citizen."[26] Given this belief, Woodhouse was skeptical of the Women's Division's kind of feminism and the approach to women in politics it was emphasizing in the 1940s. By appointing Woodhouse as Tillett's replacement, the DNC leadership—perhaps inadvertently—stepped into the debate about the nature of gender and politics, which was most often articulated through disagreements over the Equal Rights Amendment. That debate was always simmering under the surface with political women at midcentury and was particularly prominent in the mid-1940s.[27] The Democratic Party endorsed the Equal Rights Amendment for the first time in its 1944 platform. The war had increased support for the ERA, as more women entered the paid labor force and encountered discrimination in hiring and pay.[28] But in spite of the amendment's inclusion in the party platform, women remained very much divided. A dismayed Molly Dewson lamented that the party was "pledged to Emma Guffey's amendment."[29] Woodhouse was an equality feminist and an ERA supporter. It is no surprise that someone with her politics did not wholeheartedly embrace working for women voters as a distinct group. Woodhouse's leadership of the WD, had it persisted, would have represented a major shift in the group's beliefs.

ERA advocates were almost the only women who called themselves feminists in these decades, but they were a minority of politically active women during the early Cold War.[30] Woodhouse, however, may have been surprised by their weakness within the DNC and the WD. The majority of WD leaders and active workers believed that, while equal rights was a good goal, eliminating the laws that regulated women's working conditions would do more harm than good. But this was not a clean partisan split, and the relationships around the ERA within the Democratic Party were always delicate. Woodhouse was not the only ERA advocate on the Democratic side, as the persistent work of Emma Guffey Miller and her allies over the previous decade shows. India Edwards, however, was not in favor of the amendment. In 1946 she noted, "I am not a feminist and I am not for the Equal Rights Amendment (as written) but I am an advocate of the school of thought that advises against under-estimating the power of women."[31]

This sentence reveals a great deal about Edwards's thoughts on women, gender, and politics. She thought of women as a group with common attributes, and she thought the DNC ignored them at its peril. It was precisely because she understood women as different from men but not unequal with respect to political power and opportunity that she was such a fierce advocate for women in politics, for special attention to be paid to women voters, and for not underestimating women's abilities. This statement closed a letter in which she excoriated Hannegan for the DNC's lack of attention to women voters during the midterm. Believing in women and men as different did not, for Edwards or most other political women who agreed with her, mean that she believed women could do less than men. They did things differently, they thought, and in that very difference was power.

The ideological conflicts between Edwards and Woodhouse, combined with Woodhouse's apparent disinterest in doing her job, came to a head in early 1948. On January 2 of that year, Edwards detailed her complaints about Woodhouse and her vision for the Women's Division. She told Chairman McGrath:

> The reason why I felt impelled to write this is that before she left for Connecticut on Dec. 24 CGW told Kay Foley that when she submitted her report about her trip to you she was going to recommend that the Women's Division be dissolved. I do not for one moment think you would consider doing this but it

> seems to be a good time for me to have my say on the subject of the W.D. and the importance of the women's vote. . . .
>
> I've always thought that the ideal set-up would be to have no differentiation as to sex in the [Democratic National] Committee but until there is less discrimination against women I believe it is essential that the Committee have a Women's Division.[32]

The idea of dissolving the WD was incomprehensible to Edwards. To her mind there was still so much sexism in society, and the Democratic Party, that treating women differently was a necessary step. That separation, she believed, helped women eventually secure equal footing. Eliminating the WD would eliminate women's power within the party. Different treatment ensured more equality.

By laying out her position so clearly, Edwards was demanding that the DNC pick a side in the debate over feminist tactics and philosophies. By forcing the DNC to choose between her and Woodhouse, Edwards was asking them, indirectly, to decide if the changes in the approach to women voters that had occurred because of the demographics of a wartime election would be permanent, or if politicians would return to Depression-era norms in which female votes were not treated as a distinct voting bloc.

It is possible that McGrath and the other men with whom Edwards butted heads did not fully understand this fight, but she did not take the time to explain in detail. Instead, she went to work. Edwards had an ally in DNC executive director Gael Sullivan. Sullivan was the second-in-command at the DNC and strongly supported Edwards and her position. At the same time she was firing off this angry letter to McGrath, she also wrote a far more personal letter to Sullivan: "I will fight for the W.D. to the last ditch, for I think it would be suicide to abolish it, but I'm not fighting for myself. I'm so darn tired and discouraged as of this moment that I would welcome the chance to stay in the country and forget politics."[33] Sullivan took up Edwards's side and began pushing McGrath to do more about women voters. In February 1948 he told McGrath that state-level party leaders were not doing enough to involve women: "I think National Committeemen and State Chairmen should be advised that the national committee hopes that they will give the strongest possible representation to women—consistent with the ballot delegates—throughout the state. I have just seen the list of a couple of states [committees]—and the delegates are all men, with just a sprinkling of women among the officers. The latest figures disclose a two million vote majority of women over men. Shall I prepare the letter?"[34] In just a few sentences, Sullivan exposed how thoroughly the party's organization of women had fallen apart in the previous several years. From 1945 to 1948, male party leaders at the state level had stopped including women in the ways they had been included since the 1920s. No wonder the rank-and-file women were writing angry letters and were so disappointed in Woodhouse in particular. The lack of attention to women voters and party workers by the national office had allowed exactly the kind of discriminatory backsliding Edwards warned about. Sullivan was worried it would cost the Democrats the presidency.

McGrath, however, wasn't so sure. He seemed exasperated by both Edwards and Woodhouse. His response to Sullivan's encouragement to write a letter to the state-level party leaders was not what Sullivan had hoped for: "I do not think we ought to write about this matter," the party chairman declared. "However, if the Women's Division care to prepare this letter," they were free to do so.[35] McGrath didn't want to have to think about the Women's Division or women voters. By ignoring both Woodhouse's suggestion to dissolve the division and Edwards's threat to quit if Woodhouse stayed, he probably hoped the whole conflict would go away. But with India Edwards on the job, that was never going to happen.

With an absentee boss and no immediate threat of being fired, Edwards simply ran the Women's Division her way and began gearing up for the 1948 election. She quickly began to clash with the campaign's publicity chair, Jack Redding. In March, Redding angrily informed Chairman McGrath that, "It has come to my attention that the Women's Division is now carrying on a publicity campaign. None of this material has ever been seen by anyone in the Publicity Division." He urged McGrath to instruct the Women's Division to stop or at least require them to get the approval of the Publicity Division before they mailed anything.[36] Redding either did not know or did not care about the historical autonomy of the WD. The division had always put out its own material, going back to Dewson and the first set of rainbow fliers in 1932. In requesting approval power over the Women's Division's materials, Redding threatened the core of Edwards's vision of the division. She recalled in a 1960s oral history that Redding had "no conception" of the goals of the division and what she was trying to do.[37]

McGrath informed Edwards that he was "in accord with Mr. Redding," but Edwards ignored them both. Three months later, Redding again complained to McGrath, declaring that, "the problem of proper clearance of material from the Women's Division of the Democratic Committee is still a problem." But by the time Redding lodged this complaint in June, Edwards was officially Women's Division director and, perhaps more important, a close confidant of the president.[38]

Edwards finally got promoted in mid-April, after threatening once again to quit. That month, Woodhouse stepped down as WD head, but Edwards was only offered the directorship on an interim basis. In response, she announced that she was "completely fed up" and unwilling to become director temporarily. She planned to walk away in the middle of the campaign, in spite of her tremendous admiration for Truman, because she did not believe she had been treated respectfully. She was also angry that Woodhouse seemed to be getting promoted for her poor performance, as she had been appointed to a consultant position with a U.S. government program in Germany.[39] This threat did the trick; within a week, she was the permanent WD director. She immediately tried to patch things up with McGrath, telling him that if he ever felt he had "made a mistake" in hiring her, he "won't have to suggest more than once that I resign." McGrath responded simply, "The only mistake made was the change should have been made sooner. You understand the difficulty."[40]

There are many reasons why Edwards's vision of the Women's Division as a robust part of the party mechanism that spoke to women voters *as women* and held space for them in the life of the party carried the argument. One was her persistence in doing the work and Woodhouse's obvious disinclination to do so, even though she was being paid the director's salary. Another was the demographic factor Sullivan highlighted as he lobbied McGrath to support the division. Women had become the majority of voters during World War II, and after the war, that remained the case. Not only were there more women, there were also "more women in the independent group than there are men," at least according to Edwards. Women were a critical swing voting bloc and needed to be specifically targeted.[41]

Targeting women voters as a distinct group also fit with the political culture of the early Cold War. Historian Wendy Wall's argument that postwar politicians valued "pluralism," a belief that America was stronger when there were many different voices participating in politics, resonates with Edwards's triumph in the WD fight. While Wall identifies this support for pluralism as opening the door for religious minorities and, to a lesser extent, African Americans to enter American party politics more fully, it is clear that similar ideas applied to women. Throughout the postwar era, politicians from both parties gave speeches and wrote articles promoting the importance of women in politics.[42]

Political pluralism was also strategic, as it meshed well with the gender ideology of the Cold War. As an ideology emphasizing women's role as homemakers became more pronounced, both the DNC and the RNC turned critical attention to women as swing voters in close presidential elections. And it was *because* men and women were seen as so different that women voters were pursued as a distinct voting bloc. In these years, both Democrats and Republicans used "woman" and "housewife" as interchangeable terms in campaign materials that pursued women's votes, reflecting the American housewife's centrality to Cold War ideology. One major demonstration of America's superiority to the Soviet Union, according to politicians and journalists, was the ability of American women to stay within the home, remaining feminine and disengaged from the "affairs of men," as historian Elaine Tyler May phrased it.[43] A good mother who raised her children, participated in postwar consumerism, and provided a fulfilling sex life to her husband—that was the ideal and idealized American woman of the postwar period. But that woman, that housewife, was also an important voter in the minds of both parties, and women leaders in the parties believed that women *did* belong in the "affairs of men." How, then, to reach her? Treating her identically to men, as Woodhouse advocated, made no sense in a culture as deeply invested as Cold War America was in promoting distinct gender roles and at least rhetorically supporting diversity in politics. That diversity was not intersectional and Edwards rarely included African American women in the work of her WD. But as the 1948 campaign season got underway, she and her team created ways to speak to the (primarily white) American housewife, to convince her that the Republican Congress elected in 1946 was the root of all her domestic problems and that a vote for President Truman and the Democrats would restore the prosperity of her home.

V

Housewives for Truman

THE 1948 CAMPAIGN

Democratic women proved their value many times over during the 1948 campaign. Even before the campaign kicked off in earnest, women of the party were rallying to Truman's defense and publicly making the case for his election. In May, the *New Republic* magazine harshly criticized Truman and urged Democratic leaders to persuade General Dwight D. Eisenhower to be their candidate, rather than the incumbent president. Emma Guffey Miller took a break from criticizing the WD's lack of support for the ERA and wrote a stinging rebuttal, which was published nationally. Copies were sent to women on the WD's mailing list, so they could use Miller's talking points if the *New Republic* article came up in conversation. Edwards also forwarded a copy of Miller's response to Matthew Connelly, the president's personal secretary, noting that she "just [wanted] to let you know that the Women's Division is in there pitchin' not only for votes but for our big boss." Connelly responded warmly, "Dear Mrs. Edwards: Thank you for the material you sent. I enjoyed reading it very much. You all are doing fine work—keep it up!"[1]

In July 1948, Edwards informed the DNC leadership of her plans to do just that, by making the WD a central part of the coming campaign. She asserted once again that women voters held the balance of the election. She argued that women would continue to turn out for the Democrats only "if we can do the job that we should do during the coming months." She continued:

> Millions of those independent women voted with the Democrats when Franklin Roosevelt was alive not just because he had charm and the most marvelous radio voice in the world but because the Women's Division of the Democratic National Committee took the trouble to inform the women of the country as to what Franklin Roosevelt was trying to do. . . .

> I would like to have dozens of women out in the field during the next few months—not orating from platforms but talking to small groups, explaining to them why it will be to their best advantage to elect a Democratic President and a Democratic Congress next November.[2]

Edwards argued that informing women of the platform of the Democratic Party was essential and that they must be targeted specifically. Her emphasis on working with small groups, reminiscent of Helen Gahagan Douglas's 1944 neighborhood campaigning approach, became one of the most lasting contributions of Edwards's WD.

At the end of this speech, she eviscerated George Gallup, the pollster who made such a splash with his predictions in the 1948 campaign season and, famously, got the presidential race wrong. Gallup had recently stated that "the women's vote is a myth" because women "take their cue from the opinions or prejudices of a husband, a father, a son, or other male member of the family." Edwards argued that this common idea about women voters was completely wrongheaded: "What rot—what complete, utter, tommyrot! Mr. Gallup writes as though he were living in the 18th century. There are many women who are influenced by their husbands or their fathers or their brothers, but there are just as many men who are influenced by the women-folk with whom they come into contact. If a woman takes the trouble to inform herself about political matters and to have an opinion, she is as apt to influence her husband as vice-versa."[3]

This speech outlined the core of India Edwards's approach to women's politics. In 1948, she designed a program to reach and mobilize women voters because she believed both that the women's vote was essential on its own and that women were effective and important grassroots advocates for the party and its agenda.

Her work was made somewhat easier by the fact that one of the biggest domestic issues of the 1948 campaign seemed a perfect fit for women voters. In early 1947 the Republicans, newly in control of Congress, had ended all wartime price controls that were still in effect some eighteen months after the war's end. From almost the moment that law was passed, DNC material focused on the inflation created by the policy change. On January 2, 1948, the DNC organized a radio rally, which included speeches by Vice President

Alben Barkley and many other Democratic officials, as well as "ordinary Americans." Several of the speakers were women, including Congresswoman Mary Norton. Norton outlined the proposals that President Truman had submitted to Congress to address inflation and stated that "the session of Congress starting Monday will determine whether greed or stupidity caused the Republicans to kill price controls."[4]

Norton spoke immediately after Vice President Barkley, who had focused his remarks on "the European situation." In January 1948, the United States was in the early stages of fighting the Cold War. The president had given the speech outlining what came to be known as the Truman Doctrine less than a year earlier; the Marshall Plan, through which the government spent millions of dollars to shore up western European economies, was still working its way through Congress. Throughout the 1948 campaign, male and female Democrats talked about inflation and the high cost of living as significant domestic *and* international problems. In his Truman Doctrine speech, the president tied the appeal of communism to poverty, stating that "the seeds of totalitarianism are sown in misery and want. They spread and grow in the evil soil of poverty and strife."[5] Keeping people out of poverty was a central part of the Democratic Party's legislative agenda and its campaign rhetoric in 1948.

How politicians framed the problem of inflation did not break down neatly along gendered lines. When Democratic politicians and party leaders spoke to female audiences, they talked about *all* the ways in which inflation was a problem. They switched back and forth, sometimes in the same radio program, between a housewife struggling to make ends meet to feed and clothe her family and the global geopolitics of high prices. This blending of a housewife's budget and global political concerns was not new in the postwar era. During World War II, many women's organizations, such as women's union auxiliaries and the National Council of Negro Women, had tried to influence the rationing and pricing policies of the Office of Price Administration (OPA). These groups declared that they accepted rationing and high prices as part of their wartime sacrifice but wanted to ensure that working-class people did not bear a disproportionately high burden of rationing. Those same organizations lobbied vigorously to keep the OPA price controls in place after the war. The rhetoric around inflation that Edwards and the rest of the WD used during the 1948 campaign was another area where Edwards built on wartime foundations.[6]

Addressing inflation as both a personal and political problem was a particular focus of Helen Gahagan Douglas, now a Democratic congresswoman from California.[7] She had been elected to the House of Representatives in 1944 and served until she ran for the Senate in 1950 and lost a famously nasty campaign to Richard Nixon. In the second half of the 1940s, Douglas was among the most prominent Democrats in the House, and after her party lost control of Congress in 1946, she excoriated the Republicans for the toll their programs took on working Americans.

In April 1948, Douglas set a theme and tone that Edwards expanded on throughout Truman's campaign. Douglas often reminded the public of her status as a wife and mother of young children (her youngest child, Mary Helen, was six years old when her mother was first elected to Congress), and during the 1948 campaign her housewife identity was in full view. That April she took a photographer along with her as she went to a Washington, D.C., Safeway store and purchased basic staples of the era—ground round, pork chops, butter, soap chips, and a few other items. She then took her grocery receipt and the March 1947 OPA price list for the same items onto the floor of the House of Representatives and gave a blistering speech about how the policies of the Republicans were making it harder for families to buy food and other essentials. But she not only tied high prices to a trip to Safeway and a housewife's budget. In the speech Douglas also declared that "we are willing to spend billions to stop Communism abroad but do nothing to stop the conditions that will breed it here."[8] In this single speech Douglas incorporated the entire range of Democratic Party arguments against high prices. Edwards used the same shopping trip demonstration during her opening-night keynote address at the Democratic convention in July, taking items out of a shopping basket as she outlined high prices. Just as Douglas's had been, Edwards's was a highly effective speech. One historian has described it as the convention's "only note of optimism."[9] Edwards's optimism on all sorts of things—that high prices were a winning issue for the Democrats, that Truman would win, and that women's votes were key to his victory—sustained her through the grueling campaign. And she turned out to be right about all of it.

Edwards ensured that WD material constantly hit the major theme of the campaign, linking Republicans to high prices and sowing the seeds of communism in the process. In July the division distributed a radio program in which Edwards "interviewed" Margery Clifford, wife of White House Counsel Clark Clifford. Clifford talked about how much the price of butter, shoes, and other necessities had increased and how aware she was of the stretch on her household budget as she shopped for herself, her husband, and their three children. Edwards closed the broadcast by stating, "What can the American housewife do about high prices? The answer is to vote! And vote Democratic!"[10]

Radio programs were a favorite format for Edwards's Women's Division. In the last month of the campaign, the division broadcast two programs a week. All but one focused at least partially on the issue of high prices and the Republican Congress's responsibility for them. The program that aired on October 18, 1948, for example, featured Matilda Grepo, the wife of a Chicago steelworker, who observed: "We've got three growing kids . . . the littlest one's five and when I go to the grocery store I have to pass up lots of things I know would make them more healthy. It's on my conscience all the time. I can't do half as good by my family as I know how but my husband and I are voting Democratic again this November because it makes a lot of difference to us whether we have people in Washington who want to bring prices down and get us decent places to live."[11]

This kind of direct discussion was only one way in which the Women's Division wove the issue of prices into their radio programs. Another program, which aired the week after the one that included Matilda Grepo, featured the vice president of the Amalgamated Clothing Workers Union, a heavily female union. She focused on the problem of slow wage growth, arguing that increasing wages was just as important as lowering prices to "the woman in her kitchen as it is to her daughter who works in a factory or an office. In every case it's somebody's wages that has to be stretched to cover the high cost of living."[12] The program that aired the day before the election featured Congresswoman Mary Norton. As she had during the January radio rally, Norton again wove together the domestic and international implications of inflation. High prices, she said, were "the darkest cloud hanging over your family's plans today. But inflation in the United States is not merely a frontal attack on our *pocketbooks*—although goodness knows it is that—but in the broader sense is actually an attack on our country's security and that of the whole world."[13]

Edwards and her staff at the Women's Division wrote all of these scripts and arranged the entire series of programs. They believed that women voters would be persuaded not only by discussions of how inflation affected their personal lives but also by how it affected the world in these early days of the Cold War. The radio series was tremendously popular and effective: *Variety*, the trade magazine for the entertainment industry, declared the series "the most novel radio pitch in election campaign history."[14]

The Women's Division talked to women, connecting the dots between their experiences at the grocery store and politics in Washington. And the division also actively enlisted women's help to make that case. On September 22, the division tasked county chairwomen in fifteen cities with two additional jobs for the campaign's final push. First, each city was assigned two dates in October and a short shopping list. The local leaders were told to find volunteers who would shop for the requested items on the assigned day and send the Women's Division the price of each item via telegram. On October 14, for instance, the division wanted to know the price of pork chops, eggs, soap, and string beans in St. Louis, Salt Lake City, and Detroit. On November 1, the day before the election, they wanted the price of hamburger, milk, eggs, and cabbage in Dallas, San Francisco, and Cleveland. These details were then incorporated into the scripts of the radio addresses, giving real-life and up-to-the-minute examples of how hard it was for working-class and middle-class women to feed their families.[15]

In addition to tapping local leaders to provide the data for division talking points, Edwards also asked the county chairwomen to suggest local women who could appear in the programs. This is how Matilda Grepo and other "regular" women came to be featured. As Edwards explained to her grassroots troops:

> We need stories of housewives' trouble with their economic problems, high prices, housing, education, and any other pertinent subjects which we can use to show that the Republican party and the 80th Congress is not taking care of their problems and, therefore, cannot. Also, from this, the material will be used to show what Democratic administrations do for people. For instance, if a wife

of a veteran has had considerable trouble with housing, is paying too much for rent or cannot afford to buy and probably has to double up with relatives or live in inadequate housing, this is the kind of material we can use.[16]

In asking Democratic women throughout the country to send in these stories, Edwards built on the patterns set by Molly Dewson's Reporter Plan in the 1930s. But she was taking it one step further. Not only did Edwards want to know how Democratic policies were being received locally, she used grassroots women's experiences to shape Democratic talking points at the national level. The housewife and her home budget were deeply political things in the late 1940s, and everyone knew it. Rather than a respite from the political world, the early Cold War home was a major front in political debates. Edwards's Women's Division capitalized on that politicization, using local women and their shopping trips to create influential campaign material that helped Truman secure his upset victory.

While most WD material focused on inflation, one of the radio programs did not. Radio program number seven, which aired eight days before the election, examined President Truman's record on civil rights. Mary McLeod Bethune, the most prominent Black woman in politics in the 1930s and 1940s, was the primary speaker. Bethune urged listeners, whom she described as "women in their homes all across this great country," to endorse Truman's civil rights agenda and support him personally because he was "a man who stands for the principles of justice and fair play for *every* man and woman." Bethune was the second speaker on that day's program; the first was a woman from Atlanta named Helen Bullard, who also spoke in favor of Truman's civil rights agenda. Bullard stated, "I feel that my vote [for Truman] will be a vote for human rights. There are many southerners like myself who agree with the Declaration of Independence that *ALL* men are created equal. Like myself, they believe that the President's civil rights program is forward looking. Furthermore, they and I believe that the eyes of the world are upon us and that our sincerity will be doubted unless we redouble our efforts to wipe out racial, religious, and economic discrimination."[17] While the script does not indicate Bullard's race, the way she frames her support of Truman suggests that she is white. Having a white southern woman speaking in favor of civil rights in 1948 was a provocative step for Edwards and the WD to take, but it fits with the small cadre of southern white women like Anne Braden and Virginia Durr who wielded their white womanhood to advance racial equality in the postwar era.[18]

Having a program devoted completely to civil rights put the WD squarely within the mainstream of Truman's approach to race in 1948. Truman's support for civil rights, though something he only came to as president, was sincere and deep.[19] He had signed an executive order to integrate the military in 1947 and established a commission to investigate racial discrimination and suggest methods to combat it. The commission's report, *To Secure These Rights*, was published in December 1947. The Democratic Party also adopted its strongest civil rights plank to date at the 1948 convention, an action that caused Governor Strom Thurmond of South Carolina to lead a walkout by white southerners and to run as a third-party candidate for president in 1948. Thurmond's Dixiecrat party, grounded in white supremacy and inequality between Black and white people, had many supporters and was seen as a major threat to Truman's electoral chances.[20] One way to offset the losses in the South, Truman's staff asserted, was to shore up the African American vote in the rest of the country.[21] The Women's Division's decision to focus on civil rights for an entire radio program is an indication of how connected Edwards was to the overall ideas and tenor of the campaign. The WD was not isolated, nor was it running a special campaign on "women's issues" only—indeed, Edwards would argue that the entire party platform was composed of women's issues. The WD's task was advancing Truman's central appeal to the American people in order to elect him president.

However, while the Women's Division wrote this script, that seems to have been its only effort on civil rights. There is no evidence of targeted outreach to Black women voters while Edwards was division director. When Chase Going Woodhouse was still head of the division, she began work to organize Black women. In March 1948 she asked party chairman McGrath's permission to bring a group of Black women activists, headed by Bethune, to Washington to make plans for their work on behalf of Truman's election. Woodhouse told McGrath that the women "believe strongly in the Democratic Party, but feel that in recent years they have been very much on the outside."[22] This is the only mention I found of the Women's Division working specifically with Black women in 1948, and it seems unlikely that the meeting occurred, since

Woodhouse was out as WD director less than a month later. Like Dewson, McAllister, and Tillett before her, Edwards does not appear to have done any sort of sustained outreach or organizing among Black women. At Edwards's Women's Division, not only were "woman" and "housewife" used as synonyms, that "woman" was virtually always white. Even the radio program was not really targeted at Black women but rather designed to make white women think about why Truman's civil rights work was another reason they should support him.

The Women's Division also designed, along with the radio programs, a traveling exhibit about high prices. The program called Housewives for Truman eventually toured eight swing states scattered throughout the country, including Minnesota, West Virginia, and New York. The program was designed and organized by the Women's Division but implemented by state and local Democratic officials, as well as state and local Democratic candidates for office.

The idea of Housewives for Truman was similar to the radio addresses: the Women's Division was dramatizing the rapidly increasing cost of basic necessities, especially clothing and food. In each city, a group of local Democratic women went to a national chain grocery store and bought a bag's worth of staples. They then parked an Airstream-style trailer in a central place in town, surrounded by two or three cars hung with banners that included pictures of President Truman and slogans like "Beat High Prices," "Housewives for Truman," and "Register—Vote!" An easel placed in front of the trailer displayed the OPA-set prices of the groceries in 1946 and what the women had just paid for them that day. People could enter the trailer, look at other exhibits, and pick up fliers outlining the Democrats' position on the issues. Eventually a formal program would begin at the trailer, featuring local women talking about prices through a loudspeaker. Usually, local candidates would also give speeches, and sometimes men would join to stump for the Democrats as well. In West Virginia, for example, the group of speakers included a veteran and a coal miner in addition to a housewife.[23]

Housewives for Truman was a huge success. The chairman of the New York State Democratic Committee gushed about it to Edwards, saying, "I just want to add my bit to the acclaim which the trailer 'Housewives for Truman' has received from our workers and leaders—both men and women—all over the state. It turned out to be one of the most popular campaign techniques we have ever used. . . . My sincere congratulations to you and your staff for the tremendous contribution you made to the victory. As always, the Women's Division, nationally and here in my own state, was magnificent."[24] A female journalist from New Jersey praised the program directly to President Truman, stating that it "resulted not only in a good vote for our president but interested a number of women who had never before been identified in politics."[25] In her report on the program after the election, Edwards also described the program as a huge success, remarking "the results were electrifying" everywhere the trailers went and that "we were surprised to find that a program originally designed for the women attracted the men as well."[26]

The Housewives for Truman trailers also meshed well with other Women's Division projects, including the continued production of rainbow fliers. The 1948 fliers followed the pattern that rainbow fliers had always followed, laying out the party's argument in a gender-neutral way. One flier, *Change This Picture,* focused on growing inequality, and included two men in its images. Another flier, *Get This Straight!* included a small amount of text under the headlines "The Democrats Are for Prices You Can Afford" and "The Republicans Are for High Prices." Other fliers had titles including *Check Inflation with Your Vote, Line Up with the Democrats—and You Line Up with the Friends of the People!* and *The Democrats Are for Fair Prices: For the Housewife, for the Farmer, for the Storekeeper.*[27] The fliers were mailed to Democratic women around the country, as they had always been. But they were also distributed at the Housewives for Truman trailers. By using the Housewives for Truman trailers as a vehicle for distributing the fliers, Edwards's WD ensured that passing fliers out and striking up conversations with neighbors about politics remained primarily women's job. But having them at the trailers made them available to any woman who stopped by, not just the ones who were registered Democrats and active in party politics. Distributing the rainbow fliers in this way helped the Women's Division increase the number of women who were doing the local-level work of the party. And it was a particularly effective way of putting independent women voters, the group of women voters most likely to swing from party to party, to work for the Democrats in 1948.

From the trailers to the rainbow fliers to the radio programs, the Women's Division worked incredibly hard to turn out women's votes in 1948. They did so not only because Edwards and her staff, as political leaders, believed that women should be engaged in politics. They insisted that women were critical swing voters in the 1948 election. At the beginning of her report on the trailer program, Edwards noted that, "In 1946, the housewives of America helped defeat Democratic candidates. Most of the women did not vote. . . . This year there were about 1,579,000 more women than men eligible to vote. The women's vote *could* be decisive. But a certain lethargy existed among the women . . . particularly among the so-called independent voters. . . . Therefore our job was to excite the women and get their vote. We knew that the inflation issue was closer to the housewife's heart than federal-aid-to-education, social security, taxation, etc. Therefore we decided to dramatize the problem of high prices."[28] This report summed up the beliefs that shaped all of Edwards's work as Women's Division head: that women and men had different interests, and that women were a crucial group of voters who needed to be wooed in order to bring them into the Democratic camp and keep them there.

Edwards was not the only DNC staff member attentive to the need to bring in women voters. When Chase Going Woodhouse was still running the WD, she remarked to Truman that "the organization men at our Thursday meeting and elsewhere have stressed the importance of more work with and by women."[29] It is telling that Woodhouse does not say that *she* is stressing the importance of this work—the men in the party are, but Woodhouse still isn't sold. Also during Woodhouse's tenure, the *Washington Memo* newsletter described DNC executive director Gael Sullivan's "strategy for recapturing the women's vote, which largely deserted the Democrats last fall."[30] The fact that Sullivan was focused on turning out women voters and bringing them back into the Democratic fold in the spring of 1947, nearly eighteen months before the election, shows how seriously he took the issue. It also suggests why Sullivan supported Edwards's promotion to WD leadership during her fights with Woodhouse. Sullivan wanted Edwards because they both believed that women were a swing voting bloc and that Edwards's approach of treating women as different and distinct was the best path to victory.

Even after Sullivan left the DNC, Edwards was able to maintain her independence and fight off efforts to bring the WD's work under men's control. The primary man trying to control Edwards was Jack Redding, the DNC publicity director. Redding continued to complain about Edwards's refusal to clear WD materials with him. On June 14, 1948, he informed Chairman McGrath that "the problem of proper clearance of publicity material from the Women's Division of the Democratic Committee is still a problem. . . . You asked me to remind you of this problem so that it can be thrashed out between yourself and Mrs. Edwards."[31] Redding did not get what he wanted. A week after receiving this memo, McGrath's secretary forwarded it to Edwards with a note asking her to "take up the attached matter directly with Mr. Redding to see if this matter can be cleared up in a satisfactory manner." It is unclear if that meeting took place, but if it did, Edwards held her ground. There was no way that she was going to allow Redding to approve her materials, and their relationship remained tense throughout the campaign. Redding tried, for example, to take over the October radio shows. Edwards recalled that the two of them "fought like cats and dogs" over control of the script writing for the programs. Edwards, of course, won.[32]

One reason Edwards was able to maintain her autonomy was because of her personality and her stubbornness. But another reason was because the Women's Division materials were focusing on the same issues as the president. Notes prepared for a campaign speech President Truman gave in Flint, Michigan, in September 1948 listed "the price of meat" as the most important domestic issue for his audience.[33] Truman gave that speech at a union hall, to a majority male audience. In another speech just days before the election, Truman argued that the decision to eliminate price controls and the resulting inflation led to an increasing risk of communist influence in the United States because the elimination of price controls and other "Republican policies of the 80th Congress . . . threaten to put an end to American prosperity."[34] Women's Division programming, in other words, advanced the campaign's central domestic theme. Edwards also recalled that the president had faith in the WD's ability to get "the facts to the voters about his programs and plans." Both Truman and Edwards saw the WD filling the same role in 1948.[35]

The Women's Division also maintained its autonomy because President Truman had faith in Edwards. In the first of the October radio addresses, Edwards recounted how she had "just returned from a cross-country tour with the president on his campaign train." She went on to tell listeners about how enthusiastic the crowds were at every stop, how everywhere they went "the women who talked to me told me they are going to vote for President Truman because they know he will continue to build economic stability at home and peace for the world."[36] Although she did not say so on the air, Edwards recalled later that she participated in the famous whistle-stop train trip because the president asked her to, in order to increase outreach to women voters:

> It was my job to look after the women who rode the train. That had been the purpose of my taking the trip. The advance men would see that there were plenty of women at every stop and that they would be invited to ride the Presidential train to the next stop. I saw to it that the women met President and Mrs. Truman. I had to be quite rude to visiting men politicians who were unaccustomed to having women treated like first-class citizens. [But] I never had any trouble with the White House assistants, since they all knew I was aboard by the President's order and that women were to be given equal treatment with men on the Harry S. Truman Campaign Train.

Edwards was convinced this was critical work, because, "I was the first professional to see that women, who did much of the political work in their home communities, were given the chance to meet the candidate and his family." Not only did leading women get to meet the president, doing so empowered them to be more active throughout the campaign. "In many places where the heads of our party were doing nothing to promote the national ticket," Edwards noted, "I was able to enlist the aid of [these] dedicated women."[37] President Truman had personally invited Edwards to participate in the trip in order to ensure that outreach to women voters and locally important Democratic women was a central part of the journey, and Edwards clearly relished that part of her job.

Truman also liked having her around because of her faith in his reelection. Even other DNC staff members remembered her as the only one who always believed Truman would win. One morning during the whistle-stop tour, Edwards was eating breakfast with the president and Mrs. Truman. Truman turned to Edwards and said, "You know, sometimes India, I think there are only two people in the whole United States who really think I am going to be elected and both of them are at this table. But the Boss [his nickname for his wife, First Lady Bess Truman] is not one of them."[38] On the morning after Election Day, when the election was called for Truman and he phoned the DNC headquarters to congratulate the staff, Chairman McGrath handed the phone to Edwards first, telling the president, "I want you to talk to the person who has been certain all along that you would win." Edwards remarked in her memoir that, by letting her be the first member of the team to speak to the president, McGrath gave her "a most unusual and generous tribute from a male politician to a female one."[39]

The fact that Edwards was on the train highlights Truman's affection for her. The work she was doing there also demonstrates the importance of women voters. But the fact that she is not remembered as being part of the team on that famous trip shows how thoroughly the work of Edwards, her peers, and the Women's Division has been forgotten. In his Pulitzer Prize–winning biography of Truman, published in the 1990s, biographer David McCullough listed the advisors who were with President Truman on the whistle-stop train. According to McCullough, Bill Boyle and Matt Connelly, two senior staffers, were the people tasked with "handling political chores" during the journey.[40] Edwards is not included in McCullough's list of train passengers, nor does her name appear anywhere in the entire nine hundred page book, in spite of the fact that everyone involved in the 1948 campaign knew she was the only person who believed in Truman's victory from the beginning. Leaving Edwards out of a list of those who did the "political chores" during the whistle-stop trip is particularly glaring, since Edwards's description of her work on the train appeared in her memoir published fifteen years before McCullough's biography.

From her participation in the whistle-stop tour, to her ability to maintain control over Women's Division publicity, to the massive success of the Housewives for Truman trailers and the October radio programs, India Edwards was a critical part of Truman's election triumph. She brought women voters back to the Democratic Party in 1948, which helped Truman win his unexpected victory. A few days after the election, Dorothy McAllister sent Edwards a letter of congratulations. Her analysis of Edwards's work is important; as a former Women's Division director, she knew exactly what Edwards had done. Her praise was effusive:

> You secured more publicity than the Women's Division had ever been able to get, and it was publicity which influenced votes; you had inaugurated a radio program that everyone was talking about; and you were sending out effective

ammunition to the workers on the rise in the cost of living and the issues of special concern to women.

There is NO question in my mind but that you dramatizing the actions of the Republicans in terms of rising living costs swung the votes of many independents who were housewives to our side. I am sure that it was the women, as well as the farmers, who gave the support to Truman Dr. Gallup had not expected. And it was you who, along with the President, made it clear what women had to gain by voting the Democratic ticket. My heartiest congratulations on an outstanding contribution to one of the greatest election victories of all time![41]

VI

"*Merger or Murder?*"

THE EVOLUTION OF THE DEMOCRATIC WOMEN'S DIVISION, 1949–1953

In October 1951, President Truman called India Edwards into the Oval Office and offered her the chairmanship of the Democratic National Committee. Although flattered, Edwards declined, believing that the men of the party would not work as hard for a woman as they would for a man. Fifteen months later, the DNC eliminated its Women's Division, "integrating" women's work into the general party structure. The headline writer of the *Cleveland Plain Dealer* summed up the situation perfectly: "Democratic Gals in a Dither—Is It Merger or Murder?"

The juxtaposition of these two events shows that Edwards's impression of Democratic Party men was correct—they did not see a need to support women's work for the party. Edwards threatened to quit at least twice during Truman's full term in office, bringing her total number of written resignation offers to at least four. The rocky road that Edwards traveled during the late 1940s and early 1950s reveals that Democratic Party officials' support for women was largely superficial, despite the centrality of women's votes to Truman's 1948 victory. The lack of support also undercut Edwards's outreach efforts—in these years, she was doing less to connect the party to women at the grassroots level. And so when the DNC, out of money and out of power for the first time in two decades, eliminated its Women's Division in January 1953, that decision in many ways simply made public the headwinds Edwards had battled for years.

As soon as Truman's remarkable victory became clear in November 1948, both winners and losers began hypothesizing about how the president had pulled it off. Thomas Dewey publicly cited Truman's strong performance among farmers, a traditionally Republican group. Members of Truman's inner circle and other Democratic politicians also named farmers, along with the labor vote and African Americans, whom Truman had worked so hard to win, as the decisive groups.[1] Few other than India Edwards and other party women credited women as a decisive bloc. A month after the election Doris Fleeson, a nationally syndicated columnist, wrote a column declaring that Truman did not show "proper appreciation" for the role of women in his victory. Edwards spent weeks fielding calls and letters from unhappy grassroots activists in the wake of the article, assuring them that Truman did indeed know how much they had put into his campaign.[2] She also arranged for the president to write a letter for the December 1948 / January 1949 issue of the *Democratic Digest*, thanking the women of the party. His message was weaker than Edwards would have liked; he merely stated that "Democratic workers throughout the country helped to get informed voters to the polls, and I owe a debt of thanks to such workers for their loyal efforts." He never named women specifically.[3] Three months later, the party's lack of appreciation of its women popped up in the press again, this time in a syndicated column that declared that women's role in Truman's victory had been "completely ignored by the political analysts and commentators."[4]

In spite of this neglect, Edwards kept working hard to get women involved in politics. In the summer of 1949 she was a featured guest on the NBC political program *Pro and Con*. She spoke at length about the fact that women were more engaged in politics than ever before:

> One of the interesting things to me has been the fact that women in the cities and towns, women on the farms, housewives, workers, and professionals are becoming increasingly active politically. This was particularly evident during the last campaign. It used to be that women felt that politics was none of their business. But now the issues have come right into the home and women can't escape them any longer. . . .
>
> It is impossible to say that one issue is uppermost in the minds of women, or men either for that matter. . . . What I have been stressing is that women are becoming more active politically because they are interested in the issues.[5]

There is a tension in these statements, as Edwards insists that women were becoming more active politically while denying that there was any particular "women's issue." That apparent contradiction—that women were important political actors *as women* while denying that there were "women's issues"—

was one that Edwards worked through for the rest of her time as Women's Division leader. It was a tension that also vexed her Republican successor as women's voice in the West Wing.

One way Edwards bridged this divide was by continuing Tillett's efforts to increase the number of women in policymaking jobs within the administration. Women, Edwards believed, should be appointed throughout the government, not only into gendered jobs at the Women's or Children's Bureaus. Edwards worked every angle possible to get women into such positions. In 1948 she sent Secretary of Defense James Forrestal the names of two women who were qualified and eager to serve in the Civilian Defense program.[6] She regularly sent lists of women to the DNC chairman and to the president. Like Tillett had before her, Edwards saw women's appointments as a valuable tool in winning women's votes. Early in the 1948 campaign she urged Chairman McGrath to appoint women to four specific positions, noting that "if we could announce these appointments, preferable all but even two would help, soon we would have a powerful weapon with which to fight the anti-Truman feeling independent women have evinced on all sides."[7] She recommended a woman for the FCC, as an ambassador, as an assistant secretary of agriculture, and for the White House staff. After the election, women's appointments became even more of a focus. In 1949, Edwards's correspondence with the male DNC leadership dealt with almost nothing else.[8]

In spite of Truman's personal support for her and the importance of the women's vote in the 1948 victory, Edwards still had to fight for even a modicum of authority within the party. Throughout her time as WD director, she repeatedly had to justify her work and her approach. She recalled that "the men [in the DNC leadership] never will learn that there is truth in the slogan of the old Women's Division: 'Elections are won between campaigns.' . . . Telling people what the Administration was doing, what its goals were and what the opposition was doing day by day to thwart their achievement, would build a foundation upon which a victory in the campaign could be built."[9]

Edwards believed such consistent outreach was the most effective WD tool to turn out women's votes and make them loyal party workers. But because it was also the most expensive thing the WD did, over the course of Truman's full term she had increasing difficulty in getting her bosses at the DNC to fund such projects. Edwards always believed that sexism was largely to blame for DNC men's reluctance to support her efforts, along with their high price tag.

The treatment she continually received from leading DNC men helps explain Edwards's position on feminism and the best way to improve women's status. In the summer of 1949 Edwards gave a speech at the annual convention of the National Association of Business and Professional Women (BPW). The BPW was a bit of a tough crowd for her, as many of its members supported the ERA. Because Edwards continued to oppose the ERA, she laid out her beliefs about why workplace discrimination happened and how to fight it: "When we women remember that [work used to be an exclusively male space], we should not be annoyed, or surprised, or dismayed at the typical man's attitude towards what he considers women's invasion of what were his sacred preserves until fairly recently. More and more women are being accepted as equals by the men with whom they work and our progress in that direction is really up to us. Women themselves must behave in such a way that men will cooperate with us to do away with such discrimination."[10]

That final sentence was handwritten onto the bottom of the typed speech. In other words, Edwards herself added it after the speech had been finalized. The emphasis Edwards chose to place on women's "behavior" shows her continued disagreement with the idea behind the ERA. Edwards believed that mandating equality would not bring it about. Rather, she claimed, women need to earn it by their behavior toward men, thereby making men allies in equal treatment. She simply did not believe that a law would change behavior in any meaningful way—men were just too sexist to willingly treat women fairly. Because of that, she thought, women had to maintain their own power bases. Legislative equality would not be meaningful in her mind if women hadn't "behave[d] in such a way that men will cooperate" in the work of feminism. While Edwards did not call herself a feminist, because of that term's association with ERA support in these years, she certainly was a feminist. She was committed to improving women's standing in society and their opportunities in public life. She was deeply opposed to sex-based hierarchies. But she did not think that legislating equal treatment should be the top priority as women strove for equality.[11]

Edwards continually tried to bring more women into government, and throughout Truman's time in office, she began to include African American women a bit more. Bringing Black women fully into party life was never a major goal of hers, but on several occasions she spoke up to prevent discrimination at party functions. In 1946, she and Gladys Tillett were approached by several Black party women, requesting invitations to a dinner honoring Bess Truman at the Women's National Democratic Club. They arranged for the women not only to attend but also to be seated throughout the room, rather than at their own table at the rear. The move was not without controversy—two southern senators turned around and left upon finding out that they were expected to dine with Black women—but Edwards recounted the episode proudly in her memoirs.[12] During the 1952 campaign Edwards worked to ensure that an African American woman who had served in the Women's Division's Courier program (an updated version of the Reporter Plan) was included in a luncheon given for all couriers as the campaign wound down.[13]

Edwards also championed the government career of Edith Sampson, a Black attorney from Chicago. Sampson was part of a team of African Americans assembled by the State Department to go on international speaking tours promoting American democracy, including its work to improve the lives of African Americans. Sampson's 1949 speech in New Delhi was particularly hailed as a triumph.[14] She and Edwards were friends, most likely from their time in Chicago in the 1920s and 1930s. In 1950 Edwards recommended Sampson to President Truman as a member of the United States's UN delegation. Edwards recalled that she "did not find it difficult to persuade" the president to make the appointment and that he let her call Sampson herself to share the good news.[15] A year later, however, Edwards received word that the secretary of state, Dean Acheson, intended to "rotate [Sampson] out and include a Negro man this year." Edwards lobbied hard for Sampson to keep the position, writing to the president that "you might mention Mrs. Sampson [to Secretary Acheson] if you thought well of my recommendation that she be included again this year" and emphasizing that Helen Gahagan Douglas, whom Truman and Acheson were also considering for the post, could easily be used in any of several other government jobs.[16] The implication was that the UN delegation was a bit lower profile, and therefore a place where a Black woman's appointment was less likely to generate controversy. Indeed, since Sampson had already served a year without trouble, that was an easy case to make. While Edwards supported Sampson's career, it is also clear that Sampson's value lay at least partially in her ability to keep her head down and not attract too much attention.

In 1950 Edwards was also more attuned to the need to make the case for the Democrats directly to African Americans than she had been in 1948. In the final month of the 1950 midterm campaign, the Women's Division paid the salary of Venice Spraggs, the Washington bureau chief for the *Chicago Defender*. Spraggs wrote columns urging African Americans to get out and vote for Democrats. Edwards hired Spraggs after hearing concerning reports about apathy among Black voters. Spraggs had also written for the Women's Division during the 1948 campaign, although at that time her newspaper continued to pay her salary.[17]

In spite of these moments, Edwards's vision of women's role in politics and, especially, the role of local women in the party structure never expanded to consider the difference that race might have made. She thought of the local-level Democratic women she directed as housewives, and mostly middle-class. When Black women fit into that category, or when they were professional women like Spraggs and Sampson who could work for the party, Edwards welcomed them. But using the Women's Division to respond to the distinct problems faced by African Americans was not something Edwards ever appears to have considered. The women's organizations with which Edwards interacted most often, groups like the National Women's Party and the Business and Professional Women, had only a handful of Black members. So she was unlikely to have gotten any sustained pressure from colleagues to change her tactics or to have been around people who thought differently about this issue. These facts highlight one of the major ways white feminism perpetuated itself. White spaces and white organizations tended to remain white, creating a cycle of inattention to the needs of Black women or other women of color.

Edwards's experiences during the 1950 midterm election probably would have pushed her away from focusing on Black women even if she had considered doing so. On paper, it looked like she was getting more power. She earned the title of vice-chair of the DNC in April 1950, when Gladys Tillett stepped down from that role. In Tillett's oral history, recorded in the late 1970s, she implied that she left the vice-chair position to help run her friend

Frank Graham's Senate campaign that year.[18] But Edwards also asked her to step aside so that she could have a turn as vice-chair:

> Gladys, you told me to let you know if ever I would like to be Vice Chairman of the committee. Well, if you felt that you were willing to relinquish this title, I think that this is the only time that it would be feasible for me to have it. I do not anticipate heading the Women's Division in another presidential election for I think someone else should take over before '52 but I will work through the '50 election and I will try and get someone ready to direct the activities when I retire. So this would be the only time for me to be the Vice Chairman and I think I have earned the right to have that title for a year, don't you?[19]

Edwards became vice-chair less than a month later.

As the midterm campaign shifted into high gear, Edwards was hard at work. She envisioned a program similar to Housewives for Truman focused on the president's proposed government health insurance program. Trailers would go to certain key congressional districts, set up displays about what the health program would do, and have material for people to take with them so they could continue to discuss the facts about the program with their friends. Edwards wanted to make Truman's health plan the centerpiece of the midterm campaign in the spring of 1950. And while her plans for these trailers were detailed, they never came to fruition.[20]

One reason why Edwards's robust plans for outreach to women throughout the country never got off the ground in 1950 was money. Much of the information about the health program trailers comes from letters Edwards wrote to Mrs. Albert Lasker, wife of a wealthy advertising pioneer and philanthropist, asking her to donate a substantial sum to fund the project. It is unclear if Mrs. Lasker donated the money, but most of Edwards's plans for publicizing the health plan were never implemented.

Edwards's intention to focus on health care also got shoved aside because the Korean War began in June 1950. Edwards's speeches during the rest of the campaign season focused largely on the war, such as one in which she argued that the Truman administration had done everything it could before the outbreak of hostilities to prevent the spread of communism on the Korean peninsula and which she specifically stated at the beginning was addressed not to women but to "all Americans."[21] Many of her public remarks throughout the summer and fall of 1950 were fairly gender-neutral, focusing on how all citizens should be interested in the issues that the Democratic Party supported, not only defeating communism in Korea but also the Democratic record on natural resources and conservation, Social Security, and increasing wages.[22]

This new language from Edwards reflected a shift occurring at the grassroots. Fewer women were engaging in the work of the Democratic Party during the 1950 midterm. The only major project undertaken by the Women's Division was one that it had been doing for years: organizing "Schools of Politics" around the country to educate grassroots party activists about the policy initiatives of the party. During the first such program of the 1950 campaign, held in Wisconsin, a disturbing trend emerged: more men than women attended the program. Prior to 1950 men had never attended the Schools of Politics at all, except as presenters. Now, suddenly, there were more men than women in the audience.[23]

What caused this shift? Was it the Cold War rhetoric that women's place was in the home, and that by staying in the home they strengthened the country in its fight against the Soviets?[24] Was it the financial crunch of the DNC, which was perpetually short of cash during the Truman years? Both of these things likely fed into a third, overarching cause: work with women voters simply did not have the support among party leaders that it had had in the 1940s. In spite of the importance that some people attributed to women voters in the 1948 election, the men at the top of the DNC seem to have not believed it. They routinely undermined Edwards's authority, and after 1948 they never gave her the money she believed necessary to do her job properly. While Edwards and the women of the Democratic Party believed in the importance of a politicized middle-class home, with women as constantly engaged and important political actors, the party leadership was not convinced.

Some of this skepticism came from the top. While Truman was very supportive of Edwards, he could also be extremely sexist and was often dismissive of political women's (including Edwards's) complaints about the treatment of women in Washington. That sexism became more pronounced in 1950. In February of that year, he refused to act when Edwards asked him to urge the White House Correspondents' Dinner to include women reporters.[25] A few months later he sent an incredibly rude letter to Emma Guffey Miller, in response to a letter from her urging his support of the ERA. Truman wrote that he “appreciated very much [Guffey’s] continued interest in the equality of men and women.” He continued: “it has been my experience that there is no equality—men are just slaves and they will always continue to be. Sincerely yours, Harry Truman.”[26] After the 1950 midterm election Edwards complained to Truman about the lack of pay equity at the DNC, where women “were not paid fairly.” There is no evidence the president addressed the problem.[27] Nothing in Truman’s rhetoric echoes FDR’s beliefs that women were part of the “collective wisdom of citizens” that shaped government. Truman appreciated Edwards’s hard work and loyalty. But he does not seem to be on board with her vision of women in politics. And without the president supporting those efforts, the men of the DNC felt free to be just as sexist as Edwards always claimed they were.

Another factor contributing to party leaders’ skepticism was that not all Democratic women at the grassroots level were supporting the president and the DNC. As historian Elizabeth McRae has shown, the Truman era was a time when white supremacist southern women “built distrust of the Democratic Party” at the local level.[28] There is no evidence that Edwards reached out to these women and tried to bring them back to the party’s fold. She undoubtedly would have seen trying to bring these women around as a waste of time, since the president’s position on civil rights issues was not going to change. But to the men of the DNC, active work against the party by groups of ostensibly Democratic women provided yet another reason to not give the WD their full support. The WD structure was premised on difference feminism, which held that all women had certain things in common because they were women. Groups of women actively opposing the president challenged that foundation.

Behind closed doors, Edwards seethed over her continual dismissal by DNC leaders. In late July 1950, she angrily reported to DNC chairman Bill Boyle that two of his lieutenants had persuaded the president not to enact a Women’s Division plan that he had previously approved: “The President was definite in his approval of having the month of September as NATIONAL REGISTRATION MONTH by his proclamation when I saw him last Tuesday but this afternoon Don [Dawson] tells me he and Matt [Connelly] have talked the idea over and have decided it is not a good idea.”[29] Edwards could not get the men of the DNC to support her, even when she had the president’s blessing. In spite of her pleas for Boyle's attention to this and other matters, Edwards was largely sidelined during the 1950 midterm.

After the Democratic Party's losses in November 1950 Edwards did as she usually did after a loss. Writing directly to Truman, she ripped into the work of the DNC leadership: "The pattern [of losing seats in off-year elections] is not of such long standing that we could not break it if we used intelligence in our long-range planning. Or, perhaps I should say, if we did any planning at all. I am appalled at the lack of policy and strategy planning that goes on or, rather, does not go on. I hope that this defect can be obviated." She went on to outline deficiencies in how the party had tried to rebut McCarthyism and disapproval of the Korean War and also decried what she saw as the wishy-washy nature of many of the candidates, what she called a lack of "courage and straightforwardness in candidates."[30]

Turning to gender issues, she described the lack of respect given to women: "I do not think our leaders take the women's viewpoint into consideration enough. You, Mr. President, and the Chairman have been most cooperative in putting women into good jobs in government but there are too few on the policy level. . . . I do not feel that as Director of the Women's Division of the DNC I have any voice in making policy or planning strategy and as Vice Chairman of the DNC I am nothing but an empty title." Given all of these problems, Edwards offered to quit: "If you want a woman who is content to be a figurehead," she stated, "let's make a change."[31] At the bottom of the draft of this letter is a handwritten note—"Copy to Chairman."

Edwards was well aware of the leverage she had within the party. Had any chairman tried to remove her, Democratic women all over the country would have flooded his office with angry letters. And of course, she had President Truman's personal support, if not always his full cooperation for her initiatives. There is a reason this letter was addressed to the president and a copy sent to the chairman. Edwards was a successful politician in part because she knew who her allies were and how to use those alliances when they did the most good.

Despite all these problems—the lack of support for WD work and the corresponding decline in women's engagement at the local level in the early 1950s—Edwards stayed on the job as vice-chair and WD director and kept making the case for why the Women's Division was important. In September

1951 Edwards gave a high-profile speech focused on what she called "political education," designed to help people understand the issues. Too many people these days, she said, only "read the headlines . . . and some of those headlines are being made by unscrupulous politicians to confuse and intimidate voters." Women's Division programming was designed to counteract those "unscrupulous" headlines, and such work needed to be done constantly, not only in an election year. After all, Edwards reminded listeners, ever since Molly Dewson's day, the WD's slogan had been "campaigns are won between elections."[32]

Less than a month after giving this speech, Edwards threatened to quit once again, sending President Truman a letter on October 30, 1951, stating, in part, "I am resigning because it is borne in upon me too poignantly and unhappily that the Vice Chairmanship is an empty title and that women's status in the Democratic Party and Committee has not risen."[33] The context out of which this letter emerged, however, could not have been more different from her threatened resignation of a year earlier. Throughout the 1950 midterm, India believed she and the Women's Division had been ignored, to the detriment of the party. But since the spring of 1951, she had been assuming more power within the party.

Two critical shifts occurred in the spring of 1951 that gave Edwards increasing influence. One was the failing health of the DNC chairman, Bill Boyle. Boyle was often absent from the office for weeks at a time, and when he was out, Edwards served as acting chair of the committee. That April, for example, she took a trip to California, where she met with party officials to discuss congressional reapportionment, the 1952 presidential campaign, and other issues.[34]

Her public profile was rising rapidly. The same month as her trip to California, *Coronet* magazine published a profile of her titled "India Edwards: Queen-Maker of Washington." The article focused largely on her work in getting administration jobs for women and outlined the process in this way: "'The secret,' [Mrs. Edwards said], 'is to get the woman's name in a hurry to the White House before men can object and have their own candidates ready.' Mrs. Edwards' 'spies' are made up of a host of women government executives, hostesses, and girl reporters. They rush hints of big job openings to her. She then delves through her file, pulls out a card and proceeds to map her campaign."[35]

The article's author, Tristram Coffin, concluded his piece by noting that Edwards did not believe the time was right for a female presidential or vice presidential candidate. "If that is right," Coffin closed, "and India is usually right, she is living a generation too early for her own good. For, as the politicians in the smoke-filled rooms [would] say, India Edwards is 'a natural for the ticket.'"[36] International recognition was also coming her way. In the summer of 1951, a French magazine, *Le Jour*, published a list of the ten most influential women in the United States. Edwards came in third, behind only Eleanor Roosevelt and Bess Truman.[37]

Along with Edwards's growing portfolio of responsibilities within the party and her high profile, she was also seen by many Democratic operatives as a solution to the problem of corruption that dogged the Truman administration in its later years. Edwards explained in her memoir that she never doubted Chairman Boyle's honesty and integrity, but it was possible that President Truman "doubted the integrity of some of Bill's associates, as I did." When Boyle was out of the office, she refused to deal with his appointed deputies, "who I suspected were far from being the loyal, honest men they should have been."[38] There were investigations headed by former DNC chairman and now Attorney General Howard McGrath into kickbacks and other improper financial arrangements in many federal programs in 1951. McGrath "botched the mission so badly" that Truman forced him to resign. McGrath's failure in this project, coupled with his former time as head of the DNC and rumors about Boyle's associates, made the summer of 1951 a tense one at the party offices.[39]

As concerns about corruption grew, some in the party and the media began to float an intriguing idea. Since the suffrage movement, one justification given for increasing women's role in politics was that they would clean it up and root out corruption. Why not, therefore, give the highest job in the party to a woman, a woman whose reputation had only improved and whose visibility had only increased in the past several months? In October 1951, Bill Boyle resigned as DNC chairman, due to his poor health. President Truman offered the chairmanship to Edwards. She turned him down. As she explained to the president at the time, and to supporters in the coming weeks, she simply did not feel that the party was ready to be led by a woman. To her ally Grace Barmore she wrote, "We have a tough fight ahead and we need a strong man as the Chairman, in my estimation. I am a great believer in womanpower, as you know, but I'm also a realist."[40] In her memoir, she recalled telling President Truman, "I do not think the men of our party are ready to have a woman chairman."[41]

Edwards might have been correct about the majority of men in the party struggling to accept her leadership, but that sentiment was not universal. The chairman of the Oregon Democratic Committee sent a telegram to the president declaring that Oregon Democrats were "enthusiastic" about the prospect of voting for Edwards as party chair because she would show the party's "determination to maintain good housekeeping in our party and willingness to recognize competent leadership of an outstanding Democratic woman."[42] Many newspapers were also supportive of the idea. In her memoir, Edwards described refusing Truman's offer of leadership as "one of the great mistakes of my life."[43] It would be another twenty years before a woman became the head of either the DNC or RNC.

Given the praise that was being heaped on her from every direction, why did Edwards send a letter of resignation to President Truman just two weeks after being offered the chairmanship? Her resignation offer came because Truman did not follow her advice and gave the chairmanship to Frank McKinney, who was not among Edwards's suggestions for the post and whom she did not know. "I have never met the new Chairman so I have no opinion regarding him but I hope he is all you want and need," she told the president. "I am truly heartbroken by the necessity of this action but there is a matter of principle involved."[44] In spite of her misgivings, McKinney appears to have known how to deal with Edwards. In his first full day as chairman, Halloween 1951, he detailed his vision for the party as it moved into a presidential election year. Regarding Edwards and the Women's Division, he declared, "It is generally recognized that India Edwards, the able leader of the Women's Division, has gained more recognition for women than any other Vice Chairman. It is gratifying to me to know that she has the solid support of the women of this organization as well as of the men. And I can assure you that during my administration she shall be Vice Chairman in the full sense and meaning of the word."[45] McKinney gave that speech one day after Edwards sent her offer of resignation to Truman. She stayed on, and after six weeks of working with him, Edwards was McKinney's biggest fan: "He seems to be 'just what the doctor ordered.' . . . I feel sure that when we are reorganized and the clouds, which seem pretty dark and heavy right now, are dissipated we will have an efficient working organization."[46]

This remarkable moment, in which a woman almost became the head of a major political party in 1951, illuminates just how much popular perceptions of women in this era overlooks. The vast majority of women were housewives in these years. A higher percentage of women were married in 1950 than in any other census in U.S. history. The baby boom was reaching its peak. And yet, a small group of white women were finding professional success in Washington, D.C., in politics and journalism.

In the fall of 1951, when Truman offered the chairmanship to Edwards, there were seven women serving in the U.S. House of Representatives, and one woman in the Senate. The majority were Republicans; the Democrats were Congresswomen Elizabeth McKee of West Virginia and Edna Kelly of New York.[47] There were almost eighty women holding presidentially appointed positions within the executive branch, representing just under 3 percent of all such jobs. Some of these women were in high-profile posts, such as Anna Rosenberg, the assistant secretary of defense, and Eugenie Anderson, the ambassador to Denmark. But most were midlevel Washington bureaucrats.[48] There were also dozens of female reporters on the D.C. beat, including Bess Furman, who had worked alongside Dorothy McAllister during the 1940 campaign, Doris Fleeson, and Esther Van Wagoner Tufty, an indomitable reporter from Michigan who ran her own wire service, the Tufty News Service, which provided D.C. reports to some three hundred newspapers nationwide.[49] Most of the women reporters were veterans of Eleanor Roosevelt's women-only press conferences and they all socialized together at the Women's National Press Club, an organization founded in 1919 due to women's exclusion from the Washington Press Club, where male reporters gathered. While Edwards's opportunity to become chair of the DNC was unusual, it fit into the growing numbers and influence of professional women in Washington. And polling data suggest that Edwards might have been overly pessimistic about the general public's reaction to a woman leading a major party. The Cold War rhetoric connecting gender roles to American superiority was still developing in the Truman years, and in 1949, 51 percent of women and 45 percent of men told Gallup pollsters that they "would have voted for a woman for president."[50]

While Edwards may have underestimated the public's willingness to support women in leadership positions, DNC actions during Adlai Stevenson's 1952 campaign showed that she had the measure of many Democratic Party men exactly right. Frank McKinney, whom Edwards got along with quite well, only held the chairmanship for a few months. Once Stevenson became the nominee in the summer of 1952, he put his own man, Stephen Mitchell, in as head of the DNC. Edwards's recollections of Mitchell's work and the 1952 campaign in her memoir are blistering. "The whole campaign was dismal," she wrote. "There was so little coordination between Adlai's people in Springfield, Illinois and the DNC in Washington that it was almost as if the two factions were fighting each other instead of the real opposition. . . . I may be unfair, but I think Stephen A. Mitchell was such a poor chairman that he contributed greatly to Stevenson's defeat." She had not done her best work on the campaign either, Edwards admitted, but that was not her fault: "As vice chairman and director of the Women's Division, I must share the blame, although Steve worked hard to keep me from doing my job."[51]

Mitchell obstructed Edwards's work in ways large and small. He implemented cost-cutting measures that crippled the Women's Division's most consistent election-year work: the production and mailing of rainbow fliers. Ever since Molly Dewson introduced the fliers in 1932, they had been paid for by the national committee and mailed nationwide under the auspices (and the budget) of the Women's Division. Mitchell made the state Democratic committees pay for every item they received from national headquarters during the 1952 campaign.[52] And while Edwards rode on Stevenson's campaign train and arranged meetings for him with local Democratic women, as she had for Truman in 1948, those meetings were a flop. Stevenson never met with the women, and his sister (who took care of traditional politician-wife duties for the divorced candidate) "had little time for the political women" either.[53]

Immediately after Stevenson's defeat, Edwards summarized her ideas regarding the best steps to move the party forward in 1953. She laid out many reasons for the defeat, including voters' desire for something new after twenty years of Democratic rule, and the unpopularity of the Korean War. She noted, however, that she did not believe Stevenson's campaign had done enough to combat the allegations of "creeping socialism" that Republicans had been launching at Democrats for years. Edwards feared that "people have been taken in at last by this spurious argument of the Republicans."[54]

Part of why that argument may have finally gained hold, Edwards implied, was because of the lack of active grassroots work by the Democrats. She told Mitchell:

> The [all-female] Democratic Couriers tell me they found only the women active in many states into which they went, New York being the most glaring example. I found this to be true also not only this year but also in '48. . . .
>
> We need to revitalize the organization in states where we have old, jaded leaders, and it is my hope that we can start some sort of membership organization among women in order to keep in close touch with more of them than just state leaders. . . .
>
> Whether or not I stay as Director of the Women's Division is unimportant but it is important that there is a woman leader at the national level whom women and men respect, and who will do the sort of job that is traditional with the Women's Division.[55]

In Edwards's mind, the Women's Division was an essential cog in an effective ground game for the Democratic Party, and the fact that the WD was only in "close touch" with state leaders shows just how much that cog had atrophied in the previous few years. As Edwards noted later in the letter, many pundits credited women voters' swing to Eisenhower with his victory. She knew that Democrats had to remain vigilant in courting women's votes if they wanted to regain the White House.

Instead of taking Edwards's advice, however, Mitchell moved the DNC in the opposite direction. Just a week after Eisenhower's inauguration, Mitchell announced that the Women's Division was being "integrated into the Committee's entire operations." Edwards publicly went along with the move, stating that the move meant that "for the first time [Democratic women] will be working side by side as full partners with Democratic men." Edwards remained vice-chair of the DNC after the WD's elimination.[56]

The elimination of the Women's Division was part of a massive overhaul of the party structure in 1953. In addition to eliminating the WD, the committee also eliminated its Radio-Television Department, integrating that work into the Publicity Department.[57] The primary motivation for all of these moves was money: the DNC came out of the 1952 campaign with a "big party deficit."[58] For the Women's Division, however, there was much more afoot. Edwards never believed that Mitchell took women voters or political women seriously. And without Truman there to support her, Edwards found herself without allies in the party leadership. While she had traveled with Stevenson during the campaign, the two apparently did not get along.

Democratic women all over the country reacted in dismay to the news of the WD's elimination. Syndicated columnist Ruth Cowan quoted one "puzzled Democratic woman" as noting that "the word Mitchell should have used was 'interred.' She said he didn't have a word of praise in his press release for the work of Democratic women in the last presidential campaign."[59] This column ran under different titles in different newspapers, but the effect was the same. In the *Louisville Courier-Journal*, the headline was "Democratic Women Puzzled by Their New 'Equal' Status." The *Cleveland Plain Dealer* was even blunter: "Democratic Gals in a Dither—Is It Merger or Murder?" A year later, Bertha Adkins's partner Winifred Helmes reflected in her diary that "Mrs. Edwards made no bone about the blow Mitchell dealt to the women in spite of all the talk of absorbing them." She also recorded the gossip that "at least four women turned down the position of director of so-called 'women's activities' under Mitchell" after Edwards resigned.[60]

Eleanor Roosevelt devoted two of her nationally syndicated "My Day" columns to the change. While her first column was generally positive, calling it "a distinct step forward," her second column on the topic was much more cautious. Two weeks after the announcement she wrote:

> We all know it is one thing to announce such integration and another thing to really see it is carried out. There must be a real determination to have women consulted on every level. It is not integration when women are told that a decision on policy has been made, without their having been included in the discussions at every level. . . .
>
> This habit that men sometimes have of making decisions and then announcing them to the women is one that will require a little watchfulness on the part

> of the men. . . . This integration into the party machinery is just one sign of the time. Both men and women must work together to see that it is real integration—that women do their full share of work but that they also get their full share of recognition.[61]

She likely knew the kind of true partnership she described in this piece was unlikely to come about.

Roosevelt's pessimism proved correct. Edwards hung on for a few more months at the DNC but resigned in October 1953. In August she sent a long letter to her grassroots troops, outlining her reasons for leaving and her vision of women's participation in American society: "Can you function efficiently without organizational identity as women? Are you 'integrated' or 'interred'? These are the questions that must be answered by every woman leader who is concerned with the future of the Democratic Party—and of women's role not only in our party but in our nation."[62]

Both Roosevelt and Edwards articulated a kind of difference feminism in these writings. Both believed that women, as women, brought distinct perspectives to the political table, and that organizing around and being open to incorporating those differences, or even letting them lead the discussion, created success. As Roosevelt's column suggests, acknowledging women's different perspective did not mean making them less than or unequal. Indeed, she and Edwards were both claiming that only when those different perspectives were taken into account were women truly treated equally. In 1953, that was a losing argument among the male leaders of the Democratic Party.

VII

Reaching Republican Women

THE 1952 CAMPAIGN

In August 1952, a picture of General Dwight D. Eisenhower with three women ran in newspapers around the country. In the *Boston Herald*, the picture appeared next to the headline "Ike Appoints Strategy Staff." That article did not have any accompanying photos, creating the impression that the women were the strategy staff.[1] The women pictured with the presidential candidate were Ivy Baker Priest, the vice-chair of the Republican National Committee; Bertha Adkins, the head of the RNC Women's Division; and Mary Lord, cochair of the nonpartisan Citizens for Eisenhower. Absent from the photo but a key part of Ike's team was Katherine Howard, the secretary of the Republican National Committee who traveled on the campaign train with General and Mamie Eisenhower.

Multiple women held leadership positions in Eisenhower's campaign partially because Eisenhower believed in the importance of women in government and sought out their opinions. Because he was so supportive of women, there were far more of them with access than had been true for his Democratic predecessors. While Bertha Adkins inherited the mantle of Women's Division director, unlike previous WD directors, she was one of several women who had the president's ear in the 1950s.

Bertha Adkins did not intend to become a professional politician. Born in 1906 in Salisbury, Maryland, she was an only child. She graduated from Wellesley College in 1928 and began work as a teacher. Over the next fifteen years, working in education saw her through the economic crisis of the Great Depression. From 1934 to 1946 she served as a dean of women at two small northeastern colleges. At one of them, Bradford Junior College in Massachusetts, she met her life partner, Winifred Helmes. But a few years after she and Helmes met, life circumstances altered Adkins's path. In 1946 her mother died, and as an unmarried women and an only child, she felt compelled to return to her childhood home in Salisbury to keep house for her father.[2] Initially, Helmes stayed in Massachusetts.

Suddenly without a career and again living, for the moment, as a single woman, Adkins turned to something that ran deep in her family: politics. Both of her grandfathers had run for local office repeatedly, losing more often than they won. The family was well known among Maryland Republicans. When she returned to the Eastern Shore, she immediately began volunteering with the campaign of Republican Ted Miller, who was running for Congress. Miller won the seat, the first time a Republican represented Maryland's First District since 1920. In 1948, largely due to her work with Miller's campaign, Adkins became the Republican National Committeewoman for Maryland.[3] After Thomas Dewey's surprising loss in 1948, the RNC overhauled nearly every aspect of its work. Democrats now would occupy the White House for two full decades. Something needed to change for Republicans to reverse that trend.

Rethinking how women connected to the Republican Party was one aspect of the overhaul. Since the 1920s, Republican women had worked largely through a national network of Republican women's clubs. The clubs were overseen by the director of the Women's Division, who was also the RNC assistant chair and the president of the National Federation of Republican Women's Clubs (NFRW). Holding these three titles simultaneously had proven challenging for several WD directors. Marion Martin, who led Republican women's activities in the 1930s, believed it was her job to quash many local clubs' independence, particularly when they failed to support Republican candidates. Martin sought to turn the clubs into effective vehicles for getting out the Republican vote, as Molly Dewson was doing at the same time for the Democrats. But many grassroots Republican women proved reluctant to always follow the lead of the Washington office. Throughout the 1940s, a backlash developed within many Republican women's clubs. The tensions around Marion Martin's vision of Republican women's clubs as dutiful foot soldiers came to a head just after the 1946 midterms. In spite of the tremendous success of Republicans in that election, Martin was fired by RNC chairman Carroll Reece in December 1946.[4]

This breakup was as much ideological as it was tactical. The Republican

Party as a whole was struggling with an ideological division in the late 1940s. One faction, led by Senator Robert Taft of Ohio, was conservative. They opposed much of the legacy of the New Deal, including popular programs like Social Security. The other faction was more moderate. Led until 1949 by Thomas Dewey, the "liberal Republicans," as Dewey called himself and his supporters, believed that there was no going back to the pre-1932 world. The New Deal and the expectations of government support that came with it were here to stay, and the Republican Party had to find ways to differentiate itself from the Democratic Party without opposing everything Democrats had done.[5]

But Dewey lost the presidency twice, and throughout Truman's term in office, the Taft Republicans seemed ascendant. Many NFRW members were conservative Taft supporters, but Marion Martin was not. Grassroots leaders of the NFRW bitterly resented Martin's rules that party women should spend their time, in one's description, "saying 'aye aye, sir' and merely rubber-stamping every policy the men propose and promote."[6] Conservative women in the NFRW wanted to be supported when they spoke out against the Dewey faction of the party and, especially, when they believed their identity as women led them to differing ideas. They saw their job as promoting policies rather than a party. Martin saw it the other way: NFRW women were Republicans first and women second.[7] Doing the work assigned them by party leaders was the NFRW's primary job in Martin's mind.

Throughout 1947 and 1948, the conservative grassroots faction gained the upper hand. In 1948, the NFRW elected a new president, Betty Farrington. Farrington wanted to separate the NFRW from the RNC, in order to give women more autonomy and the ability to challenge party leadership when they disagreed. Her election as the group's president showed that the majority of NFRW members agreed with that approach. In the summer of 1952, just weeks before Dwight D. Eisenhower secured the Republican Party nomination, the split became official. The RNC Women's Division no longer had any direct relationship with the NFRW. There were now two groups representing Republican women—the NFRW and the "regular" party women who served in the Republican Party structure as county and state committee women. Those were the women who worked with the Women's Division director.[8]

This final split happened on Bertha Adkins's watch. As Betty Farrington was increasing the independence of the NFRW, Adkins was hired as the new director of the Women's Division of the RNC in March 1950. Committee chairman Guy Gabrielson, who took over as RNC head in August 1949, was impressed with a speech Adkins gave in her role as national committeewoman for Maryland at an RNC meeting. Several months later he invited her, in Adkins's words, to come to Washington and "do an organizational job to get women active in the Republican Party."[9] Adkins immediately got to work, modeling her efforts on India Edwards's programs at the DNC. Adkins traveled the country, talking to women and adding them to her mailing list so that she could send them newsletters, postcards, and everything else the Women's Division created. She also spoke to nonpartisan women's groups such as the American Association of University Women (AAUW) and the General Federation of Women's Clubs. Adkins found those events to be highly effective at bringing new women into partisan work:

> It did give us contacts, and the Republican women who were there, who maybe were not active in the party as such, would come and would bring friends, and you got an opportunity to get names of people who were interested in the Republican Party, who were not at that moment active in it. Just the fact that the Republican Women's Division was represented meant an interest in the organization, which members, whether they were Democrats or Republicans, liked. So the activity at those meetings was more the personal contacts and development of a list of people that you could call on later in the campaign.

Often she would share the stage with Edwards at these events, and in her oral history Adkins emphasized that both of them always made "nonpartisan" speeches.[10] From the moment Adkins joined the RNC Women's Division, therefore, she and Edwards were pursuing similar goals: encouraging more women to be involved in government both because that involvement was valuable in gaining voters for the party and because it generated groups of women with the skills to run for office or be nominated for political appointments.

When Adkins described this period of her life in the late 1960s, she commented on her unmarried status. She remarked that "eventually, of course, we [young women] anticipated marriage, which did not happen for me, but I think all girls anticipate it."[11] This is her only mention of her private life in the entire interview, and while it is strictly accurate—she never married—it obscures her decades-long romantic partnership with Winifred Helmes. It is unclear if the women maintained a relationship while Adkins lived with her father, but they were together by 1952 and by 1954 Helmes had secured a job in Washington, D.C., and the two were living together. They stayed together for the rest of their lives and are buried together in Maryland.[12]

Adkins's silence on her relationship with Helmes is completely unsurprising given the virulent homophobia of the early Cold War. Adkins was named director of the Women's Division at the height of the "lavender scare," a period in which LGBTQ people were being fired from federal government jobs by the dozens because their identity as gay men and women allegedly made them security risks.[13] While more men than women were fired from civilian jobs, queer women working for the government certainly felt the pressure. To give just one example, in 1948 Miriam Van Waters, who ran the Massachusetts Reformatory for Women, burned twenty-two years' worth of letters between herself and her partner, Geraldine Thompson, rather than let them fall into the hands of conservative state officials who were coming to seize her papers, searching for cause to fire her.[14] It is impossible to know how many other women made the same choice. Adkins kept her relationship with Helmes publicly invisible throughout her career, and it is possible that they were not together when she was first named to the RNC staff in 1950. But by the time of the 1952 campaign, the two were clearly a couple. Helmes's diary of their time in Washington recounts happy dinners out with groups of other women, dinner parties at home for friends, and other social events the two women attended together. While Adkins could not make her relationship with Helmes public, they were also not completely in the closet. Their friends and acquaintances knew the women were a couple and treated them as such.[15] But for Adkins to talk publicly about her relationship would have damaged her career in multiple ways. Even if she had been able to keep her job—which would have been highly unlikely—she would not have been seen as the right person to bring the American housewife into politics and into the Republican Party.

As the 1952 campaign season began, Adkins was careful not to align herself with any faction within the party. She recalled that, "As the executive director of the Women's Division of the RNC I did not feel I should be *for* any particular candidate until he had been nominated."[16] This approach meant that when Eisenhower became the nominee and Adkins started to work with him, they were starting from a very different place than any of her predecessors on the Democratic side. Molly Dewson was so proud of her early support for FDR that she had a bracelet engraved "F.R.B.C."—for Roosevelt before Chicago, the site of the 1932 Democratic convention where he became the nominee.[17] McAllister and Tillett served an incumbent president. And Edwards had been an active Truman supporter ever since 1944, when he became vice president. Not only did Adkins maintain strict neutrality prior to the convention, because Taft supporters controlled the RNC prior to Eisenhower's nomination, most people assumed she was a Taft supporter as well.[18]

The prominence of Taft supporters in RNC offices meant there was a great deal of turnover when Eisenhower, rather than Taft, became the nominee. Adkins's boss, assistant party chair Rose Mayes, left after the nominating convention, as did Guy Gabrielson. Mayes was not immediately replaced, and so Adkins continued giving speeches, talking to women's groups, and generally doing the work, even though no one was directing her. To her, her efforts were vitally important:

> Weeks went on, and we had no assistant chairman to head the women's campaign. I was carrying on the activities, but I felt that it was imperative that a woman be named to this spot. The assistant chairman was recognized as the top representative of the women's activities. . . . So I got in touch with both Arthur Summerfield [the new RNC chairman] and with General Eisenhower, and made an appointment to talk with Eisenhower in Denver, on my way back from Los Angeles. In talking with the General, I pointed out the value of his giving recognition to the women's activities, and urged that this post be filled, and not just left in abeyance. He concurred in this.[19]

But Adkins was not made assistant chairman at that point. Instead, Eisenhower appointed Ivy Priest, the Republican National Committeewoman from Utah.[20]

Adkins was not overly disappointed by not being appointed assistant chair in the summer of 1952. As Women's Division director, she had plenty to do. A structure emerged in the Eisenhower campaign in which Adkins served as a coordinator of all women's activities for the campaign, which were being carried out by multiple groups. Unlike the Democratic campaigns of the previous two decades, where all the action for women voters flowed through and was directed by the WD, Adkins served more as a liaison who made sure each group of women knew what the others were doing. This clearinghouse role sometimes proved tricky. All of the women were devoted to electing General Eisenhower as president, but their reasons for doing so varied. And those different motivations sometimes caused tension behind the scenes, even while the public face was of a well-oiled machine. Those tensions persisted throughout Ike's first term.

One group organizing women workers for Eisenhower was the NFRW, where Betty Farrington was still president. In spite of the official separation between the NFRW and the RNC, Farrington encouraged her members to participate in the programs that Priest and Adkins developed. Many NFRW members worked alongside "regular" party women who held roles as county chairwomen or precinct captains. Women from both the party and the NFRW gave speeches, held fundraisers, and both Priest and Farrington regularly reached out to "National Committeewomen and state Vice Chairmen" to get a sense of how the campaign was going on the local level.[21] It was unusual for Farrington to be contacting some of the regular party women. After all, the NFRW and the RNC had finalized their breakup just two months earlier. This moment of reconnection between the two groups of Republican women may have been due to Priest's and Farrington's different tenures in their jobs, since Priest was brand-new to national-level work. For perhaps the same reason, Priest was supportive of the NFRW and the regular party women working together in this and other projects. One of her first moves as the new assistant chair was to firmly shut down any lingering tensions about Taft's loss of the nomination: "If we are ever going to win an election," she recalled stating, "we have to bury our preconvention differences and rid ourselves of petty jealousies and bickering. Elections were not won by cliques or factions but by united effort."[22] The "preconvention differences" were effectively papered over during the campaign, but the factions remained.

One reason why the RNC and the NFRW teamed up in this way was because there were not many overlapping areas of strength around the country. In some historically Republican locations, the regular party mechanism was robust. In other areas, the more volunteer-oriented NFRW was stronger. Using the two organizations in tandem allowed the party to use its womanpower to its "best advantage," Adkins recalled, coordinating efforts "so that we weren't duplicating."[23] One place where the two groups worked together particularly well was the babysitting system organized for Election Day. As Democrats had done in 1944 and both parties in 1948, Republican Party officials directed county chairs to ask each voter canvassed, "Will a temporary baby sitter be needed on election day?"[24] Canvassers made a note of everyone who answered yes to that question, and Republican women—some from the regular party office and some from the NFRW—arranged a time to come and watch the children while their mother went to vote.

There was also a new player organizing campaign volunteers in 1952, one working totally outside of the Republican Party structures. During the primary season, a nonpartisan Citizens for Eisenhower group had spread quickly throughout the country. The Citizens, as the group was called by campaign insiders, had its own woman cochair, Mary Lord, who was responsible for organizing the women workers within that group. As a nonpartisan organization dedicated only to electing General Eisenhower as president, the Citizens were most useful in areas where the Republican Party was weak, such as the South.

Adkins's job during the campaign was not only to coordinate between the regular party women and the NFRW but also to bring the Citizens' volunteers into the fold. There was a strong potential for ideological tension between the NFRW and Citizens women. Women who came from the Citizens were working for Eisenhower because of his history, reputation, and moderate politics. NFRW women worked for him because he was the Republican nominee, but he was not conservative enough for many of them. Taft supporters were still numerous within the NFRW in 1952, and so one of Adkins's jobs was to keep personal preferences minimized in order to maintain a focus on electing a Republican president for the first time in twenty years.[25] As Adkins described it, "Ivy's job was to go out around the country, speaking; Mary Lord was working with the Citizens, you see, and I was there in the headquarters in Washington and was in touch with both organizations, keeping tabs on who was doing what, where they were, and what was happening."[26] The tensions that simmered between Adkins and the NFRW throughout her time in Washington are apparent in this statement: Betty Farrington isn't mentioned at all, even though Adkins received regular reports from her throughout the 1952 campaign.

Adkins spent the campaign in the Washington office. She was not going out on the campaign trail speaking, as Gladys Tillett had, nor was she traveling with the candidate, like India Edwards. Tillett had been both WD director and DNC assistant chair in 1944, and Ivy Priest's speaking schedule as RNC assistant chair is comparable to hers. But who was on the train with Eisenhower? How did the candidate and his inner circle know what was going on with efforts to reach women voters?

The person on the train was Katherine Howard, who had been secretary of the Republican National Committee since 1948. Howard was a Dewey supporter then but retained her position as secretary when Guy Gabrielson became chairman in 1949 and, in her words, "the Taft forces were back in the saddle."[27] She and Gabrielson maintained an icy relationship throughout their time working together. During the 1952 convention, their hotel rooms were on the same hallway. "It was arranged that way so that we would be near and could confer easily," she recalled in her memoir. "We never did."[28]

One reason Gabrielson disliked Howard was because she endorsed Eisenhower before the convention. Gabrielson believed, as Adkins did, that party officials should not publicly endorse candidates before the convention. Gabrielson supported that position even for officials working to advance a particular candidate behind the scenes, as he was doing with Taft. When Eisenhower became the nominee, the general installed a new party chairman, as was typical in the Republican Party. Both Adkins and Howard, however, were asked to stay in their roles. After he was ousted as party chairman, Gabrielson made a point to chastise Howard as he told her goodbye: "'Katherine,' he said, 'I enjoyed working with you, too, but I cannot understand how you, as Secretary, could endorse General Eisenhower.'"[29]

Despite Guy Gabrielson's preferences for behind-the-scenes dealings, Katherine Howard threw everything she had into supporting General Eisenhower. Her politics were too moderate for her to support Taft. And her husband, Charlie, had served on Eisenhower's staff for fifteen months during World War II. As he told a reporter during the campaign, "to General Eisenhower a Howard on his staff is nothing new."[30] Katherine Howard was determined to be on his staff in a meaningful way, not stuck in RNC offices taking care of correspondence as committee secretary. But gaining an active role in the leadership of the campaign was not a straightforward task.

In mid-August 1952, shortly after Adkins had gotten Ivy Priest appointed assistant chair, there was a meeting at Eisenhower's campaign headquarters of all the women responsible for women voters. Priest and Adkins were both there, representing the regular party women, along with Betty Farrington from the NFRW and Mary Lord from the Citizens. Making any of those women the person to travel with the president would have implied a preference for one of the groups over the others, and the party needed all of the women those four leaders represented to be working hard. Someone else was needed, someone who was outside of these sometimes-squabbling groups. Katherine Howard described the moment in her memoir:

> With little ado he [campaign chief of staff Sherman Adams] announced that I would be a member of General Eisenhower's staff to coordinate the women's activities; then he turned on his heel and departed as abruptly as he had come. There was an awkward silence for by implication he put me over their heads. It was up to me. I said that I knew they each had their own important spheres of work and if they would keep me informed I would channel all information to our Candidate. In turn, I promised to keep them informed of developments on the train. I could tell by the expressions on their faces and by the way Bertha nodded that harmony had been restored.[31]

Howard hit the ground running and immediately established her role as the conduit between the candidate and women workers throughout the country. She had a one-on-one meeting with Eisenhower her first full day on the job and was reassured by his emphasis not only on women voters but on women within his administration if he won the election. On her second day in her new job, she met with national committeewomen from around the country so they could bring her up to speed on local action and sent a report of that meeting to Priest, Farrington, and Lord.[32] Howard sent regular memos to Priest, Farrington, and Lord throughout the rest of the campaign. Farrington and Lord responded with updates on their work, but Ivy Priest forwarded Howard's letters on to Adkins. Most of the return mail from the RNC therefore came from Adkins, coordinating from Washington. Priest spent the campaign on the road making speeches and left the work of keeping tabs on women's work to the Women's Division director. This structure proved successful. Winifred Helmes noted in her diary that "Katherine, Ivy, Tad [her nickname for Adkins] and Mary Lord all worked well together during the 1952 election campaign. They kept in touch with each other, supported each other, and thus accomplished a lot more."[33]

Having so many people focusing on women during the campaign was partially due to the many different organizations that were working to get Eisenhower elected. But it also reflected the candidate's belief in the importance of women voters and women in government. Throughout his time campaigning, he frequently addressed the importance of women voters. In responding to a question from a female television host in Connecticut, Eisenhower stated that, "it would be impossible to carry out the responsibilities of the office without such help [from women]."[34] During a campaign event in Portland, Oregon—a city that had a female mayor in 1952—he declared, "I want to speak for just a second about my honest belief, my deep conviction, that we should have more women in public life."[35] During her first press conference—which Bertha Adkins arranged less than a week after she had been appointed to the campaign staff—Katherine Howard told reporters that the general told her, "show me an able woman, and I will see that she gets a job. . . . I think women have some of the top brains in the country."[36]

Eisenhower maintained his commitment to including women throughout his presidency. It was a "deep conviction," as he put it, born out of both politics and personal beliefs. Bertha Adkins felt that his support for women, his opposition to "putting women to one side," and his "awareness of the importance of women in the role of policy-maker as well as doer in government," stemmed from his time working with women in auxiliary military units during World War II.[37] Women had served ably with him during the war, and Eisenhower saw no reason why they shouldn't continue to do so. To him, it was as simple as that. He elevated political women throughout his time as president and, according to one biographer, even tried to convince Oveta Culp Hobby, who served as secretary of health, education, and welfare during his first term, to run for president in 1960.[38] His support for women in politics was absolute.

Beyond the candidate's personal beliefs, there were other reasons why women became a focus of the Republicans' 1952 campaign. Pure demographics were one factor, as they had been since the early 1940s. As Adkins noted,

"Today women voters outnumber the men by nearly two million. They can control the election in thirty-two states if they organize their efforts."[39] But the candidate also believed that there was a deeper reason. During a September speech in Winston-Salem, North Carolina, Eisenhower explained why he needed women to be part of his campaign: "My associates and I are engaged in a crusade that is firmly based on *ideals*, on purposes that we think reflect the highest of moral standards. In such a crusade the concern of women for that kind of value is important. Women never forget that the moral tone of the *home* is the basis of our civilization. As a consequence, they carry that kind of crusading spirit even into a campaign. I should say they instinctively carry it into a campaign; and we need exactly that at this moment."[40] Eisenhower was making a similar argument to that India Edwards had been making for the previous seven years: women are different from men, and that very difference is why they are important to politics. Edwards would not have argued that women were inherently moral, but she would have agreed that they had an inherently different perspective than men.

Adkins, like Edwards, downplayed the morality language. To her, women should be more active in politics simply because they should be. As citizens and as active members of their community, women found politics was a logical part of their lives. Writing in the AAUW's magazine during the campaign, Adkins argued that "since government now affects every phase of our living, it behooves the women to become active political workers."[41] She and Eisenhower were making the same argument about women's involvement. Both of them knew the demographics that made women voters valuable. Both of them believed that women were good at political work. And both of them were asserting that government was present in women's lives, even when they spent their lives as mothers and homemakers. The morality language in Eisenhower's speech makes it appear that he is advocating a different role for women than Adkins was, or Edwards or Tillett before her. But in fact, all four politicians are making the same claim: that women are not exempt from politics because of their status as women or as mothers. Instead, those roles make their political participation even more important. And the consistency of this message across the two major parties shows just how much supporting women's active involvement in politics was a part of the postwar political consensus.

Another similarity between the Eisenhower campaign and the Truman effort four years earlier was the lack of meaningful engagement with African American women. While Eisenhower publicly courted Black voters during his reelection campaign in 1956, they were much less of a focus in 1952. None of the sources I have examined discuss African American women during the 1952 campaign at all, with one interesting exception. In her memoir, Katherine Howard recalled inviting the new president of the National Association of Colored Women's Clubs, Irene McCoy Gaines, to join her for tea and have her picture taken with Eisenhower. Howard recalled that the photograph "had wide circulation, particularly in the black press."[42] But it is unclear if Gaines was part of Howard's meeting with midwestern women activists that preceded the tea or if Gaines had any meaningful conversation with the general.

As was true in 1948, outreach to women voters and outreach to Black voters were handled by different groups, with African American women categorized by their race rather than their sex. Eisenhower did take some small steps to gain African American voters' support. Howard noted that he did not hold indoor campaign events in the Jim Crow South, instead holding speeches and rallies "out of doors, so all could come."[43] And although Eisenhower gave a major campaign speech on civil rights in Los Angeles, pledging to desegregate every aspect of the federal government and end segregation throughout Washington, D.C., even the leading historian of African American Republicans largely skips over the 1952 campaign.[44] While the two major parties each continued to argue throughout the 1950s that they were the better party on civil rights, the difference between the priority given to African American voters by Truman in 1948 and their relative neglect by Eisenhower in 1952 shows how clearly the pendulum was swinging on race and partisan alignment. The campaigns' different approaches to civil rights makes the consistent absence of Black women across the two parties even more striking. Midcentury consensus pluralism was not an ideology that had room for people who fit into multiple boxes. The white people in charge decided which category particular "diverse" people fit into, and white women in party politics consistently saw African American women as members of their race rather than their sex.

A multifaceted approach to white women voters, however, was a central piece of Eisenhower's overall campaign. Women were still seen as swing voters, and so Adkins, Howard, Priest, and their colleagues went all-out to bring them to the Republican side. One tactic they adopted from Truman's success in 1948 was having local women visit the candidate on his train. Katherine Howard was in charge of those meetings, and she ran them somewhat differently than Edwards had four years earlier. Whereas most of the women's time on the Truman train was spent with the candidate, women visiting Eisenhower spent more time with Katherine Howard than anyone else. Howard introduced the women to Eisenhower when they first came aboard the train, then took them to a different car to chat with Mamie Eisenhower for about ten minutes. Originally the couple had met everyone together, but "it was soon found to be too exhausting" for Mamie Eisenhower to move around the train all day, from her car to the VIP lounge, and so she stayed in her car and the female visitors were brought to her. After ten minutes of "chatt[ing] gaily and personally" with the candidate's wife, the women—most of whom were local county chairwomen, state vice-chairs, or other officials within the Republican Party—would go to Howard's car to get down to business. Once they were away from the candidate and Mrs. Eisenhower, they talked "about issues, policies, and what was of particular concern to this region. This I [Howard] would relay to the Policy and Strategy Committee and to the three top women leaders," Ivy Priest, Betty Farrington, and Mary Lord.[45] These meetings were a way for the campaign to make sure it knew what women were concerned about throughout the country. The information Howard gained through these meetings then shaped speeches that Priest gave, or talking points that Adkins, Farrington, and Lord provided to the women on their various mailing lists.

The efforts to get women onto Eisenhower's side paid off: 58 percent of women's votes were cast for Eisenhower in 1952, as opposed to just under 50 percent of women supporting Dewey four years earlier.[46] Women's swing to Eisenhower was publicly discussed as one of the factors that enabled Republicans to reenter the White House after a twenty-year absence.

Once Eisenhower was elected, decisions had to be made about who would stay on at the RNC. It was at this moment that Bertha Adkins consolidated her power. Before the inauguration, the president-elect offered Ivy Priest the job of treasurer of the United States. She accepted immediately, even though she did not know what the job involved, because "if Ike wanted me to do the job and thought I could handle it, I would certainly give it my all."[47] Katherine Howard took a very different approach. She was determined not to take a job that she did not feel qualified for. And although she had spent many years working at the top level of the Republican Party, she did not consider herself qualified for most policy-making positions. She declined the leadership of both the Women's and Children's Bureaus of the Department of Labor for that reason. Eventually she became the assistant director of the Civil Defense Administration because "it seemed to me that it reached into every home in the country, and that it was the sort of job that I could do, being a woman, being a homemaker, having political experience, knowing people all over the country, and that this was something that I could do and I could do well."[48]

Howard regretted her decision almost immediately. She quickly came to feel that she wanted to be "a part of Eisenhower's administration" at a higher level, and people throughout the party frequently commented that "Mrs. Howard is looking for more to do."[49] Women Republicans were especially confused by her choice; a year later Winifred Helmes puzzled in her diary, "I wonder why Katherine Howard wasn't put on the White House staff."[50] But as 1952 turned to 1953, Howard chose to step back. And Bertha Adkins stepped in, becoming the highest-ranked woman in the RNC and one of the leading women in the Eisenhower administration.

As soon as Priest accepted the job of U.S. treasurer, Adkins became the assistant chair of the RNC, a post that both Gladys Tillett and India Edwards had held concurrently with Women's Division director in the Democratic Party. Adkins did the same and immediately outlined how the Women's Division would function within the party and the White House. She was trying to consolidate all the work with women voters under her umbrella. In a December 1952 report, she described her ambitious plans, which she called the "Program for '53." She would continue the Schools of Politics, regional meetings where women learned about issues from administration representatives and party leaders. These had first been used on the Republican side by the NFRW in 1950, but when they proved successful the RNC quickly took them over.[51] Adkins proposed seven regional meetings and one national meeting annually for all Republican Party women. The national meeting would be open to "all women throughout the country." There would be monthly meetings in Washington where leading party women could meet with administration officials to discuss policy, a new monthly publication by the Women's Division, and a weekly radio program. It was a complicated, expensive plan. Adkins requested an annual

WD budget of $500,000.[52] The speed with which she submitted these plans, even before Eisenhower's inauguration, shows that Adkins was ready to seize more power and influence as soon as she got the chance.

Beyond how quickly Adkins had the report ready, there are two other striking things about her "Program for '53." One is its similarity to Democratic Women's Division programming for the previous twenty years. The new monthly publication was clearly a copy of the *Democratic Digest.* The Schools of Politics, regional meetings, and radio programs had all begun on the Democratic side of the aisle as well. At precisely the same moment that the DNC was deciding that these structures were too expensive and not worth saving and was preparing to dissolve the Democratic WD, Adkins was busily building those same structures to serve the Republican Party.

Given the Democrats' decision to dissolve their WD, the enthusiasm for Adkins's program is also surprising. Assistant Chief of Staff Max Rabb noted that "the great merit of this program is that it represents action. It is good to harness the enthusiasm of women early, and get a jump on the next election."[53] Even the price tag did not cause Rabb to hesitate, although he did note that it was an expensive program and the price required "serious consideration." Overall, however, Rabb was enthusiastic. But he wanted to make sure that the projects Adkins and the WD undertook did not serve existing Republican women exclusively, or even primarily. "Care should be taken," he wrote, "to insure [*sic*] that this is not a case of shaking hands with one's self. The regional meetings, the Washington meetings, etc., might well be just an occasion for dyed-in-the-wool Republican women leaders to meet socially without effective political results. The emphasis should be on attracting women who are young, Independents, or Democrats."[54] This emphasis on bringing new women into the Republican Party had been a focus of Adkins's work since she joined the WD in 1950. Her speeches to nonpartisan women's organizations were designed to achieve this goal. As she stepped more fully into party leadership, Adkins continued to prioritize bringing more women into the Republican Party. And her efforts to do so would often ruffle the feathers of those "dyed-in-the-wool Republican women leaders," especially at the NFRW.

VIII

"Government Comes Right into the Home"

WOMEN'S PARTY POLITICS DURING THE BABY BOOM

Throughout the middle years of the 1950s, a perhaps unexpected scene played out weekly in the dining room of the Hotel Washington: between ten and twenty female members of the Eisenhower administration gathered for lunch. Bertha Adkins began the lunches and described them as opportunities for women to socialize and "exchange ideas." Adkins's secretary made the weekly reservation, whether Adkins herself could attend that week or not.[1] Over consommé and chicken salad, the women networked and mentored each other. Although they would not have used those words, they undoubtedly shared updates on their work and tips for navigating the overwhelmingly male world in which they lived their professional lives.

The Hotel Washington was one block east of the White House and two blocks from the Executive Office Building, where many of the women worked. Adkins originally invited the Republican women in Congress (six in the House and one in the Senate in 1953) to the lunches, but their more varied schedules and farther walk to the hotel meant that they did not come often, a fact Adkins regretted. Two blocks east of the hotel, however, was the National Press Club building, which housed the offices of the Women's National Press Club. While women reporters were not formally invited to Adkins's lunches, many of them were friendly with women politicians and administration staff. It would have been common for the executive branch women to be sharing the dining room with reporters such as Liz Carpenter, her boss Esther Van Wagoner Tufty, or veteran D.C. reporter Doris Fleeson. Undoubtedly more than a few quotes and scoops were secured in passing conversations at the Hotel Washington's lunch hour. Many of these women also socialized after work hours. On election night 1956, many of the "girls of the press" spent most of their time at Adkins's party.[2]

This vibrant, interconnected world of professional women in the nation's capital is not a typical vision of women in the 1950s. But it was a world that Bertha Adkins worked hard to create. She frequently spoke before women's organizations such as the American Association of University Women or the General Federation of Women's Clubs and encouraged their members to run for office.[3] She kept a list of women who were interested in government jobs and made sure their names were under consideration whenever political appointments were available, just as India Edwards had done.[4] Politics was Adkins's career for a decade—as Women's Division director from 1950 to 1958, and then as an assistant secretary of health, education, and welfare from 1958 to 1960. She dedicated herself to ensuring that more women entered government work and that they were supported when they got there, as she felt supported by President Eisenhower and his administration.

But Adkins also knew that the majority of American women were not pursuing careers in politics at the height of the baby boom. To Adkins, however, that did not mean that they should not engage in politics. Instead, she focused her outreach efforts on programs designed to bring politics and government "right into the home." Adkins frequently reminded Republican women leaders throughout the country that "you are the saleswomen for the Administration."[5] This emphasis on women's role in partisan politics, their vital contribution to winning elections, and the synergy (rather than conflict) between that work and their role as homemakers was at the center of Adkins's political vision since she began working for the Republican National Committee in 1950. During the 1952 campaign, she had declared: "I am a politician—and so are you. Today it is essential that every citizen of the United States realize that we're all politicians."[6] Two years later Ellen Harris, the new Citizens cochair, argued that women's involvement in women's clubs and politics showed that "women recognize that a homemaker of today is also a citizen."[7] Eisenhower's staff, especially those working on campaigns and elections, took women voters and the politics of the home very seriously.

As she built up the work for and by women within the Republican Party, Adkins modeled her efforts on what the Democratic Women's Division had done over the previous twenty years. The DNC's decision a week after Eisenhower's inauguration to disband its WD did not alter her choices. Instead, she doubled down on developing the same kinds of networks, meetings, and publications that Molly Dewson had pioneered and her successors had refined. The Democratic-developed structure, Adkins believed, gave her the best chance to continue the progress made in 1952 toward closing the gap between Republicans' and Democrats' success in making women nationwide "saleswomen" for the parties.

The interconnected world of professional Washington women helped Adkins achieve her goals. Female members of the press and women politicians knew each other well, and so Adkins always had a group of supportive reporters every time she sent a press release. Some of the relationships dated back to Eleanor Roosevelt's women's-only press conferences, but most of the women on the D.C. beat by the 1950s had not participated in those. They were a second generation of women reporters that included Helen Thomas, Liz Carpenter, and others who would have long and storied careers. During the 1952 campaign, many members of the press (male and female) traveled on the Eisenhower campaign train and shared meals with the campaign staff. Katherine Howard recalled that everyone except General and Mrs. Eisenhower ate in the train's single dining car, and so the relationships were varied and close. Both Doris Fleeson, a syndicated columnist who covered women's politics for years, and Esther Van Wagoner Tufty were on the campaign train and spoke with Howard often.[8] Tufty was an indomitable woman. Nicknamed "the Duchess," she had started her own wire service, the Tufty News Service, before World War II. She personally covered three wars, traveling to Europe, Korea, and Vietnam, and is credited with launching the careers of many other women journalists, including Liz Carpenter, who eventually became chief of staff to First Lady Lady Bird Johnson and, in the 1970s, a leader in the ERA fight.[9] Tufty covered every president from FDR to Reagan, and Eisenhower's State Department sent her on an official visit to Australia in 1954. She came home from the trip with a pet kangaroo.[10] She was the president of the Women's National Press Club, a group which provided networking and support for women reporters for decades. Fleeson, Tufty, and syndicated columnist Ruth Cowan were the most high-profile women reporters, and they were dedicated to supporting the growing group of female journalists through the mentorship of the Women's National Press Club.[11] Women on the D.C. beat covered social events, but they also covered women politicians and their work.

And there were more women working in politics in 1950s Washington than one might imagine. The seven Republican women in Congress included Senator Margaret Chase Smith of Maine, who spent more than thirty years in the legislature and was the first woman to serve in both chambers. Smith famously denounced Joseph McCarthy in June 1950 with a speech that came to be known as her "Declaration of Conscience" speech, in which she declared that McCarthy was leading the Republican Party toward "the Four Horsemen of Calumny—Fear, Ignorance, Bigotry, and Smear."[12] Adkins tried to engage Smith in the Women's Division work but had difficulty getting access. Helmes noted in her diary that Smith's scheduler required anyone who wanted time with the senator to go through him and so Adkins could "not talk with her [Smith] directly."[13] One wonders what Smith and Adkins could have done together if they had been able to coordinate, as their politics and their investment in women having meaningful voices in Washington certainly aligned.

Eisenhower also kept his word and appointed women to his staff. His most high-profile appointment was Oveta Culp Hobby as the first secretary of health, education, and welfare. Hobby was only the second female cabinet secretary in history and the first to oversee the creation of a new federal department. He also appointed Clare Boothe Luce, who had been out of politics since 1946 when she declined to seek reelection, as ambassador to Italy.[14] Luce, Hobby, and Ivy Priest as treasurer were the most visible appointments, but by the end of October 1953 Eisenhower had named forty-two women to high-level federal jobs, from several customs inspectors up to his new director of the Women's Bureau of the Department of Labor, Alice Leopold.[15] In addition to the political appointees, there were also thousands of women in the civil service: secretaries, assistants, and others who kept the executive branch of government running smoothly. Those women were the majority of the nearly 500,000 women employed by the federal government at the end of 1953.[16] While many of the political appointees did not actually work in Washington—they were ambassadors or customs inspectors or members of the United States' UN delegation—most of those civil servants were always in town. In 1947 women made up 47 percent of the federal government's employees in the District of Columbia, and that percentage subsequently grew.[17] These midlevel Washington women—neither the secretaries nor the Secretaries—were the women who frequented the lunches at the Hotel Washington. They were the ones who might bump into Doris Fleeson on the way into the dining room or stop and have coffee with Esther Van Wagoner Tufty.

The most direct link between political women and women journalists was Anne Wheaton, the director of women's publicity for the RNC. Wheaton had assumed that position in 1939 and had done publicity work for women's organizations and Margaret Sanger's National Birth Control League for fifteen years before that.[18] She was a veteran of Washington who came into her own when the Eisenhowers were in the White House. She and Mamie Eisenhower became friends during World War II, when Mamie was living on her own in Washington while the general was overseas. According to Wheaton, in those years she and Mamie often got together for lunch at the Women's National Press Club building, which means that the women journalists knew the First Lady for a decade before she assumed that role.[19] Wheaton's connections with other Republican women were also well established. During the preconvention months in 1952, when as a member of the RNC staff she had to keep her preference for a candidate to herself, Wheaton called Mary Lord of the Citizens for Eisenhower every morning at 7:30 to let her know what she'd heard people say about the general the day before.[20] Wheaton was a valued part of Eisenhower's team throughout his presidency, and Ike rewarded her with a promotion in April 1957 when he named her associate White House press secretary.[21] She was the first woman to be part of the White House press office.

These women were all part of the world that Bertha Adkins worked in as she rose to prominence within the Republican Party and the Eisenhower administration. In spite of its high price tag, the "Program for '53" that she proposed before the inauguration was accepted. The detailed plan shows Adkins's goals as WD director and how she believed things like the radio programs and meetings would help her achieve those goals. In describing the radio program, called *Women Want to Know*, Adkins claimed that the program would "support the Division's policy of bringing all the nation's women to Washington, at least in spirit."[22] The fact that Adkins was aiming for "all the nation's women" shows just how much she saw her job as reaching out to *women*, not only

Republican women. She believed it was her role to bring more women into government. Throughout her time at the WD, that remained one of her highest priorities.

There was widespread acceptance among Republican officials that outreach to women needed to continue, and that the number of women working for the administration needed to be substantial. The RNC passed a resolution at its February 1953 meeting—the first since Ike's inauguration—in favor of appointing more women to the administration. They even recommended hiring a woman in the personnel department of each executive department to oversee the recruitment of women to every part of the executive branch. The RNC Executive Committee unanimously endorsed that idea and also unanimously agreed that Bertha Adkins, as WD head, was "the proper person to be consulted in regard to appointments for women."[23]

Adkins and other RNC leaders wanted women in Washington because they believed women brought something different to politics. Just like India Edwards before her, Adkins worked to get more women government jobs out of a desire to help professional women like her advance and a deep belief that women brought something distinct to their work. She laid out these thoughts most clearly in 1955, in the middle of her time working in the West Wing. That January, she spoke to the Long Island Federation of Women's Clubs. In front of that sympathetic crowd, she sang the praises of women in politics. "I am proud of the role women are playing today in politics," Adkins declared, "and I firmly believe that women's participation in politics has contributed greatly to the responsible operation of our government. Women make good politicians. They have a real interest in the issues, and they have a desire to learn more. Women have patience and determination, both of which are necessary in politics. And women have the energy and enthusiasm which makes them good workers."[24]

Six months later, she addressed the national convention of the AAUW and made similar comments. Here, however, she was even more pointed, and called for the college-educated women in the audience to join the administration in a professional capacity. Adkins argued that moving beyond a volunteer role focused on getting out the vote and civic education by actually running for office was a critical next step for American women. Only when they were office holders or administration staff did women have the opportunity to "be an integral and influential part" of political parties and, therefore, of government.[25]

Over and over again, Adkins turned to groups like the AAUW and the General Federation of Women's Clubs as a source of women to bring into Washington work and into the Republican Party. She believed that these groups—which grew rapidly during the 1950s—were vitally important in American politics, and she was not the only one who thought so. Women's organizations frequently testified before Congress in the 1950s, on a huge range of issues. Throughout the decade, women's groups made up between 30 and 45 percent of all groups testifying in congressional hearings about international affairs and foreign aid. Out of every one thousand speakers in front of Congress on all topics during the 1950s, sixty to ninety were from the seven largest women's organizations, which included frequent Adkins hosts the AAUW and the GFWC.[26]

Adkins's most concrete effort to woo the members of nonpartisan women's groups to work on behalf of Eisenhower was a series of breakfasts she arranged in the first half of 1955. The meals were held at the Sulgrave Club, a private women's club established during the Great Depression and housed in a Dupont Circle mansion.[27] Adkins drew up the guest list and invited women active in their community regardless of their party affiliation. She recalled that she organized the breakfasts because they were an efficient way for the president to be "more knowledgeable on the things which women's organizations were doing." Even though not all of the women were Republicans, Adkins saw a partisan benefit: "of course, I was interested in having the women of these national organizations know that the Republican President and his administration were interested in what they were doing."[28] Each invited woman took a couple of minutes to summarize her organization's activism, and Eisenhower was an attentive guest. In the archives there are two folders' worth of personalized thank-you notes he sent to each attendee. They are remarkable letters, as they all mention his interest in each woman's specific project or activism. The fact that the president believed sending these kinds of notes was a valuable use of his secretary's time is telling—he believed wooing these women was important.[29]

At the end of the first round of breakfasts, Eisenhower thanked Adkins profusely for arranging the meals. "Dear Bertha," he wrote, "Since we have had the last breakfast of the current season, I want once again to tell you how much I have enjoyed and profited from the opportunity of meeting with such a splendid and representative group of Republican women. The contacts you have afforded me in this manner have been invaluable in my effort to interpret the always-changing mood of the American people. . . . Incidentally, I can't tell you how many people have written me of late to tell me of the fine contribution you are making to the Republican Party, and how effective your work has been." He signed the letter, "with warm regard, Dwight D. Eisenhower."[30]

Other RNC staffers also believed the breakfasts were a good use of Ike's time. In the fall of 1955, Adkins asked the keepers of the president's schedule to restart the breakfasts. Congressional liaison Wilton Persons told Eisenhower that the "consensus of opinion at the White House is that they represent the only effective way of maintaining your contacts with that important (ahem) group of the population. If you feel you can take them, the boys feel they are productive of the highest possible reward."[31]

The "ahem" aside in Persons's memo gives a glimpse of the attitude some male staffers had about Adkins's work and the outreach to women voters in general. One Eisenhower staffer who worked in PR responded to a lengthy 1954 document produced by the Citizens for Eisenhower vice-chair Ellen Harris by stating that supporting Harris's data on the importance of women voters "is like being against sin."[32] In other words, everyone supports this, and you don't need to spend so much time convincing people. Persons's "ahem" and the "against sin" quip suggest that some of the men in the West Wing were not completely on board with the president's emphasis on hearing women's opinions and courting women voters. They were doing it because the boss told them to. But the boss was insistent. Eisenhower never wavered from his belief that women should be involved in government and that their opinions were valuable. Early in his administration Eisenhower sent his chief of staff, Sherman Adams, to speak to a national gathering of nonpartisan women's clubs.[33] And he repeatedly praised Adkins for her work and made himself available when she needed him. As Adkins recalled nearly a decade after she left the RNC, Eisenhower "didn't put them [women] to one side. He was interested in and aware of the importance of the role of women as policy-maker as well as doer in the government."[34]

Because of Eisenhower's personal belief in the importance of women in government, Adkins had a relatively free hand throughout her time as the head of the WD. But she didn't get everything she wanted. During the 1954 midterm campaign, there was no nationally distributed radio or television program targeting women voters, in spite of the emphasis given that kind of programming by both Adkins and the Citizens for Eisenhower. Adkins had proposed weekly radio programs as part of her "Program for '53," and a campaign clinic event attended by party regulars and Citizens for Eisenhower members in April 1954 also emphasized radio. Presenters at that event argued that radio was particularly important for reaching women voters, more so than television, because "the housewife can listen to the radio while working, but the TV requires a letdown in her household chores."[35] In spite of this, there were no regular radio addresses targeting women voters. RNC chairman Len Hall explained their absence by noting that the committee "simply [has] not had the funds to pay for them." The president gave a special radio address to women voters on October 28, roughly a week before the election.[36] But there was not a series of radio programs like those India Edwards had done in 1948 and Adkins and the Citizens had lobbied for.

The absence of regular radio programming hints at the declining scope of WD work in the middle years of the 1950s, even though Eisenhower valued the work of the division. One of the problems that Adkins encountered was the multiplicity of groups organizing the work of Republican women. The WD, the NFRW, and the Citizens all continued to do their own programming throughout the Eisenhower years. Dividing the work across multiple groups meant that more women were probably reached by Republican activists than had been reached by Democratic women in the late 1940s. But it was easier for people not directly involved in the work to have an incomplete picture of who was doing what, for initiatives to be overlooked, and for time and money to be spent on duplicate efforts. This became clear in the early months of 1954, during planning for the midterm campaign. The Citizens for Eisenhower structure was still completely disconnected from the RNC and the Women's Division. Ellen Harris, the cochair of Citizens in 1954, wrote a three-page memo that January outlining the need for a "women's telecast," a TV program in which Eisenhower spoke directly to women.[37] Harris seemed unaware of Adkins's consistent efforts to get a similar radio program going throughout 1953 or the obstacles she faced in doing so.

Influential men associated with the Citizens also appear unaware of the Women's Division of the RNC. In February 1954 Henry Cabot Lodge Jr., the U.S. ambassador to the United Nations who had been a founder of the Citizens in 1952, urged the president to support Harris's telecast and then suggested that "Mary Lord, Katherine Howard, and Ivy Priest should start going to women's meetings . . . with a speech approved by the White House showing exactly what the Eisenhower program means to women." Lodge continued that "some woman should be made responsible for all this, perhaps Katherine Howard, who is eager to take on some more work."[38] It is clear that Lodge had no idea what Adkins's job was, or perhaps even that she existed. The program he was suggesting as a new development for the 1954 midterm campaign was exactly what Adkins had been doing for over a year. Charlie Willis, a member of the West Wing staff who was a cofounder of the Citizens group along with Lodge, sent all this material to Chief of Staff Sherman Adams with a note that "this is a fine idea. The timing should be such that the local organizations are all ready when the telecast is made so that these women workers have some tangible spot to which to report and work."[39] Willis's vision of this program as something run by the Citizens and separate from regular party structures is revealing, as he corresponded with Adkins occasionally. For whatever reason—a belief that they were more efficient than the party structure, or more appealing to independent voters than the party structure, or some other reason entirely—the Citizens crowd was determined to maintain their autonomy, even if that meant duplicating projects.

The Citizens' efforts did nothing to diminish Adkins's work. As she rolled out her plans for the 1954 midterm, she prepared a wide range of materials for the campaign, continuing to build on the patterns established by Molly Dewson and her successors at the DNC. The clearest parallel was a series of postcards titled *Let's Talk about It!* Inspired by the rainbow fliers, the postcards were mailed to Republican women around the country. They included talking points about Eisenhower's policies on a range of topics. With titles like "Security," "Taxation," and "Human Needs," each postcard provided women with three to five major accomplishments in each area. The first full run of cards was sent to county vice-chairs and other RNC women leaders in June. Adkins told the ten thousand women who received the cards, "I hope this summer you will all take advantage of every opportunity that arises to spread the story of the Republican Administration and the 83rd Congress. Enclosed you will find a sheet outlining summer activities and projects you should undertake. . . . The [*Let's Talk about It!*] cards can be used for postcards, enclosures for mailings, handouts on neighborhood calls or at meetings. At a dinner meeting in one state, a card was placed at each person's plate. The cards formed the basis for lively discussion."[40]

Many of the women who received these postcards were also among the 1,400 who came to Washington for an April 1954 meeting Adkins organized. Like at other institutes since 1940, attendees heard speeches from administration and congressional officials and met with the First Lady. Excerpts of the speeches were mailed to participants, providing them with material several months before the *Let's Talk about It!* cards were first distributed.[41] A statement from the president was part of the postmeeting packet. In it, he praised political women, stating that "they have come as dedicated people, ready to work, appreciating the seriousness of their job. I could wish that kind of attitude, that kind of spirit, was shared by every single American."[42]

While she was giving women the tools to be the "saleswomen" of the Republican Party at the local level, Adkins also continued to encourage them to run for office. In the summer of 1954 Adkins told her lieutenants: "Women's role in politics today is steadily growing. Women can, and often do, bring to politics the kind of idealism which makes politics the high profession it should be. Therefore, do all you can to encourage qualified and capable women to file for public office. Talk with your county chairman, and get his support for women candidates. *Let's make this a winning year for the women as well as the Republican Party*."[43] Adkins always believed these efforts supported each other. More women officeholders made politics seem like an appropriate place for women and enabled women politicians to thrive. Women working to get out the vote and doing other behind-the-scenes work of partisan politics helped women win elections. And both of those things, in Adkins's mind, helped the Republican Party to grow.

Adkins worked hard throughout the campaign season, sending out postcards and letters to party women around the country and urging them to remain active at the local level. She also traveled extensively, giving speeches and attending planning meetings all over the country. In the second half of September, for example, she attended seven meetings in New Mexico in three days, then traveled to California where she did eleven events in six days.[44] Eisenhower appreciated and praised her work, writing her an encouraging, deeply personal note a month before the election (and just ten days after that grueling stretch of events): "I send you this note simply to let you know my awareness of the heavy burdens you are carrying in our common struggle for victory in November. I think I have some appreciation of the sacrifices and the strains and difficulties coincident to your efforts and I know that all the members of our Party are grateful for your leadership and dedication in our cause.... I am acutely aware that what you are doing is crucial to our success—and I just wanted you to know I appreciate it. Sincerely, D.E."[45] Adkins made a total of ninety-five different appearances during the election year, not counting the regional and national meetings she organized.

The size of the WD's mailing list, however, shows that Adkins's influence was comparatively small during the 1954 campaign, in spite of Eisenhower's support for her. Her summer mailing, including the first run of *Let's Talk about It!* cards, went to only 10,000 women.[46] By contrast, a small print run of rainbow fliers in 1940 was 750,000. Adkins's mailing list did not grow over the course of the campaign, because it was made up entirely of women who held official positions within the Republican Party. Women who were simply interested in working for Eisenhower but perhaps did not identify strongly as Republicans were more likely to support the president through volunteering with the Citizens for Eisenhower, or by showing up at the local RNC office and receiving the material that Adkins mailed to RNC officials. The lack of radio or television broadcasts also restricted her ability to reach women who were not already plugged into the RNC in some way.

The Citizens for Eisenhower team was also directly competing with the WD in its recruitment of women to get out the vote for Eisenhower and run for office. A Citizens' pamphlet from the midterm campaign used almost identical language as WD products but cast a broader net, reflecting the distance between the Citizens and the RNC. Next to stick-figure drawings of a man and a woman, each of whom carry a briefcase, the text read, "Who are these people? They are a Republican Congressman and Congresswoman, on their way to Washington, pledged to support the Eisenhower administration. They have been elected in marginal Congressional districts as a result . . . of their hard work and the enthusiastic support given them by the local Citizens for Ike. Who put them in office? We didn't ask . . . Republicans, Democrats, Independents, Fence-Sitters . . . but primarily people interested in sending to Washington representatives pledged to support Ike."[47]

The emphasis on women as officeholders in the Citizens' pamphlet matches Adkins, and the work of getting out the vote is described here as not being gendered at all, but rather work that men and women do. While these distinctions are important, the main point is that there were many avenues into supporting Eisenhower. This was a clear difference from the Democratic side of the aisle, where everything flowed through the DNC. And the biggest grassroots network supporting Eisenhower, the Citizens, actively distanced itself from the RNC in order to maintain its appeal to independent voters and others who didn't identify as Republicans but liked Ike.

Because Adkins was only speaking to the official party women, and the Citizens were talking to Ike supporters of all stripes, the leaders of the NFRW saw an opening for their group to do more to organize rank and file Republican women. While NFRW leaders argued frequently that women were the best local troops of the party, they did not support increasing the ranks of professional political women. Indeed, Adkins's identity as a single woman with a career seemed to rankle NFRW leaders, as did her loyalty to Eisenhower. Historian Catherine Rymph has argued that Adkins's identity as a professional, paid by the RNC, was a source of tension and that "several women leaders in the Federation privately identified their enemies not only as the Democrats, the liberals, and the communists, but also the women in the Women's Division," especially Adkins and Anne Wheaton.[48] NFRW leaders, particularly Nora Kearns, the organization's president during Eisenhower's administration, claimed that NFRW members were the "true" Republican women. As housewife volunteers, they did not rely on the Republican Party for their income and therefore could push the party to pursue the "moral" position on issues, something they felt the Eisenhower administration rarely did.[49] It is impossible to know if Adkins's lesbianism also contributed to this animosity, since it is unclear how many people outside of her immediate circle knew about her relationship with Helmes. But even her public identity as a single woman without children likely increased NFRW leaders' sense that Adkins was not like the women they worked with throughout the country.

Kearns and Adkins clearly had a tense relationship, though they were careful not to disparage each other publicly. Adkins would always talk about the NFRW as a partner in her goal of mobilizing Republican women, but she rarely included them or their leaders in her work. This was most clear during the 1955 breakfasts. Adkins saw the breakfasts as a way for Eisenhower to get to know what women were doing, regardless of their party affiliation, and also a way to bring women who did not identify as Republicans to their side. She therefore did not consult Nora Kearns about the invite list, nor inform her when NFRW women attended. Kearns was furious at the slight. She fired off several angry letters to Bernard Shanley, Eisenhower's appointment secretary. "I wonder on what basis the selections are being made" for whom to invite to breakfast, she fumed. "Would it be possible," she continued, "when such breakfast are set up in the future that some might be arranged under the auspices of the National Federation of Republican Women so that all our state presidents, elected officers and committee chairman, who are the leaders of the vast army of volunteer workers of the Party, might be included?"[50] Shanley forwarded the letter to Adkins, who instructed him to write back to Kearns saying that he had passed her letter along to Adkins and that the breakfasts "have been arranged by me as the Assistant to the Chairman of the Republican National Committee and Director of Women's Activities." Adkins added a handwritten note to the bottom of this memo: "as of the moment I am paying for the breakfasts too!"[51]

Kearns would not be put off, however. A month later she again informed Shanley that not only was she not getting to shape the invitation list, she was not even informed when NFRW officials were included. "I still regret," she tersely told Shanley, "that I have not been informed of the women chosen to represent the Federation in advance of their coming to Washington because I have had no opportunity to make plans to take advantage of their time and travel costs. Naturally, they have been amazed when they have come to my office and realized that I have not been informed of their coming. . . . Though a press release [naming the attendees] is given out a day or two in advance and our office is next door, we have only recently been included in the distribution."[52]

In the polite world of women's midcentury politics, this exchange was as heated as it gets. Adkins was clearly being a little bit petty by not even sending Kearns a list of whom she was inviting. And Kearns never liked Adkins, objecting both to the visibility of and support for a professional woman instead of women volunteers and to Adkins's politics, which were too moderate for Kearns. But this was not just a clash of personalities. Just like the tension around Chase Going Woodhouse's appointment nearly a decade earlier, what seems like a personal squabble actually reveals much deeper conflicts about women and politics. Kearns and Adkins had substantively different ideas about the appropriate role of women in government and about what policy positions "women" favored.

NFRW women were, as a group, more conservative than Adkins, anyone in the Citizens', or indeed most of the Eisenhower administration. This ideological division was widely known at the time, a "general impression," as Catherine Rymph has written, "that the Republican women who joined the Federation (as opposed to joining other party organizations, holding Republican offices, or merely voting) were among the party's more conservative (or right-wing) women."[53] Many NFRW women opposed anything that "smacked of communism, subversion, or immorality," a position they shared with women in far-right groups such as the Minute Women of the U.S.A.[54] Right-wing women frequently sent angry letters to the Eisenhower administration, such as a note from Mrs. J. Davidige Warfield to Len Hall, the RNC chairman, in 1954, which excoriated Adkins and other members of the RNC who claimed to speak for Republican women in support of Eisenhower: "At the Republican strategy meeting recently in Washington, we heard Bertha Adkins say, 'We the women who elected Ike . . . women are on the march to back up Ike and bring to him a Congress he needs for his program.' How wrong can she get? Women all over the nation . . . are up in arms against the so-called Ike program, and Republican Women want a Republican Program not a rubber stamp of New Dealism or appointment of New Dealers and One Worlders to positions. . . . you will do well to stop these Ike Clubs, which are hurting our party."[55] Adkins's office attached a note to this letter, telling Hall that her office had received so many complaints and angry letters from Mrs. Warfield that they had stopped responding.

Warfield's mention of who was getting appointments within the administration hit another sore point between Adkins and the Republican women further to her right. Both right-wing women like Warfield and NFRW women were disappointed by many of the women Eisenhower appointed to high office. The NFRW felt snubbed when its outgoing president, Betty Farrington, got no job at all in 1953.[56] And they were angry that Eisenhower's most high-profile female appointee, Oveta Culp Hobby, wasn't even a Republican. Hobby had been the head of the Women's Army Corps during World War II, and so Eisenhower knew and respected her, and did not particularly care that she was a Democrat. Katherine Howard recalled intervening in this situation to ensure that a high-profile Republican woman was announced at the same time as Hobby. But that appointment went to Ivy Priest as U.S. treasurer, rather than to Farrington as the NFRW women had hoped.[57]

Because the relationship between Adkins's WD and the NFRW was so tense, in 1955 Nora Kearns and other NFRW leaders began to make independent plans to support Eisenhower's reelection. Their biggest project, begun in April 1955, was the NFRW Kitchen Kabinet. This program named one NFRW leader as responsible for each cabinet department of the federal government. Those leaders would "clearly interpret to the housewives of America the job that is being carried out in each department under the Republican administration." This "interpretation" took the form of "monthly recipe cards," written up by the NFRW leaders and distributed throughout the country.[58] NFRW leaders further explained that, "the typical citizen in the individual community served by the Federation clubs does not spend much time considering politics as such but does measure the accomplishment of government in action. . . . For that reason, the neighbor-to-neighbor type of political activity, conducted by well-informed women of the Party, over a cup of coffee in the kitchen or by sharing a new recipe with the lady next door, will provide a voters eye view of the Republican Party to the man or woman casting a 1956 election ballot."[59]

The job of NFRW women, therefore, was to take the information summaries provided by their leaders and use those talking points to begin conversations with their friends and neighbors about the Republican administration. In other words, it was the same goal Adkins had for the *Let's Talk about It!* postcards, using virtually identical tactics.

Had NFRW women been dissatisfied with the way issues were framed on the postcards for the 1954 election? Were Nora Kearns and her team simply trying to make sure they were being active, in hopes of getting more credit within the party? Kearns announced the Kitchen Kabinet program the same month that she was complaining about being shut out of the breakfasts. This timing suggests that she may have feared the NFRW becoming more isolated from the channels of power if she did not act aggressively to position her members as the foot soldiers of the party. In announcing the Kitchen Kabinet, she described NFRW members as the ones who worked for the party, stating that "a more extensive job of salesmanship had to be done by the Republican Party and that the women of the Federation, through its year round political education and study programs, could set the machinery into operation among its 500,000 members."[60] In other words: we are your best tools, not the regular party women and professionals working with Adkins. And there are far, far more of us than Adkins's party women.

This fight between the NFRW and the WD in some ways echoed the tension between India Edwards and white supremacist Democratic women in the Truman years. The WD and its staff of professional women espoused positions that were more liberal than those supported by a portion of the party's grassroots women. As was true then, fights among women within the party opened up the entire WD structure to questions. It once again highlighted the fundamental flaw of difference feminism: women do not all think alike. And when that fact became increasingly obvious, structures built on difference feminism, like the WD, lost support. In the second Eisenhower term, this was just one of many factors contributing to a decline in women's influence within the Republican Party.

IX

Fundraisers and Pollsters

THE 1956 ELECTION AND THE DECLINE OF THE WOMEN'S DIVISION

The women on Bertha Adkins's mailing list received a new kind of request in November 1955: they were tasked with raising money for the 1956 campaign. Julie Kirlin, the Women's Finance Program director of the RNC (and a longtime friend of Katherine Howard's), informed regular party women that they "can and will" do the work of door-to-door fundraising because it would create "goodwill, good workers, grassroots support, [and] more campaign funds."[1]

By halfway through the campaign season, however, Kirlin was fed up. In June 1956 she told RNC chairman Len Hall that the fundraising program was not going well. Volunteers in Kansas City, for example, "encountered a great deal of resistance in persuading the women to work." Their experience was typical of regular party women all over the country. "I've never worked so hard in my life on anything," Kirlin continued, "yet I've never been associated with a drive that produced less or was more discouraging in its results."[2]

Why was the fundraising program such a flop? After years of happily going out and striking up conversation with their friends about the benefits of the Republican Party and the Eisenhower administration, why were women suddenly resisting doing the work that the party asked them to do? The exact reason is never discussed in the archival material. But it is clear that fundraising was seen by grassroots women as a different kind of work than what they had done for the Republican Party before.[3] Casually striking up a conversation about taxes or foreign policy while waiting in line at the grocery store or getting kids from the bus stop was one thing. Organizing meetings in one's home to talk about politics was also a comfortable, respectable project. But knocking on the doors of friends or strangers and asking them for money? The poor response to the fundraising program suggests that, for many women, that was something they would not do, even for Eisenhower. Even the regular party women seem to have been less comfortable being political activists outside of their homes or other gendered spaces. The fact that the money went to Washington, rather than staying locally as Democratic women's fundraising had in the FDR years, may also have been a problem.

In spite of Kirlin's alarm bells, fundraising remained the focus of the Women's Division's work throughout the 1956 campaign. While they did print and distribute seven different *Let's Talk about It!* postcards and other traditional material, the WD also printed more practical guides for women on how to do the work of campaigning. With titles like *So You're Planning a Rally* and *How Women Win*, the WD was pushing Republican Party women to take on different tasks during the 1956 campaign.[4] If the poor results of the fundraising effort paralleled the overall work of the WD, then it definitely declined in 1956.

Adkins may or may not have noticed the drop-off in regular party women's effectiveness. During the 1956 campaign she was working as the assistant chairman, a title she had held since the beginning of 1953. Adkins recalled that Len Hall "gave me the responsibility of coordinating and meeting with the heads of all the divisions in the national headquarters, and not just the women's division." She supervised the work of every part of the campaign, not only women but also the publicity and finance divisions, the Young Republicans, and outreach to Black voters. Hall instructed her to meet with the head of every subgroup of the campaign weekly, in order to make sure everyone was working together smoothly. In many ways this work was similar to her work in 1952, where she coordinated all the groups working to turn out the women's vote. But in 1956, she had many more groups to coordinate across a wide range of issues and tasks. It was a huge responsibility, but one Adkins clearly relished. More than a decade after the campaign she proudly recounted that, "As the title implies, I was the assistant chairman. This was the first time we had done this." When asked if the Democrats had ever used a similar structure, Adkins was quick to point out that India Edwards "worked just with women's activities."[5]

Hall leaned on Adkins in other ways during the campaign season. In July 1956 Harold Stassen, who had briefly been a front-runner for the GOP nomination in 1948 and was Eisenhower's special assistant for disarmament, made headlines by publicly suggesting that Eisenhower replace Vice President Nixon on the 1956 ballot. Stassen created major headaches for the RNC, even going so far as to publicly attack party chairman Len Hall. Hall and Stassen decided to have breakfast in order to calm the situation, and as Adkins "persuaded Len he needed a witness when he talked with Stassen, Len amazed her by telling her she could come and be that witness."[6] Adkins was truly working as the second-in-command of the RNC throughout the 1956 campaign. It was an important promotion and shows Republican leaders' faith in Adkins. But it created problems with outreach to women.

Two groups picked up the slack created by Adkins's promotion and the corresponding drop-off in WD activities. One was professional pollsters and public relations men. Eisenhower had always used PR professionals, ever since the 1952 campaign. That year, a member of the staff of Madison Avenue advertising firm BBDO was on the Eisenhower campaign train at least occasionally. Katherine Howard remembered having breakfast with "a man" from that firm aboard the train one October morning.[7] McCann Erickson, another PR firm, wrote the scripts for the campaign's television ads in 1952. Four year later BBDO, Y&R, and other famous Madison Avenue companies of the *Mad Men* era were doing frequent work for the RNC. Many of their assignments, including local polling and media script writing, had been WD jobs in the past.

As professional men became the main conduits for learning what people at the local level thought about policies and politics, the task of organizing women to spread the word of the campaign at the local level fell increasingly to the National Federation of Republican Women. With the NFRW at the helm, women's work in 1956 emphasized voluntarism over the development of professional political women and was more conservative in content than the rest of the campaign. While Adkins was thrilled with her promotion and worked hard as the assistant chairman, the ties connecting the party offices in Washington and women around the country frayed during Eisenhower's second campaign and his second term. All of these shifts also meant that the white women of the Eisenhower team were not discussing racial issues and African American voters, whom the overall campaign focused on far more in 1956 than it had four years earlier. Where India Edwards incorporated Truman's new emphasis on civil rights into her 1948 work to a modest degree, none of the women's work in 1956, from either the WD or NFRW, did the same.

Adkins did not prioritize outreach to Black women voters or do anything to turn the work of regular party women to the issue of civil rights. The reason for that omission, whether due to lack of engagement in the day-to-day running of grassroots campaign activities or a deeper hostility to civil rights work, is impossible to determine. But both of those factors likely contributed. This lack of action put her at odds with others within the campaign team who were urging Eisenhower and the RNC to do more to pursue African American voters. In the context of southern Democrats' massive resistance to the *Brown v. Board of Education* decision, prominent Black Republicans argued that the time was ripe to bring African American voters back to the party of Lincoln. In July 1955 E. Frederick Morrow was appointed the White House officer for special projects and a presidential advisor on racial issues.[8] He joined Val Washington, head of the "Negro Division" of the RNC since 1946. The two men pushed Eisenhower and the RNC to make civil rights a focus of the 1956 campaign by promoting a "direct program of action" to advance civil rights and economic opportunity.[9]

Adkins and the WD, however, did not engage with this part of the campaign. None of the *Let's Talk about It!* postcards for 1956 discuss civil rights in any way.[10] There was one African American woman included among seven women featured in a television program called *The Women Ask the President*, which aired a week before the election. The press material for the program, however, emphasized the extraordinary educational accomplishments of her children and grandchildren and did not dwell on her race. She was also from Adkins's hometown, suggesting that Adkins did not put much effort into locating a Black woman for the program.[11] Helen Edmonds of North Carolina, an African American woman, seconded Eisenhower's nomination at the convention, but her appearance was arranged by Morrow and Washington, not Adkins.[12] Adkins did recruit at least one African American young woman to serve as a page at the convention, but overall, she did little to reach out to Black women voters.[13] Looking back on the campaign, Adkins listed women and "the so-called minorities group" as two separate entities that she oversaw during the 1956 campaign.[14] The tendency of many white women working at the highest levels of politics to see "women" as a group that did not include racial and ethnic minorities clearly persisted into the late 1950s.

The lack of connection between Black and white Republican women continued after Eisenhower's reelection. In the spring of 1958, Helen Edmonds informed Val Washington that the Black Republican women of North Carolina "don't know what is going on" with the NFRW in the state, or with RNC work for women.[15] In spite of Washington asking Adkins months earlier to ensure that Edmonds and her friend Elreta Alexander, an African American lawyer, were invited to the National Republican Women's Conference, Edmonds did not hear of the meeting until just a few days before the conference.[16] Washington's frustration boiled over. He argued to Chief of Staff Sherman Adams, "How long can the Republican Party survive and completely ignore our own party workers? This is a new day and when people of Dr. Edmonds' stature are treated so lightly, what hope can they find in the party? Miss Adkins has always worked with me. I do not know whether this was an oversight or intentional. It is certainly the kind of mistake that can be very costly."[17]

There is a handwritten notation at the bottom of this memo, asking Washington to make sure that Adkins did not object to Edmonds meeting with Adams when she was next in Washington. This deference to Adkins in the face of Washington's clear anger is surprising. But as the assistant chairman, Adkins outranked Washington within the RNC organizational structure. That may be the reason that Washington was told to confer with her before extending the invitation. Or there may have been concerns that Adkins had indeed kept Edmonds out of the loop on purpose, for reasons unknown to the chief of staff's office. Whatever the reason, the result was that a prominent Black Republican woman got the runaround from the Eisenhower administration.

The increasing prominence of the NFRW in work with grassroots Republican women also did not bode well for increasing the party's outreach to Black women. The NFRW structure was built around using neighborhood networks to spread the word about the Eisenhower administration and the GOP. In the mid-1950s, the overwhelming majority of American neighborhoods were segregated. The NFRW's 1956 campaign efforts revolved around a project called Operation Coffee Cup, where women invited their neighbors into their home. As Catherine Rymph has written, the "intimacy of the household" was critical in creating space where NFRW women felt comfortable discussing politics. That intimacy would have been shattered, in the minds of most NFRW women, by having women of different classes or races present.

By using a neighborhood-based structure, the NFRW ensured that even white Republican women who wanted to reach out to Black women would have found doing so difficult.[18]

Operation Coffee Cup was the first part of a two-step project that the group developed in 1956. NFRW leaders envisioned their members having informal chats with other women wherever they encountered them, whether those women were Republicans or not. Sometimes coffee hour open houses at members' homes were organized as well, often during the day while children were at school. The second prong of the program, the Republican Roundtable, was more formal. The materials sent to members laid out the process: "Federation members will meet 'around the table' with their neighbors to learn more about their government, the role of political parties, what the Republican Party stands for, local registration & election laws, precinct vote analysis, the accomplishments of the Eisenhower administration, and the NFRW."[19]

In spite of their more formalized agenda of topics, roundtable meetings were still intended to take place in homes. The NFRW never encouraged its members to hold open, public meetings—that was simply not the way the organization operated. And they believed that their behind-the-scenes work was a successful approach for Republican women. The headline on the back of the pamphlet describing the program declared "Women Want to Know How to Campaign Effectively!" implying that the information in the pamphlet, outlining these two projects, taught them exactly that.

The most striking thing about this program was its similarity to WD efforts, especially during the 1954 midterm and under Democratic presidents for the previous quarter century. Providing basic education about how to participate in the electoral process and moving from there to promote your party's candidates and use women to provide and analyze information about local voters and their concerns was the bread-and-butter of the Women's Division since Molly Dewson reinvigorated the structures in 1932. RNC leadership in 1956, however, signed off on the NFRW taking on these tasks early in the campaign season. Remarks from the Republican Women's National Conference, which was held every spring, show that the men at the helm of the campaign endorsed Operation Coffee Cup and saw it as a key part of the campaign's efforts, in spite of the official separation between the NFRW and the RNC.

A message from presidential press secretary Jim Hagerty to the meeting declared that the program designed by the NFRW was "a natural project for Republican Women's Clubs. We expect that it will have the co-operation in every area with the regular party officials and other leaders."[20] Hagerty emphasizing party officials' work with NFRW volunteers shows that Kearns's efforts to move her members into closer relationships with party leaders was paying off.

The NFRW doing the work the WD had done in the past meant that working for the campaign was less likely to lead a woman into a paid job in Washington. This tradition had never been as robust on the Republican side as it had been for the Democrats, where both Gladys Tillett and India Edwards moved from voluntary roles during one campaign to paid staff positions the next. Bertha Adkins and Anne Wheaton's paths as women professionals who moved into political work was far more common among Republicans. But even so, the NFRW was a group that emphasized its volunteer identity. Much of the tension between Adkins and the NFRW revolved around Adkins's identity as a professional woman, as well as her politics. Also, the separation between the grassroots women and the WD meant that those women who were employed by the RNC were less likely to hear about dynamic women coming up through the volunteer ranks. By putting the work with grassroots women under the supervision of a group devoted to voluntarism, a pipeline between local politically active women and the national party leadership eroded on the Republican side, three years after the DNC's decision to dissolve its Women's Division had had the same impact across the political aisle.

But the Republican WD still existed in 1956, and it was still connecting with the women it had always worked with: the comparatively smaller group of county and precinct chairs and state committee women of the regular party offices. These were the women Julie Kirlin and other WD staffers were trying to turn into fundraisers, with little success. Adkins seems to have focused what work she did specifically with women on producing the year's *Let's Talk about It!* cards and organizing the single time women spoke at the 1956 Republican Convention. Adkins did not give a stump speech at the convention—she could not be on the speakers' platform at all, because she was serving as a delegate-at-large for Maryland.[21] But she did not bring any other high-profile Republican woman in to give a major speech. Instead, Adkins organized a program to "present the women of the GOP." This was a series of brief remarks by a number of Republican women running for office in 1956.[22] Its goal—to promote Republican women running for office—could not have been more different than Tillett's and Edwards's convention speeches of the previous decade. They both took to the stage to persuade women to vote for their candidate because they felt the Democratic Party was better for women. They were not speaking to or about professional political women—they were trying to turn out the women's vote. While Adkins may have thought highlighting the number of Republican women seeking office would appeal to women voters, the persistent tension with NFRW leaders around issues of professionalism versus voluntarism suggests that was not universally true.

Adkins also had to fight to keep even this little bit of attention to women included in the convention telecast. The day before the spot was planned, she learned that Len Hall intended to cut it. It was scheduled to occur at the same time that the president would be landing in San Francisco for the convention. Given Eisenhower's recent health problems, Hall wanted the television cameras at the airport, to capture the president getting off of the plane. Adkins put her foot down. Winifred Helmes recalled that:

> When Tad [Helmes's nickname for Adkins] was asked to see Len Hall, she marched into his office and really let him see how she could lose her temper. . . . Everyone but Tad believed the women's program would be cut and there would be no help for it. But Tad changed the whole picture. She flatly refused to have her program out or shortened in any way or taken off the air. It was to go on as planned or she would resign right then and there! She didn't resign and her program went on the air. . . . Robert Montgomery [who handled TV for Eisenhower] called the President's plane and told them to delay landing for half an hour.[23]

There are many mentions in Helmes's diary about Adkins's frustrations with the RNC men throughout this campaign season. The television program mentioned above, featuring a group of women and airing a week before the election, occurred so late because Adkins could not get the RNC men to agree to it earlier. As Helmes recalled, "All this [details about the program] Tad wanted [to have] decided two months ago, but she got nowhere with Len and the White House boys before today."[24] That entry is dated October

17; the program was broadcast a week later, because the campaign was almost over.

Adkins was also frustrated with Katherine Howard, and according to Helmes, she was not the only one. As early as July 1956, Helmes noted that "Katherine Howard [is] still wanting a 'title,' and Len and Tad [are] trying to think up a good one."[25] By September they had put Howard in charge of a project to celebrate the president's birthday, which appears to be the only thing the Citizens network did during the 1956 campaign. The idea was to get people excited about the election by, essentially, throwing a birthday party for the president with cakes, parades, and special events. While it garnered good media attention, it is hard to say how much of an effect the event actually had on the outcome of the election.[26] What it clearly did do was alienate Katherine Howard from the RNC leadership even more. In Helmes's diary and elsewhere, Howard comes across as a woman who regretted not taking the big appointment when it was offered to her after the 1952 election and trying to fight her way into a prominent role four years later without any clear allies. Helmes noted that Howard "has worn out the patience of Sherman Adams, Len Hall, and Tad" by constantly wanting to make sure she had a prominent role.[27] The personality clashes with Howard, which may have led to her taking on something as insignificant as the birthday celebrations, meant that another avenue of having women be central to the campaign was lost in 1956. Baking cakes for the president didn't do anything to help sell the administration and its accomplishments the way that Citizens and WD work had done in 1952. It showed the administration's appreciation for women's traditional housewife roles but did little else.

So how did the accomplishments of Eisenhower's first term get sold? If the previous sources of grassroots campaign workers weren't serving in that role, who was? In large part, the work was taken over by professional PR firms hired by the administration. The 1956 election was a pivotal one in cementing the professionalization of political campaigns by public relations companies. The president of Madison Avenue firm BBDO, Ben Duffy, was most likely the man Katherine Howard met on the train in 1952. He remained a close advisor four years later. Duffy and the other ad men were in a position of great strength in 1956 because of the unusual circumstances of the campaign. Eisenhower suffered a massive heart attack in the fall of 1955. In February 1956, when he announced his intention to seek reelection, his doctors still did not believe he was healthy enough for a traditional campaign schedule. And so he announced that he would use "mass communication" to let people know about the accomplishments of his administration. There would be no train tour, no public speeches by the president. Instead, the American people would hear from him only through their television sets.[28] This was the reason Len Hall so badly wanted TV audiences to see him getting off of his plane.

Eisenhower's necessary reliance on television to conduct the 1956 campaign helps explain the Women's Division's turn to fundraising. There were no groups of local women politicians to host on the train, none of the grassroots work that had occurred every four years for the previous two decades. Money to pay for television spots was the campaign's greatest need, and so the WD tried to meet that need.

Professional companies also took over the internal polling work. BBDO conducted weekly polls and provided Len Hall with detailed breakdowns in the last few months of the campaign.[29] In spite of this robust polling structure, campaign insiders were not happy with the quality of information they were getting. A memo sent to Hall on October 15, a few weeks before the election, complained that in seven critical swing states, "One of our greatest weaknesses is lack of political intelligence. Such intelligence can only come from those on the spot and cannot be accurately ascertained by outsiders."[30] Eisenhower had been concerned with the reliance on professional pollsters for months, telling a member of the RNC public relations staff in August that he thought the RNC "placed altogether too much reliance on them."[31]

The fact that the president's unhappiness with the polling data did not lead to an increase in work for the WD is telling, because the WD had piloted a polling program the year before. In the fall of 1955, regular party women had gone door-to-door in their neighborhood and asked questions to "find out what the men and women in your neighborhood are thinking so we can better gear our Republican policies to the needs and wishes of the people."[32] The WD office prepared a breakdown of the results, divided by region, and provided it to the RNC leadership.[33] The structure was in place for regular party women to work as pollsters during the 1956 campaign. But there is no evidence that anyone thought to use that structure. Even when she was introducing the program, Adkins described it as a tool to help "us here in National Headquarters in formulating our national campaign plans."[34] So why did the WD not step into the breach if Eisenhower was unhappy with the data he was getting from BBDO? Given Adkins's absence from the day-to-day running of the WD, it is likely that there was no one at the RNC office who could connect the dots. Without a full-time Women's Division director, the local party women did not have an effective way of communicating with the party offices in D.C.

Eisenhower's health and the related rise in professional PR men's work on the campaign could have been a one-time emergency. Those factors did not necessarily mean that women's time as critical campaign workers and sought-after voters were over. But during the 1956 campaign and throughout Eisenhower's second term, there was also a clear shift away from a vision of women as a special, distinct group that needed to be courted by politicians. The highly gendered rhetoric that had been present in at least some material produced by each winning presidential campaign since 1944 was absent in 1956. The gender norms of the era, however, had not changed. It was still the height of the Cold War, the height of the baby boom. Women were still understood as fundamentally different from men. So where did gendered appeals to women voters go?

The prominence of professional advertising men offers one explanation for this absence. The fact that the Women's Division was no longer creating much written material or other media—they were not writing scripts, they were only producing a handful of *Let's Talk about It!* postcards, and they were not doing a tremendous amount to activate grassroots women—is another piece of the puzzle. Finally, the 1954 quip that supporting a focus on women voters was like "being against sin" suggests that the idea may have become so accepted by campaign men that none of them believed it was their job to attend to outreach to women voters. Everyone was doing it, they believed, which in practice meant that almost no one was. While the NFRW programs and materials were clearly built to work within the structures and schedules of housewives' lives, none of their materials made claims that Eisenhower's reelection would be good *for women* in distinct ways.

Eisenhower's rhetoric during his second term also transitioned away from his earlier focus on promoting the interests of women. In March 1958, he addressed the annual gathering of women who worked within his administration, for Republicans in Congress, or for the RNC. After speaking to this group of professional political women about economics, foreign policy, and other issues, he concluded, "I have talked to you not as women but as American citizens with a real responsibility in public affairs. You see, there is no 'women's angle' to the great issues of our day."[35] This statement is quite different than the ones he made during the 1952 campaign, when he sang the praises of the moral values women brought to politics. Eisenhower's rhetoric clearly moved away from supporting the idea of women as a distinct bloc of voters that brought special traits to government. In many ways, this quote would have made sense coming from FDR, and it resonates with his statement that women's opinions were part of the "collective wisdom of citizens" but not distinctly important in any particular way.

The president also appeared to be shifting his policy preferences on women's issues in his second term, although that appearance may have been deceiving. In his 1957 budget message to Congress, delivered just a few days after the State of the Union, Eisenhower declared, "The platforms of both major parties have advocated an amendment of the Constitution to insure [*sic*] equal rights for women. I believe that the Congress should make certain that women are not denied equal rights with men."[36] Pro-ERA women like National Women's Party president Nina Broderick Price took that statement as an endorsement of the ERA, and they were disappointed when the president did not follow up with active support for that amendment.[37] But Eisenhower's support for the ERA was an illusion—his statements were always vaguely in support of "equal rights" and never explicitly in support of the amendment. Historian Rebecca DeWolf has gone so far as to argue that he "did not fully understand the purpose of the amendment."[38] In spite of his lack of actual support, however, by making statements that could be interpreted as supportive of the ERA, he was articulating a different vision of women's role in society than he had during the 1952 campaign. Whether he was doing so intentionally or not—and it may well have been unintentional—the tone about women in politics was shifting in the late 1950s.

By the time of the 1960 election, the situation regarding women voters had changed dramatically from just eight years earlier. The DNC had been without a Women's Division for seven years. Even had that structure still been robust, John F. Kennedy ran his campaign largely with his own people, outside of official DNC channels, especially during the primaries.[39] Bertha Adkins also recalled Richard Nixon's 1960 campaign as a "lone wolf operation," unwilling to use Eisenhower people who were ready to go to work for the vice president.[40] By 1960 Adkins herself was no longer in the RNC. In the fall of 1958 she had moved out of the political wing of the Eisenhower administration and into a policy role as under secretary of health, education, and welfare. Oveta Culp Hobby had left the cabinet in 1955, so when Adkins took her new job, she became the highest-ranking woman in the Eisenhower administration. While Adkins was replaced at the WD by Clare B. Williams, and the RNC kept a Women's Division until at least 1962, under Williams's leadership the WD's work focused even more narrowly on the regular party women.[41]

The focus on women as a distinct voting group was gone by the early 1960s, and so was the high profile of professional political women. In 1963 Kennedy administration staffer Clayton Fritchey argued hard that the administration should pay attention to women in their reelection efforts. He appears unaware that his arguments were commonplace assumptions just a decade earlier. Fritchey noted that, "Women now compose the majority of the electorate, and that majority is constantly increasing. Women are also rapidly becoming strong political activists. . . . Currently, we have not only no Mrs. Roosevelt but no Mrs. Perkins, or Anna Rosenberg, or India Edwards, whose names became household words in previous Democratic regimes. Even the Eisenhower regime had its Clare Luce and Oveta Hobby. Today there are no really famous women serving in government."[42] The loss of these "famous women" indicated a broader loss of thinking about women by leading male politicians. Eisenhower's second term saw a rapid decline in the focus on women as a separate political force. And that decline had ripple effects for decades to come.

Epilogue

Clayton Fritchey's lament about the lack of "famous women" in politics in 1963 overlooked many important women in Congress at that time. Most notably he did not count as famous Democratic congresswomen Edith Green and Martha Griffiths. Those two would, over the next few years, write or cowrite some of the most important feminist legislation in American history. They worked alongside the many newly elected congresswomen who joined them throughout the next decade, including Shirley Chisholm, Bella Abzug, and Patsy Takamoto Mink. Griffiths ensured women's inclusion in Title VII of the 1964 Civil Rights Act. Green coauthored the bill that became Title IX with Mink. And many of the women staffers and journalists who worked alongside WD leaders were still working in Washington as the women's movement geared up.

But Fritchey was not wrong. One clear example of the rise and fall of women's power within parties and campaigns was visible at the presidential libraries where I did my research. FDR, Truman, and Eisenhower's libraries hold the papers of influential women who worked on campaigns for those men—Molly Dewson, India Edwards, and Bertha Adkins—in addition to Women's Division papers. At the Kennedy, LBJ, and Nixon presidential libraries, there are no equivalents. Researching the role of women in campaigns there led me to the papers of men like Frederick Panzer at the LBJ library and Jeb Magruder at the Nixon library. The women disappeared from campaign structures in the 1960s. By that decade, politicians no longer saw value in having a separate space for women. They had all come to agree with the Democratic Party leaders who claimed, when they dissolved their WD in 1953, that integrating women into the overall structure of the party was the better path. Difference feminism, which had been a dominant mode of feminism since the nineteenth century, saw its influence fall sharply in the 1960s. As it waned, however, a feminist vision based on treating men and women the same, especially in law and policy, came into its own.

The paradox at the end of this story is that feminist policies gained more traction while structures for women's partisan inclusion declined. Just a few months after Clayton Fritchey complained about the lack of women in the party, JFK's President's Commission on the Status of Women issued its report, documenting hundreds of ways in which the federal government discriminated against women. The culmination of more than two years' research, the PCSW report led to important policy changes in areas like civil service hiring. It also spawned state-level commissions that became critical pieces of the 1960s and 1970s feminist landscape.[1] The PCSW is often credited as one starting point for the women's movement that blossomed over the next fifteen years. That same year, Congress passed the Equal Pay Act, a law that many women legislators and their allies had been working to pass for more than a decade. The declining influence of the WD, therefore, was part of the overall declining influence for difference feminism that valued treating women differently in favor of an equality-based vision that, over the following fifteen years, created enormous improvements in women's legal status and their lives.

As women's rights slowly became a more prominent topic over the course of the 1960s, women throughout the country learned about the movement through a variety of channels. But the two major parties did not serve as channels for feminist change in the 1960s, as they might have done had a national feminist movement emerged in the 1940s or 1950s when the WD structure was thriving. This fact created space in the 1960s and 1970s for groups ranging from NOW to Phyllis Schlafly's Eagle Forum (a direct spin-off of the National Federation of Republican Women's Clubs) to mobilize politically active women—some of whom likely would have worked for the major parties a generation earlier—both for and against feminism.

This loss of behind-the-scenes channels tied to national party structures is, of course, not an entirely bad thing. Women had a great deal of power and prominence in the 1970s, more than they likely would have had within the parties, and much more than they had at midcentury. The experiences of Phyllis Schlafly and her fellow conservative women clearly demonstrates how much could be gained by stepping outside of the parties.[2] But just because the women of midcentury were held down by a glass ceiling does not mean their stories are unimportant. Showing that women's role in government was debated throughout the twentieth century, that women and feminism did not simply vanish from Washington for several decades, and that politicians took women voters seriously are vital correctives to our understanding of women in politics.

The collapse of party-run women's politics also eventually opened the door for more African American women to move into electoral politics. Throughout the middle of the century Black women had built up political power outside of the major parties. They engaged in civil rights work in both mixed-sex groups like the NAACP and SNCC and women's groups like the National Council of Negro Women. In 1944, as Gladys Tillett gave a keynote address at the Democratic National Convention, Rosa Parks was investigating the assault on Recy Taylor for the Alabama NAACP. Septima Clark was teaching in South Carolina, developing the curriculum she would use to train civil rights workers at the Highlander Folk School. Mary McLeod Bethune directed the National Council of Negro Women, which she had founded nine years earlier, to continue lobbying at the state and national level on a wide range of issues. By the 1960s, African American women had decades of political organizing experiences that had occurred outside of the parties, which they were able to use to advance Black women within party politics beginning in the late 1960s.[3]

Highlighting the extensive political work of Black women outside of the party structure emphasizes the WD's role in perpetuating the segregation within women's politics. The WD was one of several structures that bridged the segregated women's politics of the late nineteenth century into the still-substantial segregation of 1960s and 1970s feminism. There were many racially integrated feminist groups during the women's movement, but there were also many groups that were white only. White women in both segregated and integrated groups often struggled to understand the different perspectives that women of color brought to feminist activism, especially on topics such as reproductive justice, rape, domestic violence, and other issues of bodily autonomy.[4] FDR's quashing of an explicit push for racially integrated women's politics during World War II is therefore the most tantalizing "what if" of this book. The segregation of women's politics continues to trouble feminism today. What if Eleanor Roosevelt had been able to put her substantial influence behind breaking it down eighty years ago? Instead, the WD structure—with its assumption of lots of free time and postwar reliance on neighborhoods and homes as the sites of politics—helped make "women's politics" mean white women and embed that white women's politics further into the foundations of both parties.

The world of the WD, therefore, had substantial limitations. It was segregated. It did not lead to legislation that tangibly improved women's lives. It did little to increase the number of women in paid political roles, although not for lack of trying. But it is also a remarkable story. It is a story of women who broke many of the boundaries of their time. They thrived in the male world of Washington politics, even as working mothers or as lesbians. They empowered tens of thousands of women throughout the country to educate themselves about policy and have political conversations with friends and strangers. They built the postwar political culture of facts that guided the country during a period of unprecedented prosperity. Molly, Dorothy, Gladys, India, and Bertha were at the heart of one of the most consequential periods of American history. We should know their names.

NOTES

INTRODUCTION

1. Edward, *Pulling No Punches*, 141–42. Emphasis in original.

2. Finding Aid, Dorothy Smith McAllister Papers, Bentley Library, University of Michigan, https://quod.lib.umich.edu/b/bhlead/umich-bhl-87150?view=text.

3. The details of how McAllister managed to balance her roles as a working mother are largely unknown. There is only a small collection of McAllister's papers at the University of Michigan; according to the finding aid they are largely focused on her work. Due to the coronavirus pandemic, researchers not affiliated with the University of Michigan have been barred from those archives at least through this writing in March 2022, and so I was unable to access what little survives of McAllister's own papers. Family stories and oral history are also not an option, as neither of her daughters had children.

4. Sara eventually enrolled in Chatham Hall, a girls' boarding school in southern Virginia. While she was closer to her mother, the school is still over two hundred miles from Washington, D.C. See Tillett to Dr. E. J. Lee, President of Chatham Hall, April 13, 1942, folder 1209, box 28, Gladys Avery Tillett Papers, University of North Carolina Wilson Library (Special Collections).

5. Mary Rickett to Frank McHale, October 14, 1947, folder 3, box 1, India Edwards Papers, Harry S. Truman Presidential Library.

6. Johnson, *The Lavender Scare*; Freedman, "'The Burning of Letters Continues.'" The rate of arrest statistic is from Cervini, *The Deviant's War*, 4.

7. Winifred Helmes diary, October 5 and 24, 1956, box 1, Winifred Helmes Papers, Edward H. Nabb Research Center, Salisbury University (hereafter cited as Helmes diary).

8. Clipping, "Both Parties Woo Women as Decisive Election Factor," *Washington Star*, February 20, 1944, in DNC Women's Division Scrapbook, box 138, DNC Women's Division Papers, Franklin D. Roosevelt Presidential Library (hereafter DNC WD Scrapbook). Clipping, "Key Political Force—the Ladies," *New York Times Magazine*, March 11, 1956, folder 13, news clipping file series box 640, Republican National Committee Papers, Dwight D. Eisenhower Presidential Library. The consensus that women's votes were not a focus in these years is present in both political science and historical scholarship. See Anderson, *After Suffrage*; Corder and Wolbrecht, *Counting Women's Ballots;* and Harvey, *Votes without Leverage*. One historian has examined women as voters in the 1928 election. See Balogh, "'Mirrors of Desire,'" 222–49.

9. Historians of women's political activism have documented women's political engagement outside of the two major parties and have written biographies of female elected officials. There is one chapter on the Women's Divisions in Jo Freeman's *A Room at a Time*, which briefly narrates the story this book tells. Cynthia Harrison's *On Account of Sex* also discusses some of these women, especially Edwards and Adkins. But her book was published before Edwards's papers at the Truman Library were processed, and so there is much new material here. Freeman, Harrison, and the other works can be found throughout the notes and in the bibliography of this book.

But like so much historical scholarship, none of this work has altered the perception that most people outside of academia hold of white women in these years. Twenty-first-century media such as *Mad Men*, *Revolutionary Road*, and *Don't Worry Darling* have only reinforced beliefs about white women's domesticity in the middle decades of the twentieth century.

10. For example, Jill Lepore includes a paragraph of discussion about women's work for the Republican Party in the 1950s in her recent synthesis of U.S. history, but she does not interrogate the meaning of that work or discuss its Democratic precedents (*These Truths*, 557).

11. The exceptions to this are the several wonderful histories of right-wing women in these years, such as Nickerson's *Mothers of Conservatism* and McRae's *Mothers of Massive Resistance*. The women studied in those books clearly understood their homes as political spaces and grounded their politics in a defense of the home. Because all of the works that make these connections are about right-wing women, the impression has been created that they were the only white women who saw the home as an appropriate place for politics in these years.

12. FDR to Dorothy McAllister, November 12, 1940, folder 3, President's Personal File 603, Franklin D. Roosevelt Presidential Library (hereafter FDR PPF).

13. On the New Deal's pursuit of union voters see Cohen, *Making a New Deal*, chap. 6. On labor women see Twarog, *Politics of the Pantry*, chaps. 1 and 2; and Cobble, *The Other Women's Movement*, 51–55.

14. Charlie Willis to Jim Hagerty, April 26, 1954, folder 8, box 587, Eisenhower Official File, White House Central Files, Eisenhower Presidential Library.

15. On white women's politics in this period see Newman, *White Women's Rights*; Skelton, "'Women in a Changing World'"; and Sneider, *Suffragists in an Imperial Age*, among others.

16. On this disagreement and split see Tetrault, *Myth of Seneca Falls*, chap. 1.

17. On the YWCA, see Robertson, *Christian Sisterhood;* and Blair, *Revolutionizing Expectations*. On the WCTU see Gilmore, *Gender and Jim Crow*. The American Women's Suffrage Association was racially integrated but also included many male members and so was an outlier in women's political organizing in multiple ways. We also know very little about the AWSA's daily work in these years, for reasons Lisa Tetrault describes in *Myth of Seneca Falls*.

18. The foundational book on Black women's clubs is Giddings, *When and Where I Enter*. Other important works include Lindsey, *Colored No More*; Parker, *Unceasing Militant*; Tuuri, *Strategic Sisterhood*; and Deborah Gray White, *Too Heavy a Load*.

19. The best general overview of segregation and the struggle against it outside of the South is Sugrue, *Sweet Land of Liberty*.

20. Wall, *Inventing the "American Way,"* 7.

21. Cobble, *The Other Women's Movement*, 3–4. Cobble identified the "equal rights teleology" in histories of American women and feminism as a problematic approach more than two decades ago. Women's history is still struggling to break out of that teleology, and I hope this book is another step in that direction (7).

CHAPTER ONE. "AN INSTRUMENT TO ATTAIN THEIR HOPES AND DREAMS"

1. "The Attitude of Democratic Women," April 15, 1936, p. 2, folder 7, OF 300, White House Central Files, Franklin D. Roosevelt Presidential Library (hereafter FDR WHCF).

2. Ibid., p. 4.

3. For examples of this logic among women politicians in the 1920s see Cott, *The Grounding of Modern Feminism*, 106–11; and Schuyler, *The Weight of Their Votes*, chap. 4.

4. Andersen, *After Suffrage*, 80.

5. Trigg, *Feminism as Life's Work*, 3.

6. Andersen, *After Suffrage*, 84–87.

7. Quoted in Corder and Wolbrecht, *Counting Women's Ballots*, 4.

8. Andersen, *After Suffrage*, chap. 4.

9. McGirr, *The War on Alcohol*, 164–88.

10. Quoted in Balogh, "'Mirrors of Desire,'" 232.

11. Michaelis, *Eleanor*, 260.

12. Balogh, "'Mirrors of Desire,'" 235.

13. Ibid., 235, 238.

14. Michaelis, *Eleanor*, 260–61.

15. For more on Moskowitz see Perry, *Belle Moskowitz*.

16. Michaelis, *Eleanor*, 261.

17. Ibid., 262.

18. Ware, *Partner and I*, 158–59.

19. Molly Dewson, "An Aid to the End," (unpublished memoir held at FDR Library), quoted in Ware, *Partner and I*, 160.

20. Ibid., 161.

21. Ibid., 163–64.

22. Dewson, "An Aid to the End," 43–44, quoted in Ware, *Partner and I*, 167.

23. Ware, *Partner and I*, 163.

24. Handwritten note by Molly Dewson, p. 1, scrapbook, box 26, Mary W. Dewson Papers, Franklin D. Roosevelt Presidential Library.

25. Quoted in Ware, *Partner and I*, 170.

26. *Your Electric Bill*, flier, folder 1, box 107, DNC Women's Division Papers, Roosevelt Presidential Library.

27. On Chamberlain's work see handwritten note by Molly Dewson, p. 1, scrapbook, box 26, Dewson Papers.

28. Dewson to "Campaign Worker," October 24, 1932, folder 6, OF 300, FDR WHCF.

29. *Why Women Want Roosevelt*, folder 1, box 107, DNC Women's Division Papers, Roosevelt Presidential Library.

30. "The Attitude of Democratic Women," April 15, 1936, p. 3, folder 7, OF 300, FDR WHCF.

31. Ware, *Partner and I*, 170.

32. Quoted in ibid., 171.

33. Ibid.

34. Quoted in ibid., 173.

35. *Ibid.*, 182–83.

36. Quoted in ibid., 197.

37. DeWolf, *Gendered Citizenship*, chap. 3.

38. Ware, *Partner and I*, 197.

39. For more on Eleanor's press conferences see Beasley, "Eleanor Roosevelt's Press Conferences."

40. Ware, *Partner and I*, 198.

41. "The Reporter Plan: Its Essence," p. 1, folder 6, OF 300, FDR WHCF.

42. Ibid., p. 2.

43. Political scientist Kristi Andersen has identified "disinterestedness and intelligence" as part of women's political culture since the 1910s. Andersen, *After Suffrage*, 33.

44. Ware, *Partner and I*, 196.

45. For examples of the argument that the political culture valuing facts and expertise was a new, postwar development see Balogh, *Chain Reaction*; Herman, *The Romance of American Psychology*; and Zelizer, *Taxing America*, among others.

46. Molly Dewson to Eleanor Roosevelt, January 26, 1934, folder 6, OF 300, FDR WHCF.

47. Quoted in Ware, *Partner and I*, 201.

48. Molly Dewson to Eleanor Roosevelt, February 23, 1934, folder 12, box 10, DNC Women's Division Papers, Roosevelt Presidential Library.

49. Ware, *Partner and I*, 199.

50. FDR to Carolyn Wolfe, February 20, 1936, FDR PPF 603.

51. Charles L. Murray to Mary Dewson, August 22, 1937, reprinted and circulated to

all state committeewomen and state *Digest* directors, August 27, 1937, folder 8, box 111, DNC Women's Division Papers, Roosevelt Presidential Library.

52. Ware, *Partner and I*, 199.

53. "Senior Reporters under the Reporter Plan," pp. 1–2, folder 6, box 10, DNC Women's Division Papers, Roosevelt Presidential Library.

54. "Winning Account Duties of the Precinct Vice-Chairman," folder 6, box 10, DNC Women's Division Papers, Roosevelt Presidential Library.

55. Molly Dewson to FDR, May 29, 1935, folder 6, OF 300, FDR WHCF.

CHAPTER TWO. "WOMEN HAVE INDEED COME OF AGE POLITICALLY"

1. The university became known as the Women's College in 1932, its third name during Elliot's career. For the sake of consistency this name will be used throughout. For more on the college and its relationship to UNC-G, see "History of UNCG," https://www.uncg.edu/about-uncg/why-uncg/history-of-uncg/.

2. Ware, *Partner and I*, 202–3.

3. "Radio Transcript—A New Deal for Women," folder 5, box 110, DNC Women's Division Papers, Roosevelt Presidential Library. There is no author listed on the speech, but the archival copy bears pencil edits in McAllister's handwriting. The original author may have been Elliott, but it is more likely that it was either McAllister or her frequent collaborator Bess Furman.

4. Molly Dewson to Charley Michelson, July 17, 1936, p. 1, folder 6, OF 300, FDR WHCF.

5. Michelson's name is written as both Charley and Charlie at various points in the archives. For consistency, the more common spelling is used throughout the text, but varied spellings are preserved in the notes, as above.

6. Molly Dewson to Charley Michelson, July 17, 1936, p. 2.

7. A full list of 1936 Rainbow Flier titles is in the pamphlet, *Dedicated to Mrs. County Leader*, p. 11, folder 3, box 107, DNC Women's Division Papers, Roosevelt Presidential Library.

8. Ware, *Partner and I*, 221.

9. "Kentucky" Rainbow Flier response sheet, folder 1, box 107, DNC Women's Division Papers, Roosevelt Presidential Library.

10. "Iowa" Rainbow Flier response sheet, folder 1, box 107, DNC Women's Division Papers, Roosevelt Presidential Library.

11. "California" Rainbow Flier response sheet, folder 1, box 107, DNC Women's Division Papers, Roosevelt Presidential Library (emphasis in original).

12. Carolyn Wolfe was technically the WD director in 1936. However, the archival material makes it clear that Dewson was still in charge. For example, the introductory text

of her speeches described below reads, "Miss Dewson will be in charge of the activities of Democratic women throughout the country during the campaign." Note attached to Molly Dewson to Gladys Tillett, June 3, 1936, folder 688, box 14, Tillett Papers.

13. *Dedicated to Mrs. County Leader*, pamphlet, p. 14, folder 3, box 107, DNC Women's Division Papers, Roosevelt Presidential Library.

14. Carolyn Wolfe to Gladys Tillett, January 6, 1936, folder 685, box 14, Tillett Papers.

15. "The Attitude of Democratic Women," April 15, 1936, p. 5, folder 7, box 44, OF 300, FDR WHCF.

16. J. Wallace Winborne, state chairman, to Gladys Tillett, June 5, 1936, folder 688, box 14, Tillett Papers.

17. Gladys Tillett oral history, interview by Jacquelyn Dowd Hall, March 20, 1974, University of North Carolina Southern Oral History Project, https://docsouth.unc.edu/sohp/G-0061/G-0061.html, transcript p. 40.

18. Gladys Tillett to state leaders, July 17, 1936, folder 688, box 14, Tillett Papers.

19. Mamie Geraldine Bledsoe to Gladys Tillett, November 2, 1936, folder 691, box 14, Tillett Papers.

20. Cohen, *Making a New Deal*, 260.

21. All of the speeches are in folder 708, box 14, Tillett Papers.

22. Transcript of speech, "A Future for the Farm Family," folder 708, box 14, Tillett Papers.

23. *Dedicated to Mrs. County Leader*, p. 3, folder 3, box 107, DNC Women's Division Papers, Roosevelt Presidential Library.

24. Ibid., p. 8.

25. Ibid., p. 15.

26. Ibid., p. 16.

27. Quoted in Ware, *Partner and I*, 201.

28. Molly Dewson to Gladys Tillett, July 23, 1944, folder 716, box 15, Tillett Papers.

29. Ware, *Partner and I*, 202.

30. Quoted in Ware, *Partner and I*, 216.

31. Elisabeth Chrisman, secretary-treasurer of the NWTUL, to the Chairman of the Resolutions and Platform Committee, June 8, 1936; Frederick Libbey, executive secretary, National Council for the Prevention of War to Democratic Convention Delegates, June 10, 1936: both folder 5, box 107, DNC Women's Division Papers, Roosevelt Presidential Library.

32. "Recommendations of the Women's Committee for Suggestions on the Democratic Platform," pp. 1–3, folder 5, box 107, DNC Women's Division Papers, Roosevelt Presidential Library.

33. Ibid., p. 1.

34. Molly Dewson to Charl Ormond Williams, July 10, 1936, folder 5, box 107, DNC Women's Division Papers, Roosevelt Presidential Library.

35. For more on the employment discrimination married women faced in the 1930s see Kessler-Harris, *In Pursuit of Equity*, 56–61.

36. Kennedy, *Freedom from Fear*, 286.

37. Molly Dewson to "Democratic Vice-Chairmen," February 24, 1937, p. 1, folder 3, box 110, DNC Women's Division Papers, Roosevelt Presidential Library.

38. "Party Workers—Re-organize Now!" folder 3, box 110, DNC Women's Division Papers, Roosevelt Presidential Library.

39. "The Favored State Party Set-Up for Democratic Women," folder 3, box 110, DNC Women's Division Papers, Roosevelt Presidential Library.

40. Ware, *Partner and I*, 232.

41. Molly Dewson to FDR, April 14, 1937, folder 6, box 44, OF 300, FDR WHCF.

42. "Thomas Francis McAllister," Federal Judicial Center Biographies, https://www.fjc.gov/node/1384491.

43. "Progress Report on the Women's Division," November 9, 1937, pp. 1, 5, folder 7, box 111, DNC Women's Division Papers, Roosevelt Presidential Library.

44. Dorothy McAllister, "What Women Can Do for Their Party," reprint of August 1938 *Democratic Digest* article, folder 4, box 107, DNC Women's Division Papers, Roosevelt Presidential Library.

45. FDR to Dorothy McAllister, August 20, 1938, folder 2, FDR PPF 603.

46. FDR to Dorothy McAllister, August 9, 1939, folder 2, FDR PPF 603.

47. FDR to Dorothy McAllister, April 4, 1938, folder 2, FDR PPF 603.

48. FDR to Dorothy McAllister, July 17, 1939, folder 2, FDR PPF 603.

49. Milkis, *The President and the Parties*, 98–100.

50. On FDR's criticism of machine politics see Suri, *The Impossible Presidency*, 144.

51. Suri, *The Impossible Presidency*, 147.

52. FDR to Dorothy McAllister, September 7, 1939, folder 2, FDR PPF 603.

53. Background information on Dorothy McAllister, attached to Gladys Tillett to Sumner Wells, undersecretary of state, May 18, 1943, folder 1, box 1, Tillett Papers.

54. Dorothy McAllister to Reporter Plan directors and reporter group leader, n.d., folder 10, box 107, DNC Women's Division Papers, Roosevelt Presidential Library. A reference to the war in Europe and the fact that it is clearly not yet 1940 date the letter to the fall of 1939.

55. A full set of the fliers are in folder 4, box 108, DNC Women's Division Papers, Roosevelt Presidential Library.

56. Draft and final of *That Third-Term Bugaboo*, n.d., folder 5, box 109, DNC Women's Division Papers, Roosevelt Presidential Library.

57. On the third-term issue, see Jeffries, *A Third Term for FDR*, chap. 3.

58. Regional Conferences, flier, n.d., folder 11, box 107, DNC Women's Division Papers, Roosevelt Presidential Library (emphasis in original).

59. Dorothy McAllister to "Fellow-Democrats," March 26, 1940, folder 10, box 107, DNC Women's Divisions Papers, Roosevelt Presidential Library. Molly Dewson mentioned Carolyn Wolfe's original suggestion for this kind of event to Eleanor Roosevelt in 1935. See Dewson to Eleanor Roosevelt, November 7, 1935, folder 12, box 10, DNC Women's Division Papers, Roosevelt Presidential Library. Dewson noted that she was sharing this with Eleanor "just to put it in your mind to simmer."

60. The Director of the Speakers' Bureau, flier, n.d. [late 1939], folder 7, box 109, DNC Women's Division Papers, Roosevelt Presidential Library.

61. Dorothy McAllister to state vice-chairmen, March 1, 1940, folder 10, box 107, DNC Women's Division Papers, Roosevelt Presidential Library.

62. Dorothy McAllister, Plans for Campaigning, August 1940, folder 7, box 109, DNC Women's Division Papers, Roosevelt Presidential Library.

63. FDR to Dorothy McAllister, August 15, 1940, folder 3, FDR PPF 603.

64. FDR to Jim Farley, April 8, 1940, folder 8, box 44, OF 300, FDR WHCF.

65. "Answer to the Propaganda against the Women's Division Organization," folder 20, box 110, DNC Women's Division Papers, Roosevelt Presidential Library.

66. Dorothy McAllister to state vice-chairmen, February 28, 1940, p. 2, folder 10, box 107, DNC Women's Division Papers, Roosevelt Presidential Library.

67. All data about numbers of women and length of service are from Rutgers's Center for American Women and Politics, https://cawp.rutgers.edu/.

68. "Women Elected Officials by Party," Center for American Women and Politics, Rutgers, https://cawpdata.rutgers.edu/women-elected-officials/party?party%5BDemocrat%5D=Democrat&current=2&years%5B1941%5D=1941&level%5BState%20Legislative%5D=State%20Legislative&items_per_page=50&yearend_filter=All&page=1.

69. Dorothy McAllister to state vice-chairmen, February 28, 1940, p. 1, folder 10, box 107, DNC Women's Division Papers, Roosevelt Presidential Library.

70. All the speeches are in folder 6, box 109, DNC Women's Division Papers, Roosevelt Presidential Library.

71. Dorothy McAllister to Nan Wood Honeyman, July 1, 1940, folder 6, box 109, DNC Women's Division Papers, Roosevelt Presidential Library.

72. Dorothy McAllister to Gladys Tillett, July 10, 1940, folder 6, box 109, DNC Women's Division Papers, Roosevelt Presidential Library.

73. Report of the Democratic Women's Platform Advisory Committee, p. 7, folder 2, box 108, DNC Women's Division Papers, Roosevelt Presidential Library.

74. Ibid.

75. Delphine Thomas, "Some Facts about Alabama Poll Tax Laws," *Ashland (Ala.) Progress*, December 1, 1938, 5, https://www.newspapers.com/clip/63478954/some-facts-about-alabamas-poll-tax/.

76. Ibid.

77. On tensions between southern Democrats and FDR see Milkis, *The President and the Parties*, 87–92.

78. Dorothy McAllister, form letter, September 29, 1939, folder 10, box 107, DNC Women's Division Papers, Roosevelt Presidential Library.

79. Crystal Bird Fauset to Eleanor Roosevelt, telegram, September 1940, Digitized Correspondence of Eleanor Roosevelt, accessed October 29, 2021, http://www.fdrlibrary.marist.edu/_resources/images/ersel/ersel041.pdf.

80. Lela Walker Jones to Gladys Tillett, November 11, 1940, folder 20, box 1, Tillett Papers.

81. Crystal Bird Fauset to Gladys Tillett, December 22, 1940, folder 20, box 1, Tillett Papers.

82. Ibid.

83. Report of the Democratic Women's Platform Advisory Committee, p. 6, folder 2, box 108, DNC Women's Division Papers, Roosevelt Presidential Library.

84. Dorothy Crook, BPW legislative director, to Dorothy McAllister, February 23, 1940, folder 1, box 108, DNC Women's Division Papers, Roosevelt Presidential Library.

85. Susan Kingsbury to Dorothy McAllister, June 28, 1940, folder 1, box 108, DNC Women's Division Papers, Roosevelt Presidential Library.

86. For a full history of this first ERA battle see DeWolf, *Gendered Citizenship*.

87. Dorothy McAllister to Dorothy Crook, March 6, 1940, folder 1, box 108, DNC Women's Division Papers, Roosevelt Presidential Library.

88. "Emma Guffey Miller," in Sicherman and Hurd, eds., *Notable American Women*, 477.

89. Emma Guffey Miller to FDR, July 14, 1940, folder 8, box 44, OF 300, FDR WHCF.

90. Lorena Hickok to Eleanor Roosevelt, July 14, 1940, folder 1, box 8, Lorena Hickok Papers, Franklin D. Roosevelt Presidential Library. On Eleanor and Hickok's relationship see Quinn, *Eleanor and Hick*.

91. FDR to Dorothy McAllister, November 12, 1940, folder 3, FDR PPF 603.

CHAPTER THREE. "THE CONSENSUS IS THAT WOMEN WILL SWING THE PENDULUM"

1. Weintraub, *Final Victory*, 206–9.

2. Number of total service members is from the National World War II Museum, "Research Starters: U.S. Military by the Numbers," https://www.nationalww2museum.org/students-teachers/student-resources/research-starters/research-starters-us-military-numbers. Number of soldiers' votes is from Weintraub, *Final Victory*, 209.

3. Jane Eads, "Both Parties Woo Women as Decisive Election Factor," *Washington Star*, February 20, 1944, box 138, DNC WD Scrapbook.

4. Charles N. Wheeler, "Both Parties Change Tune to Win Votes of Women," *Chicago Daily News*, June 16, 1944, in DNC WD Scrapbook.

5. The two books that ignore women voters are Weintraub, *Final Victory*, and Davis, *Politics as Usual*. Biographers of women active in the era do somewhat better. Sylvia Jukes Morris's biography of Luce and Susan Quinn's recent book on Eleanor and Hick's relationship both devote a chapter to the campaign, although Morris does not discuss the broader context of women's votes. Morris, *The Price of Fame*, chap. 9; Quinn, *Eleanor and Hick*, chap. 22.

6. FDR to Ed Flynn, November 23, 1940, folder 6, box 44, OF 300, FDR WHCF.

7. Lorena Hickok to Eleanor Roosevelt, November 7, 1940, pp. 3, 6, folder 3, box 8, Lorena Hickok Papers, Franklin D. Roosevelt Presidential Library. On Hick leaving the AP to be with Eleanor, see Michaelis, *Eleanor*, 279–80.

8. Lorena Hickok to Eleanor Roosevelt, November 11, 1940, pp. 1–2, folder 3, box 8, Hickok Papers.

9. Molly Dewson to Gladys Tillett, December 11, 1940, p. 2, folder 713, box 14, Tillett Papers.

10. Molly Dewson to Gladys Tillett, Tuesday, 1940, p. 1, folder 713, box 14, Tillett Papers (emphasis in original).

11. McEuen, *Making War, Making Women*.

12. Dewson to Tillett, Tuesday, 1940, pp. 8–10, folder 713, box 14, Tillett Papers (emphasis in original).

13. On FDR's foreign policy preferences and the relationship between his action in that realm and the 1940 campaign, see Reynolds, *From Munich to Pearl Harbor*, chaps. 4 and 5.

14. Gladys Tillett to "Democratic Leaders," June 2, 1943, folder 26, box 1, Tillett Papers.

15. Memorandum to the president from Mrs. Charles Tillett, n.d., in possession of Elizabeth Avery Thomas (Tillett's granddaughter), Pittsburgh, Pa. Shared with author August 25, 2021.

16. Secretarial memo, March 1943, folder 8, OF 300, FDR WHCF.

17. Undersecretary Sumner Wells to Gladys Tillett, April 26, 1943, folder 1, box 1, Tillett Papers.

18. Gaining policy appointments remained a major focus for WD directors and has, up to now, been seen as their primary activity. See Harrison, *On Account of Sex*, chap. 4.

19. Louisa Wilson to "Radio Directors," June 7, 1944, in DNC WD Scrapbook.

20. FDR to Robert Hannegan, July 10, 1944, p. 1, folder 3, FDR PPF 603. For more on FDR's actions during this campaign see Weintraub, *Final Victory*.

21. Gladys Tillett, opening remarks for the Campaign School, July 19, 1944, folder 3, box 111, DNC Women's Division Papers, Roosevelt Presidential Library.

22. All of the speeches given at the school can be found in folder 3, box 111, DNC Women's Division Papers, Roosevelt Presidential Library.

23. Jean Poletti, "The Street-Corner Speaking Technique," July 21, 1944, folder 3, box 111, DNC Women's Division Papers, Roosevelt Presidential Library.

24. Dorothy McAllister, "Campaign Time Is Speaking Time," July 19, 1944, folder 3, box 111, DNC Women's Division Papers, Roosevelt Presidential Library.

25. Helen Gahagan Douglas, "Campaigning in Neighborhoods," speech, July 19, 1944, folder 3, box 111, DNC Women's Division Papers, Roosevelt Presidential Library.

26. Statement by Gladys Tillett, April 7, 1944, folder 607, box 12, Tillett Papers.

27. Gladys Tillett to "Democratic Leaders," September 30, 1944, folder 6, box 1, Tillett Papers.

28. Campbell, *The Year of Peril*, 263–67.

29. Davis, *Politics as Usual*, 6.

30. See the slogan, for example, on the back of flier "Plan Your Work and Work Your Plan," folder 6, box 1, Tillett Papers.

31. Gladys Tillett speech in Detroit, April 13, 1944, folder 533, box 11, Tillett Papers.

32. Speech by Gladys Tillett in honor of Mary Norton, July 20, 1944, pp. 2, 5, folder 528, box 11, Tillett Papers.

33. Transcript of radio address, p. 1, DNC WD Scrapbook (capitalization in original).

34. Gladys Tillett convention speech, p. 1, folder 2, box 110, DNC WD Papers.

35. Tillett oral history, tape 2, side A.

36. Morris, *Price of Fame*, 6–7.

37. Ibid., 82.

38. Ibid., 84.

39. "How Women May Share in Post-War Policy Making," schedule and roster, June 1944, folder 526, box 11, Tillett Papers.

40. Morris, *Price of Fame*, 82–83, 86.

41. Speech and *New Yorker* quoted in Morris, *Price of Fame*, 87–88.

42. "The Limit of Partisanship," *New York Times*, June 29, 1944, 22.

43. Morris, *Price of Fame*, 89, 94.

44. Mary Hornaday, "Competition for Clare Luce?" *Christian Science Monitor*, May 18, 1944, DNC WD Scrapbook.

45. Mary Hornaday, "How Women Polish Politics," *Christian Science Monitor*, July 22, 1944, DNC WD Scrapbook.

46. Hazel MacDonald, "Helen vs. Clare: Torch vs. Icicle," *Chicago Times*, July 16, 1944, DNC WD Scrapbook.

47. Mary Braggiotti, "DON'T Call Her the Democrats' Clare Luce," *New York Post* magazine, July 19, 1944, 1.

48. "'Fencing' with Mrs. Luce Barred by Miss Gahagan," *New York Times*, July 16, 1944, 26.

49. MacDonald, "Helen vs. Clare"; "Douglas, Helen Gahagan," Biographical Directory of the U.S. Congress, https://bioguide.congress.gov/search/bio/D000454.

50. Helen Gahagan Douglas, speech at the Democratic National Convention, July 20, 1944, pp. 1–2, folder 3, box 111, DNC Women's Division Papers, Roosevelt Presidential Library.

51. Crystal Bird Fauset to Eleanor Roosevelt, May 25, 1944, folder "Fauset, Crystal Bird," Digitized Correspondence of Eleanor Roosevelt, accessed December 1, 2021, http://www.fdrlibrary.marist.edu/_resources/images/ersel/ersel041.pdf.

52. Crystal Bird Fauset to Eleanor Roosevelt, June 13, 1944, folder "Fauset, Crystal Bird," Digitized Correspondence of Eleanor Roosevelt.

53. FDR to Eleanor Roosevelt, memo, [June 1944], folder "Fauset, Crystal Bird," Digitized Correspondence of Eleanor Roosevelt.

54. On the uprising at the Mobile shipyards, see Nelson, "Organized Labor and the Struggle for Black Equality." On the zoot suit riots in Los Angeles, see Alvarez, *Power of the Zoot*, chap. 5.

55. Eleanor Roosevelt to Crystal Bird Fauset, June 21, 1944, p. 1, folder "Fauset, Crystal Bird," Digitized Correspondence of Eleanor Roosevelt.

56. Eleanor Roosevelt to Crystal Bird Fauset, August 22, 1944, folder "Fauset, Crystal Bird," Digitized Correspondence of Eleanor Roosevelt.

57. Gladys Tillett to Bob Hannegan, October 3, 1944, folder 52, box 2, Tillett Papers.

58. Clipping, "Crystal Bird Fauset Joins Dewey Backers," *Philadelphia Evening Bulletin*, September 8, 1944, in folder "Fauset, Crystal Bird," Digitized Correspondence of Eleanor Roosevelt.

59. For their work with the Indianapolis chapter, which did not integrate until the early 1970s, see Blair, *Revolutionizing Expectations*, chap. 3.

CHAPTER FOUR. AFTER ROOSEVELT

1. McMillen, "Gladys Avery Tillett," 155.

2. Tillett to Hannegan, August 3, 1945, folder 822, series 2 box 18, Tillett Papers.

3. India Edwards to Chase Going Woodhouse, February 27, 1947, folder 83, box 2, Tillett Papers.

4. McMillen, "Gladys Avery Tillett," 155.

5. Hickok quoted in McMillen, "Gladys Avery Tillett," 153. For more on Hick and Tillett's travels during the campaign see Quinn, *Eleanor and Hick*, 286–87.

6. I only learned that McAllister's children lived with her in Washington through census research; they are utterly absent from any archives that discuss her time in Washington. Archives.com 1940 Census Records, https://www.archives.com/1940-census/dorothy-mcallister-va-6709271?FirstName=Dorothy&ExactFirstName

=1&LastName=Mcallister&Location=VA&ExactLocation=1&BirthState=MI &folderImageSeq=26.

7. Tillett oral history, transcript pp. 42–43.

8. Gladys Tillett to Lorena Hickok, December 16, 1940, folder 14, box 17, Hickok Papers.

9. George Killion to Robert Hannegan, February 28, 1945, folder 2, box 1, India Edwards Papers, Harry Truman Presidential Library (hereafter IE Papers).

10. "Not afraid of work" is from Mabel Hill to Gladys Tillett, February 21, 1945, folder 2, box 1, IE Papers. "Not take no" and "vigor and know-how" are from Mary Rickett to Frank McHale, October 14, 1947, p. 3, folder 3, box 1, IE Papers.

11. The details of Edwards's personal life are all taken from her memoir, *Pulling No Punches*.

12. Edwards, *Pulling No Punches*, 70.

13. Ibid., 83–84.

14. Ibid., 87.

15. Gladys Tillett to Bob Hannegan, March 5, 1945, p. 1, folder 2, box 1, IE Papers. "Dumped in her lap" is from Mabel Hill to Gladys Tillett, February 21, 1945, folder 2, box 1, IE Papers.

16. India Edwards to Bess Truman, August 9, 1946, folder 2, box 1, IE Papers.

17. Speech for a County Vice-Chairman, 1946, folder 118, box 3, Tillett Papers.

18. Clipping, "Snag for Truman," *Kansas City Star,* March 2, 1947, folder 19, box 155, Democratic National Committee Papers, Harry S. Truman Presidential Library.

19. India Edwards to Bob Hannegan, November 30, 1946, p. 1, folder 2, box 1, IE Papers.

20. Democratic National Committee press release, February 14, 1947, folder 11, box 3, IE Papers.

21. India Edwards to Harry Truman, January 8, 1947, folder 3, box 1, IE Papers.

22. Mary Rickett to Frank McHale, October 14, 1947, p. 1, folder 3, box 1, IE Papers.

23. India Edwards to Howard McGrath, December 15, 1947, folder 5, box 62, Howard McGrath Papers, Harry S. Truman Presidential Library.

24. Mary Rickett to Frank McHale, October 14, 1947, p. 1, folder 3, box 1, IE Papers.

25. Edwards, *Pulling No Punches*, 100.

26. Quoted in Cobble, *The Other Women's Movement*, 114.

27. For more on midcentury ERA politics, see DeWolf, *Gendered Citizenship*.

28. Ibid., 152–61.

29. Dewson to Tillett, July 23, 1944, p. 2, folder 716, box 15, Tillett Papers.

30. On the relationship between ERA advocacy and the label "feminist" see Rupp and Taylor, *Survival in the Doldrums*.

31. India Edwards to Bob Hannegan, November 30, 1946, p. 2, folder 2, box 1, IE Papers.

32. India Edwards to Howard McGrath, January 2, 1948, folder 4, box 1, IE Papers.

33. India Edwards to Gael Sullivan, January 2, 1948, folder 4, box 1, IE Papers.

34. Gael Sullivan to Howard McGrath, February 7, 1948, folder 4, box 1, IE Papers.

35. Howard McGrath to Gael Sullivan, February 7, 1948, folder 4, box 1, IE Papers.

36. Jack Redding to Howard McGrath, March 15, 1948, folder 4, box 1, IE Papers.

37. India Edwards oral history, interview by Jerry Hess, January 16, 1969, Harry S. Truman Presidential Library Oral History Project, https://www.trumanlibrary.gov/library/oral-histories/edwards1.

38. McGrath to India Edwards, March 19, 1948; Redding to McGrath, June 14, 1948, both folder 4, box 1, IE Papers.

39. India Edwards to Sullivan, April 16, 1948, p. 1, folder 4, box 1, IE Papers.

40. India Edwards to McGrath, April 21, 1948, folder 4, box 1, IE Papers.

41. Report by India Edwards given at National Committee Meeting, July 10, 1948, pp. 1–2, folder 8, box 4, IE Papers.

42. Wall, *Inventing the "American Way."*

43. May, *Homeward Bound*, 18–19.

CHAPTER FIVE. HOUSEWIVES FOR TRUMAN

1. Packet of material regarding *New Republic* article, May 1948, folder 9, box 1083, Papers of Harry S. Truman: Official File, Truman Library (hereafter Truman OF).

2. India Edwards, press release of speech to the DNC, July 10, 1948, pp. 1–2, folder 8, box 3, IE Papers.

3. Ibid., p. 3.

4. Transcript of radio rally, January 2, 1948, p. 4, folder 14, box 201, DNC Papers, Truman Library.

5. Harry S. Truman, "Presidential Address to Congress" (Truman Doctrine speech), March 12, 1947, Miller Center of Public Affairs, University of Virginia, https://millercenter.org/the-presidency/educational-resources/truman-doctrine.

6. For more on wartime women's work on prices see Twarog, *Politics of the Pantry*, chap. 2.

7. Douglas was no longer being cast as a foil to Clare Boothe Luce, who had declined to seek reelection in 1946. On this decision see Morris, *Price of Fame*, 159–60.

8. Clipping, "Mrs. Douglas to Show Congress Economics of Market Basket," *Washington News*, April 28, 1948, folder 3, box 208, DNC Papers, Truman Library.

9. Donaldson, *Truman Defeats Dewey*, 160.

10. Transcript of radio broadcast featuring India Edwards and Mrs. Clark Clifford, July 27, 1948, folder 7, box 206, DNC Papers, Truman Library.

11. Radio script, "Democratic Record Show #4," October 18, 1948, folder 10, box 208, DNC Papers, Truman Library.

12. Radio script, "Democratic Record Show #6," October 22, 1948, folder 10, box 208, DNC Papers, Truman Library.

13. Radio script, "Democratic Record Show #10," November 1, 1948, folder 10, box 208, DNC Papers, Truman Library.

14. Quoted in "Report Made by India Edwards, October 20, 1948," p. 2, folder 4, box 3, IE Papers.

15. Memo to county Democratic chairwomen, September 22, 1948, pp. 1–2, folder 1, box 209, DNC Papers, Truman Library.

16. India Edwards, cover letter to county Democratic chairwomen memo, September 22, 1948, folder 1, box 209, DNC Papers, Truman Library.

17. Radio script, "Democratic Record Show #7," October 25, 1948, folder 10, box 208, DNC Papers, Truman Library.

18. Fosl, *Subversive Southerner*.

19. Baime, *Dewey Defeats Truman*, 72–73, 99–100.

20. On the Dixiecrats see Frederickson, *The Dixiecrat Revolt*, among others.

21. McCullough, *Truman*, 590.

22. Chase Going Woodhouse to Howard McGrath, March 18, 1948, folder "W-Miscellaneous," box 49, McGrath Papers.

23. Report on Housewives for Truman program, folder 4, box 3, IE Papers. Detail about West Virginia is on p. 5.

24. Paul Fitzgerald to India Edwards, November 9, 1948, folder 4, box 3, IE Papers.

25. Helen L. Manning to Charles Ross, secretary to President Truman, November 4, 1948, folder 5, box 162, Papers of Harry S. Truman: President's Personal File, Harry S. Truman Presidential Library (hereafter Truman PPF).

26. Report on Housewives for Truman program, p. 10, folder 4, box 3, IE Papers.

27. All 1948 Rainbow Fliers are in folder 4, box 3, IE Papers.

28. Report on Housewives for Truman program, p. 1, folder 4, box 3, IE Papers.

29. Chase Going Woodhouse to President Truman, June 23, 1947, p. 1, folder 1, box 162, Truman PPF.

30. Clipping, "Industrial State Democrats Want Liberalism as Party's '48 Platform," *Washington Memo*, April 18, 1947, folder 19, box 155, DNC Papers, Truman Library.

31. Jack Redding to Howard McGrath, June 14, 1948, folder 2, box 1, IE Papers.

32. Edwards oral history.

33. "Vital Issues in Flint Michigan," notes for speech given September 6, 1948, President's Secretary's Files, 1948 Campaign Digital Collection, Harry S. Truman Presidential Library and Museum, https://www.trumanlibrary.gov/library/research-files/vital-issues-flint-michigan.

34. Transcript of Boston campaign speech, October 27, 1948, folder 13, box 206, DNC Papers, Truman Library.

35. Edwards, *Pulling No Punches*, 106.

36. Radio script, "Democratic Record Show #1," October 11, 1948, pp. 7, 9, folder 10, box 208, DNC Papers, Truman Library.

37. Edwards, *Pulling No Punches*, 112.

38. Ibid., 1.

39. Ibid., 110–11.

40. McCullough, *Truman*, 656.

41. Dorothy McAllister to India Edwards, November 6, 1948, pp. 1–4, folder 2, box 1, IE Papers.

CHAPTER SIX. "MERGER OR MURDER?"

1. Baime, *Dewey Defeats Truman*, 346–47.

2. India Edwards to Bess Truman, December 17, 1948, folder 4, box 1, IE Papers.

3. Draft of Harry S. Truman, President's Message for *Democratic Digest*, December 1948 / January 1949, attached to Dorothy Girton to Charles Ross, December 6, 1948, folder 12, box 161, Truman PPF.

4. Clipping, "Frank Sweeney Reports: Women in Washington Spotlight," attached to letter from Sidney Yates to India Edwards, March 23, 1949, folder 5, box 1, IE Papers.

5. India Edwards, transcript of speech, July 1949, folder 12, box 3, IE Papers.

6. India Edwards to the Honorable James Forrestal, March 23, 1948, folder 4, box 1, IE Papers.

7. India Edwards to McGrath, April 26, 1948, folder 4, box 1, IE Papers.

8. Folder 5, box 1, IE Papers is her correspondence with other DNC leaders for that year.

9. Edwards, *Pulling No Punches*, 102.

10. India Edwards, remarks for the BPW, July 1949, folder 9, box 4, IE Papers.

11. Most labor feminists shared Edwards's assessment that legislation such as the ERA was not the most effective tool to improve women's lives in the early 1950s, as they were finding some success with things like maternity leave through their labor unions. Cobble, *The Other Women's Movement*, 106–9.

12. Edwards, *Pulling No Punches*, 169.

13. Jane Schmidt to India Edwards, November 28, 1952, folder 8, box 1, IE Papers. On the Courier program see India Edwards to Frank McKinney, March 13, 1952, folder 8, box 1, IE Papers.

14. Dudziak, "Josephine Baker, Racial Protest, and the Cold War," 579.

15. Edwards, *Pulling No Punches*, 169.

16. India Edwards to President Truman, July 12, 1951, folder 7, box 1, IE Papers.

17. India Edwards to Bill Boyle, October 2, 1950, folder 6, box 1, IE Papers.

18. Tillett oral history, p. 52. The one biographical article on Tillett follows the oral history and gives helping Graham as the only reason for her departure. McMillen, "Gladys Avery Tillett," 155.

19. India Edwards to Gladys Tillett, April 3, 1950, folder 6, box 1, IE Papers.

20. See India Edwards to Mrs. Albert Lasker, March 17, 1950, folder 6, box 1, IE Papers. On Truman's health plan see Chapin, *Ensuring America's Health*, 41–50.

21. Text of radio speech by India Edwards, [fall 1950], folder 14, box 210, DNC Papers, Truman Library.

22. Text of radio speech by India Edwards, ("I don't suppose very many of you"), [fall 1950], folder 14, box 210, DNC Papers, Truman Library.

23. Clipping, "Women Democrats' Head to Hold Schools across Nation on Issues; Mrs. Edwards Picks Two Subjects as Most Controversial: Brannan Farm Plan and Federal Health Insurance," *New York Times*, April 26, 1950, folder 9, box 1083, Truman OF.

24. On the importance of domesticity during the Cold War see May, *Homeward Bound*, chaps. 3 and 7, and Weiss, *To Have and to Hold*, chap. 1.

25. Truman to India Edwards, February 3, 1950, folder 12, box 1, IE Papers.

26. Harry Truman to Emma Guffey Miller, August 12, 1950, folder 6, box 1, IE Papers.

27. India Edwards to Truman, November 1950, p. 3, folder 6, box 1, IE Papers.

28. McRae, *Mothers of Massive Resistance*, 13.

29. India Edwards to Bill Boyle, July 28, 1950, folder 6, box 1, IE Papers.

30. India Edwards to President Truman, November 1950, pp. 1–2, folder 6, box 1, IE Papers.

31. Ibid., pp. 2–3.

32. Transcript of radio interview with India Edwards, September 27, 1951, folder 7, box 1, IE Papers.

33. India Edwards to President Truman, October 30, 1951, folder 7, box 1, IE Papers.

34. Marian Dennehy to Bill Boyle, April 30, 1951, folder 7, box 1, IE Papers.

35. Press release re: *Coronet* article, March 23, 1951, folder 12, box 3, IE Papers.

36. Quoted in Edwards, *Pulling No Punches*, 144.

37. Memo to the Women's Division staff, June 15, 1951, folder 7, box 1, IE Papers.

38. Edwards, *Pulling No Punches*, 141.

39. Alonzo Hamby, "Harry S. Truman: Domestic Affairs," Miller Center, University of Virginia, https://millercenter.org/president/truman/domestic-affairs.

40. India Edwards to Grace Barmore, November 9, 1951, folder 7, box 1, IE Papers.

41. Edwards, *Pulling No Punches*, 141–42.

42. Monroe Sweetland, National Committeeman for Oregon, to President Truman, telegram, October 25, 1951, folder 7, box 1, IE Papers.

43. Edwards, *Pulling No Punches*, 142.

44. India Edwards to President Truman, October 30, 1951, folder 7, box 1, IE Papers.

45. Speech by Frank McKinney, October 31, 1951, folder 7, box 1, IE Papers.

46. India Edwards to President Truman, December 11, 1951, folder 7, box 1, IE Papers.

47. "Women Elected Officials," Center for American Women and Politics, Rutgers, https://cawpdata.rutgers.edu/omen-elected-officials?name=U.S.+congress&current=2.

48. Harrison, *On Account of Sex*, 58.

49. On Tufty see Beasley, *Women of the Washington Press*, 110.

50. Harrison, *On Account of Sex*, 57–58.

51. Edwards, *Pulling No Punches*, 160–61.

52. Ibid., 103.

53. Ibid., 161.

54. India Edwards to Stephen Mitchell, November 7, 1952, p. 2, folder 8, box 1, IE Papers.

55. Ibid., p. 1.

56. Press release, January 27, 1953, folder 11, box 3, IE Papers.

57. Clipping, "Radio-TV Host Is Discharged by Democrats," *Washington Times-Herald*, February 11, 1953, folder 9, box 156, DNC Papers, Truman Library.

58. Ibid.

59. Clipping, Ruth Cowan, "Democratic Gals in a Dither," *Cleveland Plain Dealer*, February 9, 1953, folder 14, box 156, DNC Papers, Truman Library.

60. Helmes diary, January 29, 1954, pp. 4–5.

61. Clipping, Eleanor Roosevelt, "My Day: New Role for Women," *Chicago Sun-Times*, February 10, 1953, folder 14, box 156, DNC Papers, Truman Library.

62. Draft of letter by India Edwards to local Democratic women, August 1953, folder 11, box 3, IE Papers.

CHAPTER SEVEN. REACHING REPUBLICAN WOMEN

1. Clipping, "Ike Appoints Strategy Staff," *Boston Herald*, folder 1, box 19, Bertha Adkins Papers, Eisenhower Presidential Library.

2. Bertha Adkins oral history, interview by John T. Mason, December 18, 1967, Columbia University Eisenhower Administration Project, https://dlc.library.columbia.edu/catalog/cul:wm37pvmfxz/details?initial_page=1, pp. 2–3.

3. Ibid., pp. 4–5.

4. Rymph, *Republican Women*, 70–71, 94.

5. Bowen, *The Roots of Modern Conservatism*, 4–5.

6. Rymph, *Republican Women*, 93.

7. Ibid., 90–92.

8. Ibid., 100–101.

9. Adkins oral history, pp. 5, 23.

10. Ibid., pp. 23–26.

11. Ibid., p. 3.

12. Finding Aid, Winifred Helmes Papers, Edward H. Nabb Research Center, Salisbury University.

13. Johnson, *The Lavender Scare*.

14. Freedman, "'The Burning of Letters Continues.'"

15. Helmes's diary opens, for example, with a description of the reception Adkins organized for Alice Leopold, the new director of the Women's Bureau of the Department of Labor, which was held at a D.C. women's club and which Helmes attended to represent the couple because Adkins was ill. Helmes diary, January 7, 1954, p. 1.

16. Adkins oral history, p. 26 (emphasis in original).

17. Ware, *Partner and I*, 159.

18. Adkins oral history, p. 32.

19. Ibid., pp. 33–34.

20. Ibid., p. 34.

21. Memo, Katherine Howard to General Eisenhower, Sherman Adams, et al., August 23, 1952, p. 1, folder 6, box 18, Katherine Howard Papers, Eisenhower Presidential Library.

22. Priest, *Green Grows Ivy*, 172–73.

23. Adkins oral history, p. 35.

24. Form letter, Dwight D. Eisenhower to county vice chairmen, September 23, 1952, p. 1, folder 2, box 872, President's Personal Files, White House Central Files, Eisenhower Presidential Library (hereafter Eisenhower PPF).

25. Rymph, *Republican Women*, 154.

26. Adkins oral history, p. 35.

27. Howard, *With My Shoes Off*, 111.

28. Ibid., 130.

29. Ibid., 153.

30. Ibid., 171.

31. Ibid., 158.

32. Ibid., 160–61.

33. Helmes diary, January 20, 1954, p. 5.

34. Eisenhower to Vivian Kellems, August 16, 1952, folder 14, box 710, OF156-G, Eisenhower Official File, White House Central Files, Eisenhower Presidential Library (hereafter Eisenhower OF).

35. Excerpts from speeches by Gen. Eisenhower on the role of women in his campaign, p. 2, folder 8, box 18, Howard Papers.

36. Howard, *With My Shoes Off*, 165–66.

37. Adkins oral history, pp. 48–49.

38. Smith, *Eisenhower in War and Peace*, 756. Although Jean Edward Smith includes this mention of Ike's encouragement of Hobby, neither his book nor the other recent biography of Eisenhower, William Hitchcock's *The Age of Eisenhower*, deal in any detail at all with his feminism. Adkins, Howard, Priest, and Wheaton are all absent from the indexes of both books, as is the term "women."

39. Adkins, "You Can Elect a President," p. 1, folder 11, box 14, Adkins Papers, Eisenhower Presidential Library.

40. Howard, *With My Shoes Off*, 198 (emphasis in original).

41. Adkins, "You Can Elect a President," p. 1, folder 11, box 14, Adkins Papers.

42. Howard, *With My Shoes Off*, 175.

43. Ibid., 197.

44. On the Los Angeles speech see Howard, *With My Shoes Off*, 205. For the 1952 campaign's place in the general trajectory of African Americans within the Republican Party see Rigueur, *The Loneliness of Black Republicans*, 27–28.

45. Howard, *With My Shoes Off*, 180–81.

46. The 1952 number is from a memo by Mrs. J. Ramsey (Ellen) Harris to President Eisenhower, April 1, 1954, p. 3, folder 8, box 587, General File, White House Central Files, Eisenhower Presidential Library (hereafter Eisenhower GF). The 1948 number is from Wolbrecht and Corder, *A Century of Votes for Women*, 111.

47. Priest, *Green Grows Ivy*, 187.

48. Katherine Howard, interview by John T. Mason, July 30, 1968, Columbia University Eisenhower Administration Project, pp. 167–68.

49. Howard, *With My Shoes Off*, 241.

50. Helmes diary, January 20, 1954, p. 5.

51. On the NFRW starting the Schools of Politics, see Rymph, *Republican Women*, 135–36.

52. Cover letter, Max Rabb to Sherman Adams re: Women's Division, January 3, 1953, p. 1, folder 4, box 476, Eisenhower GF.

53. Ibid., p. 2.

54. Ibid.

CHAPTER EIGHT. "GOVERNMENT COMES RIGHT INTO THE HOME"

1. Adkins oral history, pp. 53–54.

2. Helmes diary, November 7, 1956, p. 271.

3. For a direct appeal to AAUW women, see press release, speech to AAUW Annual Convention, June 29, 1955, p. 1, folder 9, box 18, Adkins Papers.

4. Adkins oral history, pp. 50–51.

5. Adkins to "Republican Leaders," March 1954, folder 6, box 476, Eisenhower GF

6. Bertha Adkins, "You Can Elect a President," *AAUW Journal*, 1952, p. 1, folder 11, box 14, Adkins Papers.

7. Ellen Harris to James Murphy, January 29, 1954, p. 2, folder 14, box 710, Eisenhower OF.

8. Howard, *With My Shoes Off*, 187.

9. On Carpenter's role in the Johnson White House see Sweig, *Lady Bird Johnson*, 39–40 and 329–30.

10. Esther Van Wagoner Tufty obituary, *Washington Post*, May 5, 1986, https://www.washingtonpost.com/archive/local/1986/05/05/obituaries/a7d90017-0013-4735-89ab-b61891be9267/.

11. For more on the Women's National Press Club see Beasley, *Women of the Washington Press*.

12. Margaret Chase Smith, "Declaration of Conscience" speech, June 1, 1950, United States Senate, https://www.senate.gov/about/powers-procedures/investigations/mccarthy-hearings/a-declaration-of-conscience.htm. For more on Smith, see Sherman, *No Place for a Woman*.

13. Helmes diary, May 27, 1957, p. 348.

14. On Luce's appointment, see Morris, *Price of Fame*, 309–12.

15. "Top Women Appointees of the Eisenhower Administration," October 30, 1953, folder 14, box 710, Eisenhower OF.

16. Press release by the RNC, December 4, 1953, p. 1, folder 5, box 476, Eisenhower GF.

17. The percentage is cited in Storrs, *The Second Red Scare*, 28.

18. On her earlier work with the League of Women Voters and Margaret Sanger, see Anne Wheaton oral history, interview by John T. Mason, January 31, 1968, Columbia University Eisenhower Administration Project, https://dlc.library.columbia.edu/catalog/cul:vmcvdncmv2, pp. 9–11.

19. Ibid., p. 34.

20. Ibid., p. 40.

21. Harrison, *On Account of Sex*, 61.

22. Women's Division "Program for '53," p. 3, folder 4, box 476, Eisenhower GF.

23. Wes Roberts to Sherm Adams, March 4, 1953, p. 2, folder 11, box 1056, Eisenhower GF.

24. Bertha Adkins, speech to the Long Island Federation of Women's Clubs, January 31, 1955, folder 9, box 18, Adkins Papers.

25. Bertha Adkins, speech to annual AAUW meeting, June 29, 1955, p. 1, folder 9, box 18, Adkins Papers.

26. Goss, *The Paradox of Gender Equality*, 79, 94.

27. Sulgrave Club, "Club History," accessed August 23, 2021, https://www.sulgraveclub.org/the-club/club-history.

28. Adkins oral history, p. 49.

29. Breakfast thank-you notes, folders 4 and 5, box 872, Eisenhower PPF.

30. President Eisenhower to Bertha Adkins, May 26, 1955, folder 5, box 872, Eisenhower PPF.

31. Wilton Persons, memo to President Eisenhower, September 1955, folder 5, box 872, Eisenhower PPF.

32. Charlie Willis to Jim Hagerty, April 26, 1954, folder 8, box 587, Eisenhower OF.

33. Anne Wheaton to Sherm Adams, October 21, 1953, folder 4, box 476, Eisenhower GF.

34. Adkins oral history, p. 48.

35. Campaign Clinic report, April 1, 1954, p. 1, folder 8, box 587, Eisenhower OF.

36. Len Hall to Maude Cudworth, October 27, 1954, folder 5, box 208, RNC Office of the Chairman Papers, Eisenhower Presidential Library.

37. Ellen Harris to James Murphy, January 29, 1954, folder 14, box 710, Eisenhower OF.

38. Henry Cabot Lodge to President Eisenhower, February 16, 1954, folder 14, box 710, Eisenhower OF.

39. Charlie Willis to Governor Adams, February 25, 1954, folder 14, box 710, Eisenhower OF.

40. Jim Hagerty to Bertha Adkins, June 24, 1954, folder 6, box 476, Eisenhower GF; Bertha Adkins to "County Vice-Chairman, City, Town, Ward, and District Leaders," June 21, 1954, pp. 1–2, folder 6, box 476, Eisenhower GF.

41. Bertha Adkins to "County Vice-Chairman, City, Town, Ward, and District Leaders," April 20, 1954, folder 6, box 476, Eisenhower GF.

42. Highlights of the Republican Women's Centennial Conference, April 1954, p. 1, folder 6, box 476, Eisenhower GF.

43. Packet of materials mailed to Republican women leaders, June 1954, p. 8, folder 6, box 476, Eisenhower GF (emphasis in original).

44. Bertha Adkins travel schedule, January to November 1954, folder 7, box 476, Eisenhower GF.

45. President Eisenhower to Bertha Adkins, October 6, 1954, folder 12, box 14, Adkins Papers.

46. Jim Hagerty to Bertha Adkins, June 24, 1954, folder 6, box 476, Eisenhower GF.

47. "Citizens for Eisenhower Congressional Advance," June 1954, p. 2, folder 33, box 600, Eisenhower OF.

48. Rymph, *Republican Women*, 154.

49. Ibid., 146.

50. Nora Kearns to Bernard Shanley, March 21, 1955, folder 5, box 872, Eisenhower PPF.

51. Bertha Adkins to Bernard Shanley, April 5, 1955, folder 5, box 872, Eisenhower PPF.

52. Nora Kearns to Bernard Shanley, April 25, 1955, folder 5, box 872, Eisenhower PPF.

53. Rymph, *Republican Women*, 125.

54. For more on right-wing women in the 1950s and 1960s see Nickerson, *Mothers of Conservatism*.

55. Mrs. J. Davidige Warfield to Len Hall, February 16, 1954, folder 5, box 208, RNC Office of Chairman Papers, Eisenhower Presidential Library.

56. Rymph, *Republican Women*, 147.

57. Howard, *With My Shoes Off*, 243.

58. Peter Edson, "The Kitchen Kabinet," *Washington Daily News*, April 22, 1955, clipping in folder 1, box 894, Eisenhower PPF.

59. NFRW press release, April 15, 1955, pp. 2–3, folder 1, box 894, Eisenhower PPF.

60. NFRW press release, April 15, 1955, p. 2, folder 1, box 894, Eisenhower PPF.

CHAPTER NINE. FUNDRAISERS AND POLLSTERS

1. Julie Kirlin to Republican Party Women, November 18, 1955, attached to Bertha Adkins to Sherm Adams, November 28, 1955, folder 9, box 476, Eisenhower GF.

2. Julie Kirlin to Len Hall et al., June 16, 1956, folder 19, box 104, RNC Office of the Chairman Papers, Eisenhower Presidential Library.

3. Indeed, political scientists have shown that female Republican candidates have more difficulty raising money during primaries than their male peers into the 2010s. Democratic women show no such difficulties, and in fact often outraise male candidates, suggesting a partisan aspect to the failure of the 1956 fundraising by the Republican WD (Kitchens and Swers, "Why Aren't There More Republican Women in Congress?)."

4. List of Women's Division pamphlets, folder 6, box 208, RNC Office of Chairman Papers, Eisenhower Presidential Library.

5. Adkins oral history, pp. 55–56.

6. Helmes diary, July 26, 1956, p. 230.

7. Howard, *With My Shoes Off*, 201.

8. Rigueur, *The Loneliness of Black Republicans*, 29.

9. Ibid.

10. The full run of cards is in folder 14, box 718, Republican National Committee Papers, Eisenhower Presidential Library.

11. "Participants in October 24th Women's Program," folder 29, box 600, Eisenhower OF.

12. Rigueur, *The Loneliness of Black Republicans*, 31.

13. The page was Patricia Ann Spaulding, daughter of Asa Spaulding, the wealthy president of North Carolina Mutual Life Insurance Company. Asa Spaulding to Bertha Adkins, August 22, 1956, folder 6, box 15, Adkins Papers.

14. Adkins oral history, p. 56.

15. Helen Edmonds to Val Washington, March 15, 1958, folder 3, box 477, Eisenhower GF.

16. For more on Alexander see Summey, *The Life of Elreta Melton Alexander*.

17. Val Washington to Sherm Adams, March 18, 1958, folder 3, box 477, Eisenhower GF.

18. Rymph, *Republican Women*, 139.

19. Republican Roundtable, pamphlet, p. 3, folder 2, box 894, Eisenhower PPF.

20. Remarks by Jim Hagerty to Sixth Republican Women's National Conference, 1956, p. 2, folder 7, box 15, Adkins Papers.

21. Helmes diary, August 1–19, 1956, p. 235.

22. Ibid., August 1–19, 1956, p. 236; September 24, 1956, p. 256.

23. Ibid., August 25, 1956, p. 240.

24. Ibid., October 17, 1956, p. 262.

25. Ibid., July 25, 1956, p. 229.

26. Ike Day material is in folders 2 and 3, box 20, Howard Papers.

27. Helmes diary, September 12, 1956, p. 244.

28. Parry, *Eisenhower*, 52–55.

29. BBDO analysis of polling data, September 1956, folder 9, box 104, RNC Office of the Chairman Papers, Eisenhower Presidential Library.

30. Unsigned memo to Len Hall, October 15, 1956, p. 2, folder 18, box 104, RNC Office of the Chairman Papers, Eisenhower Presidential Library.

31. Len Hall to Richard Guylay (RNC PR head), August 11, 1956, folder 18, box 104, RNC Office of the Chairman Papers, Eisenhower Presidential Library.

32. Form letter, Bertha Adkins to "Poll Worker," August 19, 1955, folder 3, box 15, Adkins Papers.

33. Poll results are in folder 4, box 15, Adkins Papers.

34. BA to Republican Women Leaders, August 11, 1955, folder 3, box 15, Adkins Papers.

35. Remarks of the president delivered at luncheon meeting of the Sixth Annual Republican Women's National Conference, March 18, 1958, p. 7, folder 2, box 596, Eisenhower OF.

36. Eisenhower 1957 budget message to Congress, The American Presidency Project, accessed September 3, 2021, https://www.presidency.ucsb.edu/documents/annual-budget-message-the-congress-for-fiscal-year-1958.

37. Nina Broderick Price to President Eisenhower, August 9, 1957, folder 5, box 1059, Eisenhower GF.

38. DeWolf, *Gendered Citizenship*, 200.

39. White, *Making of a President 1960*.

40. Adkins oral history, p. 40.

41. Women in Politics newsletter, February 1959, p. 1, folder 1, box 21, Adkins Papers.

42. Clayton Fritchey to President Kennedy, July 22, 1963, pp. 1–2, folder HU3–

Equality for Women–General, box 374, White House Central Files, John F. Kennedy Presidential Library, Boston, Mass.

EPILOGUE

1. For more on the PCSW see Harrison, *On Account of Sex*, chaps. 7–9.

2. On Schlafly and her fellow conservative women, see Critchlow, *Phyllis Schlafly and Grassroots Conservatism;* Rymph, *Republican Women*, chaps. 6 and 8; and Spruill, *Divided We Stand.*

3. On Taylor and Parks see McGuire, *At the Dark End of the Street*, chap. 1. On Clark see Charron, *Freedom's Teacher*. On Bethune and the NCNW, see Tuuri, *Strategic Sisterhood.*

4. On feminists of color's critiques of white feminists' approach to rape, see Thuma, *All Our Trials*. For their critiques on reproductive justice see Levenstein, *They Didn't See Us Coming*, chaps. 6 and 9; and Theobald, *Reproduction on the Reservation*, chap. 6.

BIBLIOGRAPHY

ARCHIVAL SOURCES

Dwight D. Eisenhower Presidential Library, Abilene, Kans.
- Bertha Adkins Papers
- Katherine Graham Howard Papers
- Republican National Committee Papers
- RNC Office of the Chairman Papers
- White House Central Files

Edward H. Nabb Research Center, Salisbury University, Salisbury, Md.
- Winifred Helmes Papers

Franklin D. Roosevelt Presidential Library, Hyde Park, N.Y.
- DNC Women's Division Papers
- Eleanor Roosevelt Papers
- Lorena Hickok Papers
- Molly Dewson Papers
- President's Personal File
- White House Central Files

Harry S. Truman Presidential Library, Independence, Mo.
- Democratic National Committee Papers
- India Edwards Papers
- Howard McGrath Papers
- Papers of Harry S. Truman: Official File
- Papers of Harry S. Truman: President's Personal File

University of North Carolina Wilson Library (Special Collections), Chapel Hill, N.C.
- Gladys Tillett Papers

SECONDARY SOURCES

Alvarez, Luis. *The Power of the Zoot: Youth Culture and Resistance during World War II*. Berkeley: University of California Press, 2009.

Anderson, Kristi. *After Suffrage: Women in Partisan and Electoral Politics before the New Deal*. Chicago: University of Chicago Press, 1996.

Baime, A. J. *Dewey Defeats Truman: The 1948 Election and the Battle for America's Soul*. New York: Mariner Books, 2020.

Balogh, Brian. *Chain Reaction: Expert Debate and Public Participation in American Commercial Nuclear Power, 1945–1975*. New York: Cambridge University Press, 1991.

———. "'Mirrors of Desire': Interest Groups, Elections, and the Targeted Style in Twentieth-Century American Politics." In *The Democratic Experiment: New Directions in American Political History*, edited by Meg Jacobs et al., 222–49. Princeton, N.J.: Princeton University Press, 2003.

Beasley, Maurine H. "Eleanor Roosevelt's Press Conferences: Case Study in Class, Gender, and Race." *Social Science Journal* 37, no. 4 (2000): 517–28.

———.. *Women of the Washington Press: Politics, Prejudice, and Persistence*. Evanston, Ill.: Northwestern University Press, 2012.

Blair, Melissa Estes. *Revolutionizing Expectations: Women's Organizations, Feminism, and American Politics, 1965–1980*. Athens: University of Georgia Press, 2014.

Bowen, Michael. *The Roots of Modern Conservatism: Dewey, Taft, and the Fight for the Soul of the Republican Party*. Chapel Hill: University of North Carolina Press, 2011.

Campbell, Tracy. *The Year of Peril: America in 1942*. New Haven, Conn.: Yale University Press, 2020.

Cervini, Eric. *The Deviant's War: The Homosexual vs. the United States of America*. New York: Farrar, Straus, Giroux, 2020.

Chapin, Christy Ford. *Ensuring America's Health: The Public Creation of the Corporate Health Care System*. New York: Cambridge University Press, 2015.

Charron, Katherine Mellen. *Freedom's Teacher: The Life of Septima Clark*. Chapel Hill: University of North Carolina Press, 2010.

Cobble, Dorothy Sue. *The Other Women's Movement: Workplace Justice and Social Rights in Modern America*. Princeton, N.J.: Princeton University Press, 2004.

Cohen, Lizabeth. *Making a New Deal: Industrial Workers in Chicago, 1919–1939*. New York: Cambridge University Press, 1990.

Corder, J. Kevin, and Christina Wolbrecht. *Counting Women's Ballots: Female Voters from Suffrage through the New Deal*. New York: Cambridge University Press, 2016.

Cott, Nancy F. *The Grounding of Modern Feminism*. New Haven, Conn: Yale University Press, 1987.

Critchlow, Donald T. *Phyllis Schlafly and Grassroots Conservatism: A Woman's Crusade*. Princeton, N.J.: Princeton University Press, 2005.

Davis, Michael. *Politics as Usual: Thomas Dewey, Franklin Roosevelt, and the Wartime Presidential Campaign of 1944*. DeKalb: Northern Illinois University Press, 2014.

DeWolf, Rebecca. *Gendered Citizenship: The Original Conflict over the Equal Rights Amendment*. Lincoln: University of Nebraska Press, 2021.

Donaldson, Gary A. *Truman Defeats Dewey*. Lexington: University Press of Kentucky, 1999.

Dudziak, Mary. "Josephine Baker, Racial Protest, and the Cold War." *Journal of American History* 81, no. 2, (1994): 543–70.

Edwards, India. *Pulling No Punches: Memoirs of a Woman in Politics*. New York: G. P. Putnam's Sons, 1977.

Fosl, Catherine. *Subversive Southerner: Anne Braden and the Struggle for Racial Justice in the Cold War South*. New York: Palgrave Macmillian, 2002.

Frederickson, Kari. *The Dixiecrat Revolt and the End of the Solid South, 1932–1968*. Chapel Hill: University of North Carolina Press, 2001.

Freedman, Estelle. "'The Burning of Letters Continues': Elusive Identities and the Historical Construction of Sexuality." *Journal of Women's History* 9, no. 4 (1998): 181–200.

Freeman, Jo. *A Room at a Time: How Women Entered Party Politics*. New York: Rowan and Littlefield, 2000.

Giddings, Paula. *When and Where I Enter: The Impact of Black Women on Race and Sex in America*. New York: Morrow, 1984.

Gilmore, Glenda Elizabeth. *Gender and Jim Crow: Women and the Politics of White Supremacy in North Carolina, 1896–1920*. Chapel Hill: University of North Carolina Press, 1996.

Goss, Kristin A. *The Paradox of Gender Equality: How American Women's Groups Gained and Lost Their Public Voice*. Ann Arbor: University of Michigan Press, 2013.

Harrison, Cynthia. *On Account of Sex: The Politics of Women's Issues, 1945–1968*. Berkeley: University of California Press, 1988.

Harvey, Anna L. *Votes without Leverage: Women in American Electoral Politics, 1920–1970*. New York: Cambridge University Press, 1998.

Herman, Ellen. *The Romance of American Psychology: Political Culture in the Age of Experts*. Berkeley: University of California Press, 1995.

Hitchcock, William I. *The Age of Eisenhower: America and the World in the 1950s*. New York: Simon and Schuster, 2018.

Howard, Katherine G. *With My Shoes Off*. New York: Vantage Press, 1977.

Jeffries, John W. *A Third Term for FDR: The Election of 1940*. Lawrence: University Press of Kansas, 2017.

Johnson, David K. *The Lavender Scare: The Cold War Persecution of Gays and Lesbians in the Federal Government*. Chicago: University of Chicago Press, 2004.

Kennedy, David M. *Freedom from Fear: The American People in Depression and War, 1929–1945*. New York: Oxford University Press, 1999.

Kessler-Harris, Alice. *In Pursuit of Equity: Women, Men, and the Quest for Economic Citizenship in Twentieth-Century America*. New York: Oxford University Press, 2001.

Kitchens, Karin L., and Michele L. Swers. "Why Aren't There More Republican Women in Congress? Gender, Partisanship, and Fundraising Support for the 2010 and 2012 Elections." *Politics and Gender* 12, no. 4 (2016): 648–76.

Lepore, Jill. *These Truths: A History of the United States*. New York: W. W. Norton, 2018.

Levenstein, Lisa. *They Didn't See Us Coming: The Hidden History of Feminism in the Nineties*. New York: Basic Books, 2020.

Lindsey, Treva B. *Colored No More: Reinventing Black Womanhood in Washington, D.C.* Champaign: University of Illinois Press, 2017.

Link, William A. *Frank Porter Graham: Southern Liberal, Citizen of the World*. Chapel Hill: University of North Carolina Press, 2021.

May, Elaine Tyler. *Homeward Bound: American Families in the Cold War Era*. New York: Basic Books, 1988.

McCullough, David. *Truman*. New York: Simon and Schuster, 1993.

McEuen, Melissa. *Making War, Making Women: Femininity and Duty on the American Home Front, 1941–1945*. Athens: University of Georgia Press, 2011.

McGirr, Lisa. *The War on Alcohol: Prohibition and the Rise of the American State*. New York: W. W. Norton, 2016.

McGuire, Danielle. *At the Dark End of the Street: Black Women, Rape, and Resistance—A New History of the Civil Rights Movement from Rosa Parks to the Rise of Black Power*. New York: Vintage, 2011.

McMillen, Sally. "Gladys Avery Tillett: White Gloved and Iron-Willed." In *North Carolina Women: Their Lives and Times*. Vol. 2, edited by Michele Gillespie and Sally McMillen. Athens: University of Georgia Press, 2015.

McRae, Elizabeth Gillespie. *Mothers of Massive Resistance: White Women and the Politics of White Supremacy*. New York: Oxford University Press, 2018.

Michaelis, David. *Eleanor*. New York: Simon and Schuster, 2020.

Milkis, Sidney M. *The President and the Parties: The Transformation of the American Party System since the New Deal*. New York: Oxford University Press, 1993.

Morris, Sylvia Jukes. *The Price of Fame: The Honorable Clare Boothe Luce*. New York: Random House, 2014.

Nelson, Bruce. "Organized Labor and the Struggle for Black Equality in Mobile during World War II." *Journal of American History* 80, no. 3 (1993), 952–88.

Newman, Louise Michele. *White Women's Rights: The Racial Origins of Feminism in the United States*. New York: Oxford University Press, 1999.

Nickerson, Michelle. *Mothers of Conservatism: Women and the Postwar Right*. Princeton, N.J.: Princeton University Press, 2012.

Parker, Alison M. *Unceasing Militant: The Life of Mary Church Terrell*. Chapel Hill: University of North Carolina Press, 2020.

Parry, Pam. *Eisenhower: The Public Relations President*. Lanham, Md.: Lexington Books, 2014.

Perry, Elisabeth Israels. *Belle Moskowitz: Feminine Politics and the Exercise of Power in the Age of Alfred E. Smith*. Boston: Northeastern University Press, 2002.

Priest, Ivy Baker. *Green Grows Ivy*. New York: McGraw-Hill, 1958.

Quinn, Susan. *Eleanor and Hick: The Love Affair that Shaped a First Lady*. New York: Penguin, 2017.
Reynolds, David. *From Munich to Pearl Harbor: Roosevelt's America and the Origins of the Second World War*. Chicago: Ivan R. Dee Publishing, 2001.
Rigueur, Leah Wright. *The Loneliness of Black Republicans: Pragmatic Politics and the Pursuit of Power*. Princeton, N.J.: Princeton University Press, 2015.
Robertson, Nancy Marie. *Christian Sisterhood, Race Relations, and the YWCA, 1906–1946*. Champaign: University of Illinois Press, 2010.
Rupp, Leila J., and Verta Taylor. *Survival in the Doldrums: The America Women's Rights Movement, 1945 to the 1960s*. New York: Oxford University Press, 1987.
Rymph, Catherine E. *Republican Women: Feminism and Conservatism from Suffrage through the Rise of the New Right*. Chapel Hill: University of North Carolina Press, 2006.
Schuyler, Lorraine Gates. *The Weight of Their Votes: Southern Women and Political Leverage in the 1920s*. Chapel Hill: University of North Carolina Press, 2006.
Sherman, Janann. *No Place for a Woman: A Life of Senator Margaret Chase Smith*. New Brunswick, N.J.: Rutgers University Press, 2001.
Sicherman, Barbara, and Carol Green Hurd, eds. *Notable American Women: The Modern Period*. Cambridge, Mass.: Belknap Press, 1980.
Skelton, Victoria. "'Women in a Changing World': The International Council of Women, Global Power, and the Boundaries of Sisterhood, 1888–1966." Ph.D. diss., Auburn University, 2021.
Smith, Jean Edward. *Eisenhower in War and Peace*. New York: Random House, 2013.
Sneider, Allison L. *Suffragists in an Imperial Age: U.S. Expansion and the Woman Question, 1870–1929*. New York: Oxford University Press, 2008.
Spruill, Marjorie J. *Divided We Stand: The Battle over Women's Rights and Family Values that Polarized American Politics*. New York: Bloomsbury, 2017.
Storrs, Landon R. Y. *The Second Red Scare and the Unmaking of the New Deal Left*. Princeton, N.J.: Princeton University Press, 2015.
Sugrue, Thomas J. *Sweet Land of Liberty: The Forgotten Struggle for Civil Rights in the North*. New York: Random House, 2009.
Summey, Virginia L. *The Life of Elreta Melton Alexander: Activism within the Courts*. Athens: University of Georgia Press, 2022.
Suri, Jeremi. *The Impossible Presidency: The Rise and Fall of America's Highest Office*. New York: Basic Books, 2017.
Sweig, Julia. *Lady Bird Johnson: Hiding in Plain Sight*. New York: Random House, 2021.
Tetrault, Lisa. *The Myth of Seneca Falls: Memory and the Women's Suffrage Movement, 1848–1898*. Chapel Hill: University of North Carolina Press, 2014.
Theobald, Brianna. *Reproduction on the Reservation: Pregnancy, Childbirth, and*

Colonialism in the Long Twentieth Century. Chapel Hill: University of North Carolina Press, 2019.

Thuma, Emily L. *All Our Trials: Prisons, Policing, and the Feminist Fight to End Violence*. Champaign: University of Illinois Press, 2019.

Trigg, Mary K. *Feminism as Life's Work: Four Modern American Women through Two World Wars*. New Brunswick, N.J.: Rutgers University Press, 2014.

Tuuri, Rebecca. *Strategic Sisterhood: The National Council of Negro Women in the Black Freedom Struggle*. Chapel Hill: University of North Carolina Press, 2018.

Twarog, Emily E. LB. *Politics of the Pantry: Housewives, Food, and Consumer Protest in Twentieth-Century America*. New York: Oxford University Press, 2017.

Wall, Wendy. *Inventing the "American Way": The Politics of Consensus from the New Deal to the Civil Rights Movement*. New York: Oxford University Press, 2008.

Ware, Susan. *Partner and I: Molly Dewson, Feminism, and New Deal Politics*. New Haven, Conn.: Yale University Press, 1987.

Weintraub, Stanley. *Final Victory: FDR's Extraordinary World War II Presidential Campaign*. New York: Da Capo Press, 2012.

Weiss, Jessica. *To Have and to Hold: Marriage, the Baby Boom, and Social Change*. Chicago: University of Chicago Press, 2000.

White, Deborah Gray. *Too Heavy a Load: Black Women in Defense of Themselves, 1894–1994*. New York: W. W. Norton, 1999.

White, Theodore H. *The Making of a President 1960*. New York: Athenaeum Books, 1961.

Wolbrecht, Christina, and J. Kevin Corder. *A Century of Votes for Women: American Elections since Suffrage*. New York: Cambridge University Press, 2020.

Zelizer, Julian E. *Taxing America: Wilbur D. Mills, Congress, and the State, 1945–1975*. New York: Cambridge University Press, 1998.

INDEX